CHIEF JUSTICE STONE
AND THE
SUPREME COURT

CHIEF JUSTICE STONE
AND THE
SUPREME COURT

By SAMUEL J. KONEFSKY

★

WITH A PREFATORY NOTE
By CHARLES A. BEARD

(Facsimile of the 1945 edition)

★

HAFNER PUBLISHING COMPANY
NEW YORK
1971

Published by
Hafner Publishing Company, Inc.
866 Third Avenue
New York, N. Y. 10022

Library of Congress Catalog Card Number: 75-152263

Printed in the U.S.A.

For

ROMA

FOREWORD

On January 5, 1925, President Coolidge nominated Harlan
Fiske Stone of New York to be an Associate Justice of the
United States Supreme Court. The nomination was confirmed
by the Senate, and Mr. Justice Stone ascended the Bench
on March 2. Sixteen years later, on June 12, 1941, President
Roosevelt nominated Mr. Justice Stone to fill the post left
vacant by the retirement of Chief Justice Hughes. Senate
confirmation followed on June 27, and on July 3 Mr. Justice
Stone was commissioned as Chief Justice of the United States.

In no sense is this volume an attempt to paint a life-size
portrait of the present Chief Justice. Its much more modest
purpose is to present, by means of the analysis of the great
public issues that have come to the Court for decision, Mr.
Stone's conception of the Supreme Court's special function in
interpreting the Constitution. But while the cases have been
read primarily for their revelation of this particular aspect
of his work on the Court, the discussion of them has not been
confined to it. The larger trends of constitutional development
as well as the conditions which gave rise to the controversies
have also been considered. The period covered is March, 1925,
to June, 1943, inclusive.

The exact scope of the Supreme Court's authority in applying the Constitution has persisted as a central problem for the
American plan of government ever since John Marshall first
asserted the right of that tribunal "to say what the law is."
Far from being a dormant question, recognized because it is
implicit in the Court's responsibility under the Constitution,
it has from time to time engaged the attention of numerous

Justices, including the greatest among them. For proper perspective, therefore, no appraisal of any contemporary contribution to the theory of the judicial function can be undertaken in isolation from the long history of this problem.

We have been told that "no judge writes on a wholly clean slate." (Frankfurter, *The Commerce Clause under Marshall, Taney and Waite*, 1937, p. 12.) Chief Justice Stone is no exception; he has built where others have left off. Holmes and Brandeis in particular loom large as influences.

In the eighteen years he has been a member of the Supreme Court—for sixteen years as an Associate Justice and the Chief Justice for two—Harlan Fiske Stone has made it clear that he, for one, has not taken for granted the Court's enormous power. Many of his opinions give the impression that not a few of his introspective moments have been spent in quest of the best way of discharging the judicial duty. From concern with one's own function as a judge to formal preoccupation with the role of the judiciary is a natural transition; and so it will be found that the distinctive feature of Chief Justice Stone's constitutional philosophy is his effort to develop a methodology for the exercise of judicial power. Whether he knowingly set himself this task is at the moment beyond the possibility of proof. Lacking as we do such biographically revealing material as personal correspondence, any conclusion in respect of his intentions is at best plausible conjecture.

But since it was necessary to rely almost exclusively on his judicial opinions, there was the inevitable danger that convenient inferences might be drawn from the collective judgments of the Court and attributed to the individual Justice studied. There were, however, several factors which minimized this intellectual peril of the undertaking. First and foremost is the fact that in the years the liberals on the Bench were in a minority, Harlan Fiske Stone was with them in most of the significant constitutional differences that divided the Court.

As a result, he wrote or concurred in dissenting opinions, many of which were in part concerned with the relation of the Court to the other branches of the government, particularly the legislature. The fight for greater judicial toleration of legislation led him to champion pragmatic tests of constitutionality; and dissents are far more reliable guides to the distinctive thought of the individual judge than is "the opinion of the Court." The very frequency of his dissents, furthermore, with their reiteration of views articulated earlier, is the second factor which made less hazardous the job of culling from them precepts to which he was personally committed. Finally, when what was once expressed in dissent came to prevail as law, his votes and opinions in the new cases helped to confirm otherwise tentative conclusions.

The Supreme Court's status as the final legal arbiter of our federalism is the one phase of its jurisdiction about which there has been practically no dispute. But general acceptance of this function of the Court has not precluded disagreement as to the way in which it should be performed. The first three chapters of the present study will examine Chief Justice Stone's views with respect to the principles and methods by which the Court may best harmonize our dual system of government. Chapters IV, V, and VI deal with the Court's role in enforcing constitutional limitations in behalf of private rights. In the main, the inductive approach has been followed, allowing the opinions and their authors to speak for themselves, as it were, before general conclusions are drawn. Except for the concluding chapter, Mr. Stone will be referred to according to his official title at the time the case was decided.

My first obligation is to Professor Noel T. Dowling, under whose expert and genial guidance this study has been prepared. As one who has known the Chief Justice and has followed his labors for nearly a quarter of a century, Professor Dowling was the ideal person to have supervised the research.

But he has been more than an adviser to whom one comes for occasional consultation. He has given lavishly of his time and ideas, and even when officially on leave from the University. In his capacity of "devil's advocate," as he is fond of calling his role, he has endeavored to anticipate questions which blunter critics might ask. It has been a pleasure to work with him.

Grateful acknowledgment is due also to Professors Henry Steele Commager, Robert L. Hale, and Arthur W. Macmahon, for the care and interest with which they read the manuscript. Professor Joseph P. Chamberlain read the chapter on administration and suggested improvements. To all of them I am deeply indebted for many helpful suggestions and much kindness.

To Miss Margaret Gustaferro, my former teacher and now friend and colleague, I owe much for a careful reading of the entire manuscript and for characteristically forthright criticism. It was her inspired and inspiring teaching of the subject that first stirred my interest in constitutional law.

The late Raymond V. Ingersoll, Mrs. Marion C. Ingersoll, Mr. Lessing J. Rosenwald, and Dr. Abraham Flexner were all uncommonly generous in easing my path at different stages in my academic progress. No man was more fortunate in his benefactors.

For their untiring effort in transcribing into Braille for me materials not otherwise available, I shall always be very grateful to the volunteers of the American Red Cross. Without the space to name them all, I should like to single out for special thanks Miss Dorothy S. Knight and Miss Edna M. Wood, who are in charge of Braille at the New York and Brooklyn chapters, respectively. I am also deeply grateful to Miss Martha Gibbell and Mrs. Sivia F. Rosenthal for cheerfully helping with the mechanics of preparing the typescript and checking the galleys.

To acknowledge all the ways in which my wife contributed to the writing of this book would require a greater outpouring of autobiographical comment than would be appropriate in these pages. It could not have been written without her indispensable assistance and unfailing encouragement. Not even those who have watched us at work can possibly know the full measure of my devoted gratitude.

S.J.K.

Brooklyn, November, 1944.

PREFATORY NOTE

IT IS the nature of Mr. Konefsky's book that gives me some warrant for acceding to his request and writing this prefatory note. If his volume dealt merely with technical matters of constitutional law, there would be every reason for silence on my part. But Mr. Konefsky's work is primarily devoted to the study of an idea—the American doctrine of judicial review—with reference to the particular form and emphasis given to it by a powerful personality of our time, Chief Justice Harlan F. Stone. In other words, the treatise before us cuts into history and character; and, although I profess no expertness here either, it so happens that I have given a little attention to the idea of judicial review and have been fortunate enough to see Chief Justice Stone in action as a citizen and a judge, and to have claim to a slight acquaintance with him. On these grounds, I venture to add a few words to the record which Mr. Konefsky has taken great pains to prepare—a labor that renders a distinct service to all citizens of the United States who cherish the form, spirit, and substance of constitutional government.

In his treatment of judicial review as expounded by Chief Justice Stone, Mr. Konefsky confines his explorations largely to documents that are matters of public record. He wonders, however, by what inner processes of contemplation and reflection the Chief Justice arrived at his conception of the doctrine in question. After raising this intellectual problem, Mr. Konefsky prudently says that at present we lack biographical material, such as personal correspondence, and hence can make only plausible conjectures with regard to the Chief Justice's inmost thought and intention as he brought to expression his distinctive formulation of judicial review.

For imagining that somewhere in correspondence and papers yet unpublished the clue to Chief Justice Stone's inner processes of thought on judicial review may be revealed, Mr. Konefsky has some justification in disclosures provided by recent studies of former Justices of the Supreme Court; studies of John Marshall, Roger B. Taney, and Stephen J. Field, for example.

No doubt studies of this character are often revealing. This is particularly true respecting men of strong passions, who are known to have asserted various dogmas privately and later transmuted them into formulas of judicial reasoning. In searching for light on men's thinking it is fitting and proper, therefore, to inquire into the circumstances of their individual history and experience and to examine the great interests which they have been associated with or have espoused. Indeed unless we are to indulge in idle speculation or in vague psychological conjectures no other course seems open to us.

There is, in my view of things, a great deal of sense in John Locke's question as to the origin of opinions and a great deal of truth in his answer. In his *Essay on Human Understanding,* Locke asked: Whence does the mind derive "the materials of Reason and Knowledge?" Then he replied to his own question: "To this I answer in one word, from *Experiences:* In that all our knowledge is founded; and from that it ultimately derives itself. Our observation employed either about external or sensible objects, or about the internal operations of our minds perceived and reflected upon by ourselves, is that which supplies our Understandings with all the materials of thinking. These two are the Fountains of knowledge from which all the ideas we have, or can naturally have, do spring."

Locke's statement is, in my opinion, an oversimplification and by no means the whole truth of the business. I doubt whether, in a strict sense of the term, any of us actually "understands" anything. Often I am inclined to think that, as some witty philosopher has put it, understanding is that feeling of satisfaction which steals over us when any new impression coming into the mind falls easily into some category already firmly established there. Yet, even so, when we seek thoughtfully to understand a person and his ideas we are bound to take into account the circumstances of his birth, rearing, life, and work—his experience in the full meaning of that word. To come immediately to the question at hand, we are surely warranted in concluding, for instance, that had Chief Justice Stone been born and reared in Novoberdo in the fifteenth century, his character and his ideas on judicial review would have been different—to take an extreme case that illustrates the problem of "origins" before us.

It is with some such overarching conception of the probable relation between character and experience fixed in my mind that I give the following brief account of Chief Justice Stone's life as it may bear upon the intellectual issue raised by Mr. Konefsky. Harlan Fiske Stone was born in Chesterfield, New Hampshire, on October 11, 1872—the son of Frederick L. and Ann Sophia Butler Stone, a New England farmer and his wife. In Harlan's youth the family moved to Amherst, Massachuetts, where, after two years in high school, he entered the Massachusetts Agricultural College, having in mind the possibility of a career as a scientific farmer. This dream was exploded, however, when he committed a breach of academic discipline and was "rusticated."

Thereupon Harlan entered Amherst College and by outside labors of various kinds earned his living as he went along. At Amherst he made a record as a hard-working student and was elected in due time to membership in Phi Beta Kappa. For three years he was president of his class. And, let it not be forgotten, he was once chairman of the Republican club.

For a time he managed the college newspaper and on the eve of his graduation in 1894 he was voted by his class the student "most likely to become famous." At Amherst also "it so happened" that Harlan met Calvin Coolidge who later, by a "happening" of history, became President of the United States. Of this incident those who are given to speculation on the contingencies of life and history may make the most, if they so choose.

From Amherst Harlan Stone went to the Law School of Columbia University, where he supported himself by teaching *history* at the Adelphi Academy in Brooklyn. Deeply impressed by the abilities and energies of the young man, Professor George F. Canfield invited Stone, immediately upon graduation from the Law School in 1898, to enter his own law firm. Three years later Stone was made a partner in the firm Satterlee, Canfield, and Stone. Since Satterlee was a son-in-law of the elder J. Pierpont Morgan, Stone thus acquired "the Wall Street taint," which later aroused the fighting temper of my friend, Senator George W. Norris.

But Stone was no mere practicing lawyer "downtown." In 1899 he was lecturing at the Columbia Law School; in 1905 he became a full professor in the School; and in 1910 he was chosen Dean—a post which he held until 1923. As Dean of the Law School Stone dedicated generous talents to the improvement of legal instruction, carried a teaching load himself, and proved to be an efficient administrator. But he was more than efficient. He was celebrated in the University for his humanness. Any student, no matter how humble in origin, could always find in the teacher and dean a sage counsellor, never too busy to hear a recitation of troubles and to give friendly advice. And amid all these distractions, including those connected with his practice downtown, Stone found time to write articles for the *Columbia Law Review*—from which lawyers later quoted passages in efforts to prove the rightness of their cause before Stone, Justice of the Supreme Court.

In the year that Stone began to lecture in the Columbia Law School, he married Agnes Harvey, of Chesterfield, New Hampshire, the place of his birth. And his colleagues who had the good fortune of meeting Mrs. Stone, if only over teacups, soon let it be known that the teacher and dean—counsellor of students and powerful clients—had a wise and human counsellor at home. Of that, as Henry Adams once said of things in general, silence is best, at least here. But it is to be remembered, lest it be forgotten.

My acquaintance with Stone at Columbia was casual and conventional, not intimate. Yet whether I met him on the Campus or at the lunch table in the Faculty Club, I was aware that I was in the presence of talents and character. On occasions when, in the routine of university affairs, I conferred with him on academic business I found him quick to get at the essential points before us for consideration, many-sided in his way of looking at them, sparing in words, and judicial in temper, and eminently fair in judgment. I knew that in politics and jurisprudence he was reckoned a conservative—no friend of the new sociological school; but when liberty of opinion was at stake he was in favor of liberty and a judicious weighing of all the issues involved.

While Stone was dean at Columbia, the first World War came; and he was chosen by the Secretary of War, Newton D. Baker, to serve on the board of inquiry charged with the duty of examining men who claimed exemption from military service on grounds of conscientious objection to war. This was a heavy burden for him, for conscientious objectors were not popular and many people who wanted to hang the Kaiser also wanted to hang the objectors. But Stone accepted the difficult commission and gave himself without stint to the duties involved in the office. In a single sentence, he provided a clue to his operating philosophy: "Liberty of conscience has a moral and social value which makes it worthy of preservation at the hands of the State." Long afterward that sentiment entered into a dissenting opinion by Harlan F. Stone, Justice of the Supreme Court, that was within a few years to become the opinion of the Court.

It was likewise well known, at least to his friends, that Stone was strongly opposed to the "red raids" made by President Wilson's Attorney General, A. Mitchell Palmer, and to the "deportation delirium" that outraged enlightened citizens at the close of the War. In other words, he was not classed as a mere "reactionary," when his friend, President Coolidge prevailed upon him to take the post of Attorney General in 1924, amid the reeking scandals that followed the exposure of the Harding régime.

In that office, Stone dropped many "hold-overs" inherited from "The Ohio gang," abolished the prying General Intelligence Division, and dispensed with the volunteer corps of sniffers and snoopers who had aided Department officials in terrorizing citizens and aliens of unorthodox opinions for about seven years. Though he did not go as far as I then hoped he would go in "cleaning house," Stone did go far in throwing out witch-burners and restoring the supremacy of law and judicial procedure, perhaps as far as circumstances would permit. At any rate, his management of the Department showed that he stood squarely against the malevolence that marked the treatment of civil liberties under President Wilson from 1917 to 1921 and under President Harding.

When Attorney General Stone was about to launch an anti-trust suit against the Aluminum Company of America, President Coolidge suddenly nominated him to the place on the Supreme Court left vacant by the retirement of Justice Mc-Kenna. The nomination was a signal for a fight in the Senate against confirmation, with Senator George W. Norris in the

lead. It was alleged that Stone's experiences and services as
attorney for men of great wealth, such as the heirs of J. P.
Morgan, and for mammoth corporations, would prejudice him,
as a Justice, against the interests of the laboring masses in
factories and on farms. Indeed until that time, he had given
little indication to the world at large that, if confirmed, he
would not immediately and permanently associate himself, in
matters of economic and social jurisprudence, with the conservatives of the Court then under the superintendence of Chief
Justice Taft. But at the close of the debate in the Senate only
six votes were cast against Stone's appointment and he thereupon ascended the Bench, in possession of himself and facing
the future.

Justice Stone had not been long at his post when he began
to reveal opinions akin to those of his colleagues Justice Brandeis and Justice Holmes, to the surprise of former foes and the
chagrin of former clients. In fact it was said by some who had
known him for years that he had been captivated, if not captured, by Brandeis and Holmes.

On this point I venture some conjectures. Stone had slight
patience with inveterate dogmatists and it may be that en-
counters with colleagues of that type from the right wing of
the Bench helped to drive him to the other side. He had a sense
of humor and proportion that made Holmes, the wit and skep-
tic, more congenial to him than, let us say, Justice Sutherland
or Justice McReynolds. Or it may be that the New England
farmer's son had a hard-headed way of distinguishing between
abstractions and underlying facts which attracted him to Justice Brandeis' style of testing legal formulas by constant reference to pertinent and impinging realities. These I offer, not as
"explanations" of Justice Stone's "processes of thinking," but
for whatever they may be worth as relevant to the problem
posed by Mr. Konefsky.

But it may be said: "These are surmises. What can be

offered in the way of knowledge respecting the influence of
Holmes, Brandeis, and, later, Cardozo on the manner of Chief
Justice Stone's thinking?" The following relevancies may be
offered.

To a slight extent I was acquainted with Holmes and Cardozo and to a greater extent with Brandeis, and I have studied
their writings and opinions. Ties of sympathy bound this trio
together, but each was a distinct personality in his own right.
So was Stone. Undoubtedly he learned many things from
members of this little group, but he also taught them; and
whatever he learned he made it a part of himself, transmuted
it, and gave it his own cast of expression. In numerous matters
he agreed with them and was more at home with them than
with other colleagues on the Bench who could be named. He
also differed from them.

Stone worked harder at the technology of constitutional law
than did Holmes. According to report, Chief Justice Taft
declared that Holmes knew no constitutional law; and he had
a certain justification for his verdict. Holmes did not care
much about historic dicta which some of his brethren were
fond of calling constitutional law. As he once remarked to
me, he looked at the Constitution itself to see what it said on
any matter before him. On the other hand, Stone took seriously the task of studying "things that are neither true nor
relevant" for the purpose of passing an informed judgment
on them.

Unlike Brandeis, Stone did not have a holy fear of bigness.
Like Brandeis he had a zest for the facts of life surrounding
any case at law. He had that zest before he went to Washington and Brandeis probably helped to sharpen it. Neither in private discourse nor public pronouncements did Stone have
Brandeis' zeal for converting the heathen. Rather was he
inclined to leave them undisturbed unless they got into his

way and then he became interested in something more than conversion.

Who can speak of the beautiful human spirit that was Benjamin Cardozo? Not I with any assurance, so pervasive and yet unobtrusive was his presence. None could have an hour with him and go away unchanged. Stone himself could scarcely describe the consequences of his association with Cardozo. I shall certainly not venture upon it.

Speaking in the past tense of the Stone whom I encountered in old days, I can say other things out of some knowledge. Stone had a strong sense of duty; when he assumed an office, whether of teaching or administering, he sought to discharge its obligations with all his strength of mind and talents. He explored its responsibilities and fulfilled them, it always seemed, to the best of his ability. Stone had dignity, but not too much. He had perspective, refused to make mountains out of mole hills, and kept his head when little men around him went into great frenzies over passing alarms. He was not witty; but he had wit and used it with effects all the more devastating for the reason that he employed it sparingly and with deadly precision. He had the independence of the freehold farmer who, as Jefferson said, could look to the sun in heaven, the soil at his feet, and the labor of his own hands for his sustenance; but it was independence tempered by a keen awareness of social obligations, small and great. He listened to others with courteous interest, often took advice, and often went his own way after hearing it. Above all, to use a sentence that I once heard fall from the lips of Holmes speaking of himself, Stone never imagined himself to be God.

In short, Stone was no absolutist when he was at Columbia University, long before he went to Washington. He was then aware, that, as Thomas Reed Powell once phrased it, extremes are extreme after all. Thus he was prepared to learn, despite any baggage of dogmas he may have taken with him to the Supreme Bench.

In manifestations of character such as those just depicted, I suspect, lies the answer to the question which Mr. Konefsky raises: How did Chief Justice Stone arrive at his theory of judicial review? At least in such manifestations of character are clues to the answer.

It has been said that a great man is one who first does something new in the nature of greatness. If this maxim is true, then there are few great men in history. On my part I am inclined to the opinion that a great person is one who discovers something that should long have been obvious and states it with such force and clarity, in favorable circumstances, that they who run and read are astounded and cry out "of course."

If that appears to be absurdly simple, it really isn't.

When Harlan Fiske Stone became a Justice of the Supreme Court, a time-worn fiction in respect of judicial review was in general circulation among lawyers and laymen. In effect it ran as follows: When judges declare an act of Congress unconstitutional, they really exercise no power themselves; they merely place the plain letter of the statute by the side of the plain letter of the Constitution and find that as a matter of fact the statute is in contradiction to the Constitution. Justice Owen J. Roberts presented the fiction when he said, in *United States* v. *Butler*, 297 U.S. 1, that the Court has "no *power* to overrule or control the action of the people's representatives" and has "*only one duty*,—to lay the article of the Constitution which is invoked *beside* the statute which is challenged and to decide whether the latter *squares* with the former." (Italics supplied). Presto! It's as artless as that!

Justice Stone thought that the operation in question could not be so simply and exactly described in physical and mathematical terms. In his dissenting opinion he viewed the act of judicial review as an intellectual and moral operation performed by human beings, and he considered it in human terms. He accepted the maxim that "unconstitutional exercise of power by the executive and legislative branches of the government is subject to judicial restraints"; but, with a frankness that was alarming to keepers of the old fiction, he stated that the courts, as well as Congress, "unhappily may falter or be mistaken in the performance of their constitutional duty." In short, he looked upon himself and his colleagues, not as carpenters and joiners engaged in laying things side by side and "squaring" them, but as human beings engaged in the business of thinking, deciding, and exercising power. Then he added the words: "The only check upon our own exercise of power is our own sense of self-restraint."

Lest some of his brethren might miss the moral of the point, Justice Stone, after reminding them that judges are human and may err, warned them against the peril of extremes: "Interpretation of our great charter of government which proceeds on any assumption that the responsibility for the preservation of our institutions is the exclusive concern of any one of the three branches of government, or that it alone can save them from destruction is far more likely, in the long run, 'to obliterate the constituent members' of 'an indestructible union of indestructible states' than the frank recognition that language, even of a constitution, may mean what it says. . . ."

On re-reading the Chief Justice's warning to executives, legislators, and judges against going too far in the exercise of sheer power, I cannot help recalling the famous dictum of an American wit on the downfall of Napoleon the Great: He tried to do too much and did it.

Nothing in his warning note was new to the thought of Justice Stone. As long before as 1928 he had said to the American Bar Association, in speaking of the Supreme Court: "Those who bear its responsibilities now and in the future will do well . . . to recall . . . that in the course of its long history the only wounds from which it has suffered have been those which, in the words of former Justice Hughes, were 'self-inflicted.' " Then, as again in 1936, Justice Stone revealed the quality of his prescience: in 1937 a storm broke over the Supreme Court. Loose and frivolous thinkers laid all the blame for that cataclysm on President Roosevelt; but, Justice Stone having given voice to fair warning, did not forget that the responsibility for the crisis was, at least, divisible.

In the economy of things, it so befell that Harlan F. Stone became Chief Justice of the United States at a time of still greater crisis, when constitutional government and the liberties of citizens as against the State are challenged by sheer and absolute power, in wide spaces of the earth. But I am convinced that in this high office he will discharge the duties of the trust vested in him, without fear, to the uttermost, come what may.

CHARLES A. BEARD

New Milford, Connecticut,
Autumn of 1944.

CONTENTS

	PAGE
FOREWORD	vii
PREFATORY NOTE by Charles A. Beard	xiii

CHAPTER

I. THE TAXING POWER IN INTERGOVERNMENTAL RELATIONS

1. Introductory	1
2. Origin of the Doctrine: *McCulloch* v. *Maryland*	5
3. Mr. Justice Stone's First Exposition of the Immunity Doctrine	10
4. Tax-Exempt Securities	13
5. For a Flexible *Stare Decisis*	21
6. Emergence of New Doctrines	25
7. Significance of Recent Trends	41

II. THE COMMERCE CLAUSE AND STATE POWER

1. Nature of the Problem	48
2. State Regulations "Affecting" Foreign and Interstate Commerce	56
3. Fees for the Use of State Facilities and Services	65
4. Privilege or Occupation Taxes	75
5. Challenge to the "Multiple Taxation" Theory	82
6. Summary and Conclusions	91

III. SCOPE OF FEDERAL POWER

| 1. Federal Spending and the Constitution | 98 |
| 2. Federal Power over Industrial Conditions | 119 |

CHAPTER   PAGE

IV. RESTRAINING THE ADMINISTRATIVE PROCESS

    1. Relationship of Court and Agency   136
    2. Allowable Delegation   140
    3. Some Aspects of Administrative Procedure   145

V. "CENSORING" STATE REGULATION OF ECONOMIC ACTIVITIES

    1. Introductory   160
    2. Price Fixing—Regulation of Business "Affected with a Public Interest"   165
    3. Minimum Wages for Women   175
    4. The States and Economic Security   183

VI. SAFEGUARDING CIVIL LIBERTIES

    1. Property Rights versus Civil Liberties   193
    2. Protecting the Political Process   196
    3. Guardian of Liberty: Court or Legislature   215
    4. Civil-Military Relations   235

VII. CONCLUDING: AN ENLIGHTENED VIEW OF THE JUDICIAL FUNCTION   255

TABLE OF CASES   277

INDEX   285

CHIEF JUSTICE STONE

AND THE

SUPREME COURT

CHAPTER I

THE TAXING POWER IN INTERGOVERNMENTAL RELATIONS

1. *Introductory*

As A PRODUCT of experience and compelling needs, the establishment of the American Union might have been expected to suffer the least from the defects of the political blueprint. But federalism has been more than a theory of governmental organization. It has vitally affected the process of government in the United States in all of its most practical manifestations. As a factor in our social politics it has colored many of the crucial issues which have divided the American people.

"The most striking and pervading characteristic of the political system of the country," observed the late Lord Bryce, "[is] the existence of a double government, a double allegiance, a double patriotism." [1] The effort to maintain this dual system of government has given the world its most successful experiment with divided sovereignty.[2] Under federalism the power to govern "men and things" is shared by two governments, both operating in the same territory and on the same individuals, although in relation to different spheres of action. The practical operation of this essentially cooperative enter-

[1] James Bryce, *The American Commonwealth* (New York: Macmillan, rev. ed., 1922), I, 15.
[2] "In America, the powers of sovereignty are divided between the government of the Union and those of the States. They are each sovereign, with respect to the objects committed to it, and neither sovereign with respect to the objects committed to the other." Chief Justice Marshall in *McCulloch v. Maryland,* 4 Wheat. 316, 410 (1819).

prise calls for amicable relations between the partners. Machinery must be provided for harmonizing and bringing them into orderly relations. Yet not even the reduction of the fundamentals of their relationship to the terms of a written constitution can possibly avoid jurisdictional disputes. This much we can gather not only from our own experience but also from the history of other federated states. It is, therefore, vital to keep open the channels for peaceful adjustment of conflicts.[3] Sharper appreciation of this need might have forestalled the decision in the famous DRED SCOTT case,[4] a decision which, by making difficult, if not impossible, a congressional solution of the slavery issue, may have helped to push the country to the arbitrament of war.

More significant, however, than its failure to avert our major constitutional crisis is the strategic position which the United States Supreme Court has occupied as the umpire of our federal system. How indispensable has been this role of the Court?

Writing in 1913, Oliver Wendell Holmes professed to see in this function the *raison d'être* for the tribunal.

I do not think the United States would come to an end if we lost our power to declare acts of Congress void. I do think the Union would be imperiled if we could not make that declaration as to the laws of the several states. For one in my place sees how often a local policy prevails with those who are not trained to national views and how often action is taken that embodies what the commerce clause was meant to end.[5]

[3] It may be in order to recall the trenchant words of Chief Justice Marshall. Speaking of the problem raised by the "conflicting powers of the government of the Union and of its members," the Chief Justice warned that that question "must be decided peacefully, or remain a source of hostile legislation, perhaps of hostility of a still more serious nature; and if it is to be so decided, by this tribunal alone can the decision be made. On the Supreme Court of the United States has the Constitution of our country devolved this important duty." *Ibid.*, pp. 400–401.

[4] *Scott* v. *Sandford*, 19 How. 393 (1857).

[5] Holmes, *Collected Legal Papers* (New York: Harcourt, Brace & Co., 1921), pp. 295–96.

So far as the need for judicial review is concerned, there would thus seem to be some basis for differentiating between the power of the Supreme Court to invalidate acts of Congress and the Court's authority to pass upon the constitutionality of state legislation.[6] Still, the governmental entity we call the United States consists of both the national government and the states, and the survival of the Union depends on the existence of its parts. As Professor Corwin has observed: "At one time, the Constitution has been interpreted from the point of view of the desire for national unity, at another time from that of the desire for local autonomy."[7] Whatever the special emphasis, the Supreme Court has not hesitated to proclaim itself as the guardian of our federalism. Whether by intention of the framers or not, the adjustment of conflicting national and state claims has been one of the historic functions of the high court. And in the case of clauses couched in such general terms as are the Constitutional foundations of American federalism, much has depended upon the basic preconceptions with which the responsibility of interpreting the Constitution has been approached.[8]

Confronted by this necessity to construct the legal props by means of which the federal equilibrium was to continue to function as a workable system, the Justices of the Supreme Court

[6] *Marbury* v. *Madison,* 1 Cr. 137 (1803), has been the law of the land for more than one hundred and forty years. But Beveridge for one regarded the Supreme Court's power which was enunciated in that historic case as purely fortuitous. "But for *Marbury* v. *Madison,* the power of the Supreme Court to annul acts of Congress probably would not have been insisted upon thereafter," and his reason for thinking so was that "nearly 70 years would have passed without any question arising as to the omnipotence of Congress." Albert J. Beveridge, *The Life of John Marshall* (Boston: Houghton Mifflin, 1916–1919), III, 131.

[7] Edward S. Corwin, *The Constitution and What It Means Today.* (Princeton: Princeton Univ. Press, 1930), p. xxiv.

[8] In his little book on Mr. Justice Holmes, Felix Frankfurter has indicated the following as some of the factors which condition the judge's application of the federal idea:

"It makes all the difference how deeply one cares for assuring a free

have devised formal rules intended to serve as legal accommodations for a complicated structure. "Federalism means legalism," wrote Dicey;[9] and in the case of the American federal
system, this legalism has been accentuated by the prerogative
which the country's Court of last resort early claimed for itself—that of furnishing the solution for the system's frictions.

The result has been a process of judicial constitution-mak-
ing. In this process the Court has not infrequently applied
principles of an earlier day which were no longer tenable. As
the prevailing economic, social, and even political conditions
which have helped to shape the legal conceptions undergo
change, the abstractions themselves begin to lose their original
utility.[10] They must somehow be adapted to the needs of the

market throughout the country, or how discerningly one sees the economic
interrelationships upon which the attainment of such a market depends.
It makes all the difference how truly one cares that the states have the
amplest opportunity for local development as to matters clearly beyond
the legal powers of the nation. In sitting in judgment upon the attempts
of others to meet the perplexities of society, it makes all the difference
how aware one is of the complexity of modern economic problems and the
organic relation of abstractly unrelated transactions. In this as in other
vital phases of constitutional interpretation, the determining factors are
the judge's underlying conception of the Constitution and his awareness
of the psychological problems presented when he sits in judgment upon
the judgment of legislatures on issues outside the domain of logical demonstration." *Mr. Justice Holmes and the Supreme Court.* (Cambridge:
Harvard Univ. Press, 1938), pp. 74–75.

9 "Federalism, lastly, means legalism—the predominance of the judiciary in the Constitution—the prevalence of a spirit of legality among
the people.

"That in a confederation like the United States the courts become the
pivot on which the constitutional arrangements of the country turn is
obvious. . . . The Bench therefore can and must determine the limits of
the authority both of the government and of the legislature; their decision is without appeal; the consequence follows that the Bench of judges
is not only the guardian but also at a given moment the master of the
Constitution." A. V. Dicey, *The Law of the Constitution* (London: Macmillan, 4th ed., 1885), pp. 170–71.

10 Thus it would be a mistake to overlook the vital connection between
Marshall's nationalistic interpretation of the Constitution and the political
atmosphere of the years during which he presided over the Court. "Strict"
construction versus "loose" construction was the burning issue dividing
the parties. There was the controversy over the Bank of the United States

changed conditions if the new issues are to be solved in keeping with the realities of the new situation. Yet the very nature of the judicial process resists rapid changes in prevailing rules. Deference for precedent is but one of its inflexible elements.

Fortunately for the vitality of our federalism, however, some of the rigid categories that have resulted from this process of balancing the conflicting claims of the federal government and the states have been challenged from time to time by some of the Court's own members. Foremost among the judges of our own day striving to revitalize constitutional doctrines has been the present Chief Justice. From the beginning of his judicial career, Harlan Fiske Stone has sought to release the discussion of constitutional issues from the weight of legal formalism and to substitute in its place more realistic criteria. The infusion of legal abstractions into the interpretation of the Constitution has inspired some of his most vigorous protests against the use of conventional methods in the disposition of constitutional questions. Small wonder, then, that that composite of constitutional absolutes known as the immunity doctrine should have served as a natural target for his critical analysis.

2. *Origin of the Doctrine: McCulloch* v. *Maryland*

As a constitutional doctrine, the immunity of governmental instrumentalities from taxation began with the decision in *McCulloch* v. *Maryland*. The case was an aftermath of the financial upheaval following the War of 1812, and was the occasion for Marshall's ablest exposition of the nature of our Union.

which had split political forces from the beginning. The nation and the states were looked upon as hostile sovereignties. The reconciliation of their opposing claims in favor of national supremacy was considered by Marshall to be the only way in which the disintegration of the Union could be averted. The conflicts between the national and state governments were not to be allowed to ripen into causes of civil strife. All these issues form the dramatic background to *McCulloch* v. *Maryland,* and how keenly aware Marshall was of their ominous presence can be gathered from the opening words of his opinion, cited above, *n.* 3.

The Maryland tax which it invalidated was typical of the hostile action which other states also were directing against the National Bank.[11] Marshall chose to ignore the obvious fact that the Maryland law clearly discriminated against the Baltimore branch of the bank,[12] and rested the invalidation of the tax entirely upon the broader doctrine of the total want of power in the states to tax the operations of "an instrument employed by the government of the Union to carry its powers into execution."[13] In coming to this sweeping conclusion, he thought he had developed a simple formula for solving a difficult problem.[14]

The problem stemmed from one of the intrinsic sources of friction under federalism, the existence of concurrent powers. Both the federal government and the states possessed the power to tax, and inevitably the question would arise whether one government could exert that power against the instrumentali-

[11] This financial upheaval and its repercussions in the states are fully described by Beveridge, *op. cit.*, IV, ch. 4.

[12] It will be recalled that the tax was to be paid by institutions not chartered by the state. The Baltimore branch of the National Bank was the only institution not so chartered. Its authority stemmed from the charter granted by Congress.

[13] In later years the Supreme Court held that state taxes upon federal instrumentalities were invalid, even when not discriminatory. *Weston* v. *City of Charleston*, 2 Pet. 449 (1829), and *Dobbins* v. *Erie County*, 16 Pet. 435 (1842).

[14] It has become so customary to depict Marshall's opinion in *McCulloch* v. *Maryland* as composed entirely of sweeping generalizations, that it is sometimes forgotten that he actually noted certain exceptions to the principle of tax immunity which he was announcing. Thus he wrote:

"This opinion does not deprive the states of any resources which they originally possessed. It does not extend to a tax paid by the real property of the bank, in common with the other real property within the state, nor to a tax imposed on the interest which the citizens of Maryland may hold in this institution, in common with other property of the same description throughout the state. But this is a tax [the Maryland tax] on the operations of the bank, and is, consequently, a tax on the operation of an instrument employed by the government of the Union to carry its powers into execution. Such a tax must be unconstitutional." 4 Wheat. 316, 436-37 (1819).

ties of the other. If the freedom of the National Bank from interference by the states had been Marshall's sole concern, he might have limited his inquiry to the effect of the particular tax. Such was not his purpose; he was seeking principles capable of wider application. This search led the great exponent of implied powers to draw from the Constitution an implied limitation of far reaching importance. By holding that the immunity of federal institutions from taxation by the states was to be inferred from the very nature of our federal system, Marshall in effect placed this implied limitation alongside the specific prohibitions which the Constitution imposes on the states. The character of the resulting immunity doctrine merits further examination.

Marshall did not undertake any exhaustive economic analysis of the degree and effect of the tax. In this he heeded the advice of counsel for the Bank.[15] Both Webster and Pinckney were careful not to limit their assault on the Maryland tax to its consequences for the fiscal policy of the federal government. They argued that "there must be . . . an implied exception to the general taxing power of the states," and that the Supreme Court was not equipped to determine "what is an abuse and what is a legitimate use of the power." Pinckney wanted to know by what means the Court could "ascertain *a priori* that a given amount of tax will crush the Bank." He went on to say:

It is essentially a question of political economy, and there are always a vast variety of facts bearing upon it. The facts may be mistaken. Some important considerations belonging to the subject

[15] With all his reverence for Marshall, Beveridge makes it quite clear that some of the most quoted language in the opinion in *McCulloch* v. *Maryland* was lifted verbatim from the arguments of Webster and Pinckney. Thus he says: "To reproduce his [Pinckney's] address is to set out in advance the opinion of John Marshall stripped of Pinckney's rhetoric which, in that day, was deemed to be the perfection of eloquence." Beveridge, *op. cit.,* IV, 287.

may be kept out of sight. They must all vary with times and circumstances.

A reading of Chief Justice Marshall's historic opinion will reveal how fully he adopted these views of counsel.[16] Thus he said:

> If we measure the power of taxation residing in a state by the extent of sovereignty which the people of a single state possess, and can confer on its government, we have an intelligible standard applicable to every case to which the power may be applied. . . . We are not driven to the perplexing inquiry, so unfit for the judicial department, what degree of taxation is the legitimate use and what degree may amount to the abuse of the power.

Marshall agreed with Pinckney that the judiciary was not equipped for the consideration of "questions of political economy." Thereby, he rejected the use of the fact inquiry in the determination of constitutional issues. Starting with the assumption that "the power to tax involves the power to destroy," he concluded that the Maryland tax must fall because there was "a total failure" of power in the states to tax the operations of federal instrumentalities.[17] Accordingly, the facts re-

---

[16] This is not to suggest that Marshall lacked his own convictions on the issues raised by the pleadings. On the contrary, there is some evidence to show that much of the opinion (delivered by Marshall only three days after the oral arguments had come to a close) had been prepared before the case was argued. For further speculation on this point, see Beveridge, *op. cit.*, IV, 290.

[17] As a statement of political theory, this logic was inherent in Marshall's conception of the nature of sovereignty in the United States. The national government, as sovereign, was beyond the reach of the powers of the states, according to Marshall. Its institutions, he stated, were "constructively without the local territorial jurisdiction, of the individual states." Add to this theory Marshall's view of the taxing power as a potential weapon of destruction, and his conclusion was almost inescapable. That conclusion, from the long range point of view, was intended to deprive the states of any power to interfere with or frustrate valid federal functions: "If the States may tax . . . any and every other instrument, they . . . may tax all the means employed by the government, to an excess which would defeat all the ends of government. This was not intended by the American people. They did not design to make their gov-

lating to the effect of the tax in question were deemed to be irrelevant, since the economic consequences were immaterial to its constitutionality.

Up to 1870, the immunity of governmental instrumentalities was actually a one-sided principle, applicable only to the national government. In that year the Supreme Court began to expand the immunity doctrine in its reciprocal form to exempt state instrumentalities from federal taxation. In his opinion for the Court in *Collector* v. *Day*,[18] Justice Nelson relied mainly on *McCulloch* v. *Maryland* and *Dobbins* v. *Erie County*. He asked:

. . . if the means and instrumentalities employed by that government [federal] to carry into operation the power granted to it are necessarily, and, for the sake of self-preservation, exempt from taxation by the States, why are not those of the States depending upon their reserved powers for like reasons, equally exempt from Federal taxation?

This he answered by saying that state instrumentalities would henceforth be "equally exempt from Federal taxation." The majority justified carrying over the doctrine of immunity to the states with the argument that the Court's responsibility was also to maintain the separate existence of the states. It thus disregarded the important distinction drawn by Marshall in *McCulloch* v. *Maryland* between federal taxation of state instrumentalities and state taxation of federal instrumentalities. Marshall had said:

The people of all the states have created the general government, and have conferred upon it the general power of taxation. The

ernment dependent on the states." 4 Wheat. 316, 432 (1819). It was by this line of reasoning that the Court in later years classified as federal instrumentalities, and hence exempt from state taxation, United States securities, *Weston* v. *Charleston*, 2 Pet. 449 (1829), and the salaries of federal officials, *Dobbins* v. *Erie County*, 16 Pet. 435 (1842).

18 11 Wall. 113, 127 (1870).

people of all the States, and the States themselves, are represented in Congress, and, by their representatives, exercise this power. When they tax the chartered institutions of the states, they tax their constituents; and these taxes must be uniform. But, when a state taxes the operations of the government of the United States, it acts upon institutions created, not by their own constituents, but by people over whom they claim no control. It acts upon measures of a government created by others as well as themselves, for the benefit of others in common with themselves. The difference is that which always exists, and always must exist, between the action of the whole on a part, and the action of a part on the whole—between the laws of a government declared to be supreme, and those of a government which, when in opposition to those laws, is not supreme.[19]

Although Marshall's interpretations of the Constitution were not devoid of economic motive, he cast them in a form which seemingly rejected the consideration of economics in the solution of constitutional problems. Adjudication in the light of actual conditions, on the other hand, is what distinguishes the methods of the present Chief Justice from Marshall's. It is this approach which has characterized the dominant part he has played in the reconsideration and modification of the immunity doctrine recently undertaken by the Supreme Court. His opinions reveal a fundamental divergence from Marshall's method in *McCulloch* v. *Maryland*.

3. *Mr. Justice Stone's First Exposition of the Immunity Doctrine*

Less than a year after coming to the Court, Mr. Justice Stone ventured to advocate the use of the more penetrating factual analysis in the decision of constitutional questions. The

---

[19] 4 Wheat. 316, 435-36 (1819). For a discussion of Mr. Justice Stone's resurrection of these distinctions as well as Bradley's dissent from Nelson's opinion, see below, pp. 30, 34n., 52.

occasion was his first opinion in a case dealing with the tax immunity of governmental instrumentalities.[20]

This case came to the Court as an appeal against the assessment under the War Revenue Act of 1917 of a tax on the net income of consulting engineers working for states and their political subdivisions.[21] Metcalf and Eddy objected to the tax on that portion of their income which they had received as compensation for their services, rendered under contracts, in connection with water supply and sewage disposal projects. These services, they claimed, made of them state instrumentalities exempt from federal taxation. They denied that the fact that their services had been secured by contract, rather than by election or appointment, in any way affected their status as governmental instrumentalities.

After finding that the facts seemed to show that Metcalf and Eddy were independent contractors,[22] Mr. Justice Stone turned to the main question in the case: Did Congress have the constitutional power to levy the tax? He did not answer this question until he had fully delineated the attitude which should govern the Court's application of the immunity doctrine. The test of the constitutionality of the tax should be, he said,

whether its effect is such as to bring it within the purview of those decisions holding that the very nature of our constitutional system of dual sovereign governments is such as impliedly to prohibit the federal government from taxing the instrumentalities of a state government, and in a similar manner to limit the power of the states to tax the instrumentalities of the federal government.

20 *Metcalf and Eddy* v. *Mitchell,* 269 U.S. 524 (1926).

21 The War Revenue Act provided for the assessment of a tax on net income; but paragraph 201(a) listed the following exemptions: "(a) in the case of officers and employees under the United States, or any state, territory or the District of Columbia, or any local subdivisions thereof, the compensation or fees received by them as such officers or employees."

22 The Court concluded that Metcalf and Eddy had "failed to sustain the burden cast upon them of establishing" that they were officers or employees within the meaning of par. 201(a) of the War Revenue Act of 1917.

His basic premise is that the question as to which agencies of a state or the federal government are immune from taxation by the other cannot be determined "in terms of universal application." It was true that the Court had uniformly held that instrumentalities through which either government "immediately and directly exercises its sovereign powers" were exempt from taxation by the other. But the mere circumstance that a person was using his property or receiving compensation through his dealings with the federal government or a state did not make him immune from the taxing power of the other government. Such business relations did not automatically transform the individual or his property into an instrumentality of government within the meaning of the immunity doctrine.

Neither was there any formula for determining "with precision in advance" which activities having some relation to government are subject to taxation and which are immune. Nevertheless, one important guide to decision was available. The whole occasion for the rule was the need to protect each government from undue encroachments by the other, and this, its primary purpose, should remain the "guiding principle" in its application. But enforcement of the rule does not require the Court to ignore economic realities. What is important is that one government be prevented from destroying the other or curtailing "in any substantial manner" the exercise of its powers. And this can be accomplished if the effect of the tax is ascertained by the correct standard:

. . . the limitation upon the taxing power of each, and so far as it affects the other, must receive a practical construction which permits both to function with the minimum of interference each with the other; and that limitation cannot be so varied and extended as seriously to impair either the taxing power of the government imposing the tax . . . or the appropriate exercise of the functions of the government affected by it.

In passing on questions of immunity raised by persons having business dealings with government, the Court should grant or withhold the exemption, depending upon the actual effect of the tax on the activities of the government alleged to be unduly burdened.[23] With the aid of this pragmatic test Mr. Justice Stone concluded that the consulting engineers were not entitled to the tax exemption for which they asked.

One who is not an officer or employee of a state does not establish exemption from federal income tax merely by showing that his income was received as compensation for services rendered under a contract with the state; and when we . . . inquire into the effect of the particular tax, on the functioning of the state government, we do not find that it impairs in any substantial manner the ability of plaintiffs in error to discharge their obligation to the state or the ability of a state or its subdivisions to procure the services of private individuals to aid them in their undertakings.[24]

4. *Tax-Exempt Securities*

Since his opinion in this early case, Mr. Justice Stone's exposition of the immunity doctrine has run a consistent course. In 1926 he spoke for an undivided Court. The dissensions which soon developed make it clear that this first opinion is significant more for its revelation of his own approach to

[23] Prevailing theory regarded agencies through which either government "directly and immediately" carried out its sovereign power as completely immune from taxation by the other. Such an instrumentality as well as the income derived from it were fully protected. At this stage in his discussion of the immunity doctrine (1926) Mr. Justice Stone evidently subscribed to these views, although he thought that the character of the agency and the manner of its creation should be considered.

[24] In this case Mr. Justice Stone spoke for a unanimous Court. Yet as recently as 1937, four Justices dissented in an opinion by Mr. Justice Roberts from the application of these principles to independent contractors employed by the federal government. Chief Justice Hughes, as spokesman for the majority, which included Mr. Justice Stone, had held that a state was free to impose a non-discriminatory tax on gross incomes derived from contracts with the United States government. *James* v. *Dravo Contracting Co.*, 302 U.S. 134, 161 (1937).

constitutional problems than for any radically new conception to which it might have committed the Court. To judge from subsequent alignments in the Court, it would seem that some of the Justices were voting for the specific result reached in *Metcalf* v. *Mitchell* rather than accepting for future use the criteria set forth by Mr. Justice Stone. Moreover, in the MACALLEN case,[25] decided only three years later, Mr. Justice Stone found himself dissenting from a decision in which he thought the Court was actually taking a step backward.

From the standpoint of an equitable tax system, tax exemption for securities was probably the most undesirable consequence of the immunity doctrine. But the full force of the exemption has been escaped by a series of important exceptions. The Supreme Court has for a long time tolerated a great variety of "privilege" taxes measured in part by tax-exempt securities.[26]

The particular corporation franchise tax invalidated in the MACALLEN case required the inclusion of interest from national and state bonds in measuring the tax. Massachusetts had previously exempted income from such securities. It then changed its corporation law to apply to all income. As a result, the excise tax paid by the Macallen Company was meas-

[25] *Macallen Co.* v. *Massachusetts,* 279 U.S. 620, 634 (1929).

[26] As early as 1889, the Supreme Court had sustained a state corporate franchise tax measured by the capital stock, although part of the stock consisted of United States bonds. The Court pointed out that the tax was not on the bonds but on the privilege of conducting business in the corporate form. *Home Insurance Co.* v. *New York,* 134 U.S. 594 (1889). The Court has also held that a state may tax a bequest to the United States and even a bequest to the United States which consists entirely of United States bonds, for the reason that the tax was on the exercise of the privilege of transmitting property. *United States* v. *Perkins,* 163 U.S. 625 (1896). And in deciding in 1922 in an opinion by Mr. Justice Brandeis that Congress might include municipal bonds in computing the tax on the property or estate of a decedent, the Court justified its apparent deviation from the immunity doctrine by ruling that Congress was not taxing the property itself but the privilege of transmitting it. *Greiner* v. *Lewellyn,* 258 U.S. 384 (1922).

ured by its entire net earnings for the preceding year, including income derived from federal and state tax-exempt securities.

Justice Sutherland, speaking for the majority, professed to see in the Massachusetts law, as amended, an effort on the part of the state to escape the limitation on its taxing power imposed by the immunity principle. Regardless of the form it took, the whole legislative history of the amendment to the Massachusetts corporation law showed that its intent was to reach income from securities constitutionally immune from state taxation. Mr. Justice Stone, on the other hand, could discover no such "sinister purpose." According to him, the Commonwealth of Massachusetts was not discriminating against the obligations of the United States, since the income sought to be taxed was derived not only from federal bonds but also from its own securities, which formerly had been tax exempt. Furthermore, its action presented no new issue for the Court, and was in fact justified by the Court's own acceptance for more than seventy years of similar state and federal privilege taxes. The greater part of Mr. Justice Stone's dissent was devoted to a review of the cases which he regarded as having settled this question for the Court. The Court was now upsetting a well-established principle without assigning any cogent reasons. He argued that "only considerations of public policy" would justify departure from precedent, but no such attenuating circumstances had been pleaded. There was no indication that the rule on which the Massachusetts legislature was relying had in any "practical way" impaired "either the dignity or credit of the national government."

In the view of Mr. Justice Stone, the Sutherland opinion not only frustrated a policy which had its basis in "principle and authority" but also represented a dangerous deviation from the practical application of the immunity principle. Justice Sutherland, too, had argued that the Court's decision was not reached by a merely formal construction of the immunity doctrine. "Neither state courts nor legislatures by giving the tax a particular name, or by using some form of words," he maintained, can deprive the Court of its "duty to consider its nature and effect." Each Justice insisted that his construction was dictated by the realities of the situation; each claimed he had tested the legislation by its effects; each, in his own way, was adhering to the pragmatic criteria to which the Court seemed to be committed at this time. But their agreement on method did not bring them to the same conclusions. What accounts for the difference in results? The answer to this question will cast some light on the nature of constitutional interpretation itself.

The disagreement between the majority and the minority in the MACALLEN case was the outcome of their diverse views on social policy. Fundamentally, that is to say, they differed over the desirability of the particular type of tax program in question. Mr. Justice Stone examined the legislative background of the tax and found that its purpose was to prevent evasion of legitimate tax burdens. He looked at the history of similar forms of taxation, which had been allowed for more than half a century, and found that they had not unduly interfered with public borrowing. On the basis of this record he felt that the Court's use of the immunity doctrine was not justified by the needs of the situation. To the majority, this view of its function was a misconception. The motive, however disguised, was to reach otherwise tax-free federal securities. Accordingly, this effect of the tax, and not its form, was to be the decisive element in the application of the immunity doctrine.[27] Manifestly, both agreed on the necessity of estimating taxes by their practical results. Unlike the majority spokes-

[27] In a series of illuminating articles, Professor Thomas Reed Powell has fully vindicated the position taken by Mr. Justice Stone. See his "The Macallen Case—and Before," *8 National Income Tax Magazine*, 47; "The Macallen Case—and Beyond," *8 ibid.*, 91 (1930); "An Imaginary Judicial Opinion," *44 Harv. L. Rev.*, 889 (1931).

man, Mr. Justice Stone was not willing to exert the judicial veto unless he were satisfied that the activity said to be curtailed—the marketing of federal securities—needed its protection. Taxation was a matter of degree, and any "reasonably practical application" of the immunity doctrine must flow from that consideration.[28] So judged, it was clear that Massachusetts had not gone too far.

Less than two years later, Justices Stone and Sutherland were again debating the same issue, except that this time Mr. Justice Stone was speaking for the majority and Mr. Justice Sutherland was dissenting. The occasion was the Court's decision in *Educational Films Corporation of America* v. *Ward.*[29]

New York State had imposed a franchise tax on all corporations, the tax to be measured by their entire net income. In computing the tax to be paid by the Educational Films Corporation, the State Tax Commission had included royalties received by the company from its licensing of motion picture

---

[28] A similar view was expressed by Mr. Justice Holmes the year before, dissenting in *Panhandle Oil Co.* v. *Mississippi,* 277 U.S. 218, 222 (1928). Dividing five to four, the Supreme Court in an opinion by Justice Butler had invalidated a state gasoline tax collected on gasoline sold to the United States government for the use of a veterans' hospital and the Coast Guard. According to the majority, the tax was a burden upon the "transactions by which the United States secures the things desired for its governmental purposes," and was therefore a tax on the United States itself. Justice Holmes called attention to the historically important fact that legal rules were no longer regarded in the same light as they were in Marshall's time:

"In those days it was not recognized as it is today that most of the distinctions of the law are distinctions of degree. If the states had any power it was assumed that they had all power, and that the necessary alternative was to deny it altogether. But this Court which has so often defeated the attempt to tax in certain ways can defeat an attempt to discriminate and otherwise go too far without wholly abolishing the power to tax." P. 223.

It was in this case that Justice Holmes expressed the confident belief that "The power to tax is not the power to destroy while this Court sits." This would seem to be the perfect answer to those who would use the immunity doctrine as an absolute standard of prohibition. Mr. Justice Stone concurred in this dissent as did also Mr. Justice Brandeis.

[29] 282 U.S. 379, 394 (1931).

films on which it owned the copyrights. Opposing the inclusion of the royalties in the measure of the tax, the company contended that the state was in effect taxing federal instrumentalities.[30]

Distinguishing the New York statute from the law involved in the MACALLEN case, Mr. Justice Stone said for the Court that the inclusion of royalties in the measure of the tax was not forbidden by the rule that the instrumentalities of government may not be taxed. He pointed out that there was nothing to show that the New York State legislature intended to include royalties in the measure of the franchise tax. The inclusion of the income from the copyrights was "the result of the application of the general language of the statute to particular circumstances to which the statute makes no specific reference." This distinction would seem to be purely technical. Since the result reached by Mr. Justice Stone in 1931 is clearly the reverse of the conclusion announced in the MAC-ALLEN case, it is legitimate to consider the later decision as overruling the earlier one, although the Court did not expressly so state.

To avoid a "mechanical application" of the immunity principle, Mr. Justice Stone insisted, the Court must give primary consideration to the need which gave rise to the principle. It was to serve as a constitutional weapon for safeguarding each

[30] By a five to four decision, the Supreme Court ruled in 1928 that it was unconstitutional for a state to tax royalties received from a patent granted by the federal government. Citing *McCulloch* v. *Maryland* as precedent—Marshall had listed patent rights as an example of federal instrumentalities—Mr. Justice McReynolds expressed the view that taxing the royalties from federal patents would interfere with the power of the federal government to promote science and invention by issuing patents and copyrights. *Long* v. *Rockwood,* 277 U.S. 142, 148 (1928).

Justice Holmes wrote a dissenting opinion in which he was speaking also for Justices Stone, Brandeis, and Sutherland. He stressed two points. First, persons who apply to the federal government for patents do so for their own private gain, and not because they are thereby rendering a service to the government. Hence, the patent is in no sense an instrumentality of the federal government. Secondly, since the state maintains

government against "undue interference" with its functions by the other. In order to remain true to the basic intent of the rule, the Court need not ignore the "consequences to the operations of government." Mr. Justice Stone continued:

Having in mind the end sought we cannot say that the rule applied by this Court for some seventy years, that a non-discriminatory tax upon corporate franchises is valid, notwithstanding the inclusion of tax-exempt property or income in the measure of it, has failed of its purpose, or has worked so badly as to require a departure from it now, or that the present tax, viewed in the light of actualities, imposes any such real or direct burden on the federal government as to call for the application of a different rule.

The dissenting Justices took a different view.[31] Their spokesman, Justice Sutherland, it will be recalled, had joined Justice Holmes in dissenting in *Long* v. *Rockwood* against the classification of patents as federal instrumentalities. His objection to the enlargement of the immunity doctrine in that case did not, it would appear, inhibit him from taking a contrary position on a problem precipitated by the very decision against which he had voted in 1928. It may have been that he regarded the precedent set by the MACALLEN case of even greater constitutional significance.

Justice Sutherland pointed to the special reason which dictated a more rigorous application of the immunity rule. Today all governments are seeking new sources of revenue to finance ever increasing activities.[32] This circumstance makes it more

many of the institutions from which those who have been granted patents secure protection of their property, it is only just that they should contribute to the upkeep of the state government by paying it taxes on the royalties yielded by the patent rights. The Court has since overruled *Long* v. *Rockwood*. See *Fox Film Corporation* v. *Doyal*, 286 U.S. 123 (1932).

[31] Justices Butler and Van Devanter joined in the Sutherland dissent.

[32] For a discussion of the way in which Mr. Justice Stone uses this fact as a premise for a completely contrary conclusion, see below, p. 31.

imperative to keep the taxing power of either government within the limits which will adequately protect the other from direct burdens on its operations. He saw in the New York law a deliberate scheme for "exacting tribute" from an instrumentality of the federal government which New York was unable to reach in any other way. This the state would not be able to accomplish if the Court had applied "constitutional principles long respected and vital to the preservation of our dual system of government."

These views of Justice Sutherland remained in the minority and won no new converts on the Court. In fact, shortly after its decision in the EDUCATIONAL FILMS case, the Supreme Court gave renewed assurance that what was expressed as dissenting theory in the MACALLEN case had now become prevailing doctrine, and once again Mr. Justice Stone wrote the majority opinion.[33] The majority had definitely returned to the Court's earlier—that is, pre-MACALLEN case—view, namely, that franchise taxes were valid, even though income from tax-exempt securities had entered into their computation. But not all those who agreed with him in the matter of tax-exempt securities seemed to be aware of the full import of Mr. Justice Stone's approach to the immunity doctrine. In the early 1930's his success in winning support was partial and intermittent,

---

[33] *Pacific Co.* v. *Johnson*, 285 U.S. 480, 496 (1932). In addition to Mr. Justice Stone, Chief Justice Hughes and Justices McReynolds, Brandeis, Roberts and Cardozo constituted the majority. This case sustained the California Bank and Corporation franchise tax as applied to the income from federal securities. The Pacific Co. had acquired the bonds when the taxation of the interest from them was prohibited by express provision of the California State Constitution. California amended its constitution (November, 1928) to permit the legislature to use income from tax-exempt securities as part of the basis for computing the franchise tax. Speaking for himself and Justices Butler and Van Devanter, Justice Sutherland again dissented. He relied mainly on the decision in the MACALLEN case and protested that the majority was failing to see that the purpose of California was to accomplish by indirection what it was constitutionally forbidden to do directly—to tax the income from federal securities.

and with some, notably Justices Butler and Van Devanter, he made no headway at all.

5. *For a Flexible* Stare Decisis

Contemporaneously with its more practical application of the rule of immunity in some cases, the Supreme Court was extending the protective force of the rule in others. Mr. Justice Stone dissented against these extensions. He saw no need for expanding the area of immunity so long as the challenged action (federal or state) did not clearly burden the functioning of the other government. That it has been more difficult to convince Mr. Justice Stone of the existence of undue interference with governmental functions is clear from the cases. He has been particularly intolerant of claims to exemption set up by private taxpayers.

Mr. Justice Stone has persistently opposed any enlargement of immunity from taxation. To this end, he has not hesitated to plead for departures from cases deemed controlling. Thus in a case [34] which even Justice Holmes conceded was governed by an earlier decision,[35] Mr. Justice Stone was willing to rely on a purely formal distinction between the two cases, all with a view to removing the basis for immunity. Writing for all the members of the Court except Justices Stone and Brandeis, Mr. Justice Van Devanter had held that the excise tax sought to be collected under the Revenue Act of 1924 could not be imposed on the sale of a motorcycle to Westfield, Massachusetts, for the use of that city's police department. His opinion, like that in the PANHANDLE OIL case, stressed that the "instrumentalities, means and operations" by which the state and federal governments exercise their powers are immune from taxation. The immunity was not to be de-

[34] *Indian Motorcycle Co.* v. *United States,* 283 U.S. 570, 580 (1931).
[35] *Panhandle Oil Co.* v. *Mississippi,* 277 U.S. 218 (1928).

termined by the "amount of the particular tax or the extent of the resulting interference, but is absolute."

In a sharply worded dissent, Mr. Justice Stone took the position that viewed realistically the tax was on the seller and not on the buyer. The seller would be entitled to the exemption only if he were able to demonstrate that the tax substantially burdened the governmental function or instrumentality involved. Although the seller—the manufacturer of the motorcycle—was subject to the tax in the ordinary course of his business, he objected to the tax on the sale to Westfield on the theory that the burden of the tax would be shifted to the city. Mr. Justice Stone pointed to the lack of any proof that such would be the effect of the tax. It was more likely that the "practical effect" of the exemption granted by the Court would be "to relieve individuals from a tax, at the expense of the government imposing it, without substantial benefit to the government for whose theoretical advantage the immunity is invoked." The notion that recovery by a taxpayer in a case such as this would indirectly benefit the government with whom he had business relations was based on "speculation rather than reality." Mr. Justice Stone thought that it was rather significant that neither the federal government nor any state government had ever intervened before the Court to support such an argument for immunity. He felt that the opinion of the majority embodied an economic judgment in which not all economists would concur. For under certain conditions the burden represented by the tax might be retained by the seller, be passed back by him to the producer in the form of a lowering of the producer's price, and not necessarily or always shifted to the consumer by raising the seller's price. More important still was the fact that according to economists, the factors which make possible the shifting of the incidence of a tax are "so various and complex as to preclude the assumption *a priori* that any particular tax at any particular time is passed on." But if the Court had to come to a conclusion "unfounded in economic realities," it would have been preferable not to amplify the principle of the PANHANDLE OIL case. What was important was that the immunity rule should not be extended, and to that end even a "verbal distinction" between the two cases should have been made. The rule announced in the PANHANDLE OIL case should have been limited to taxes expressly imposed on sales.

Were it not for the overwhelming evidence to the contrary, this dissent by Mr. Justice Stone might create the impression that he has been willing to compromise with his own conception of the process by which the Court should adjudicate. In the interest of his major objective—perhaps because he knew that a complete reversal was not to be had—he made a temporary concession to formalism; but he has also sought outright reversals, especially where he found "blind adherence" to precedent was stifling sound judgment.

As early as 1932, Mr. Justice Stone pleaded with his brethren that they overturn accepted doctrine, albeit it had been announced in an opinion by Justice Holmes only ten years before. He made his plea while dissenting from the Court's invalidation of a federal tax imposed on the income of private persons from a lease on state-owned oil lands.[36] Basing its decision on the 1922 ruling,[37] the Court held that the lease was an instrumentality of the state. The state of Oklahoma was using the revenue derived from the leasing of the oil lands for educational purposes, a fact which led the Court to conclude that a tax on the lessee would in effect subject the state

[36] *Burnet* v. *Coronado Oil and Gas Co.*, 285 U.S. 393, 401 (1932). Justices Brandeis, Roberts, and Cardozo concurred in the dissent.

[37] *Gillespie* v. *Oklahoma*, 257 U.S. 501 (1922). Over the objection of Justices Brandeis, Clarke, and Pitney, Justice Holmes, for the majority, had held invalid a state tax as applied to the income from Indian Oil lands. The lessee was deemed to be an instrumentality of the United States "used by the United States in carrying out duties to the Indians."

itself to the burden of the tax. Mr. Justice Stone found this ruling inconsistent with the opinion he had himself delivered for the Court the previous year.[38] In that case it was held that income from the sale of gas and oil produced by a private company from land leased to it by the state of Texas was not exempt from federal taxation.[39] The Oklahoma leases were indistinguishable from the Texas leases, and both were identical with the lease involved in the GILLESPIE case. In all three instances the income for which the shelter of the immunity rule was sought had been earned by private concerns from their exploitation of property leased to them by government in the performance of its sovereign functions. And, since the effect on Oklahoma was no different from that on Texas, the decision in the GILLESPIE case confronted the Court with an "irreconcilable conflict in the theories upon which two of its decisions rest." There was only one way open to the Court for resolving the dilemma:

It is plain that if we place emphasis on the orderly administration of justice rather than on a blind adherence to conflicting precedents, the "Gillespie" case must be overruled. . . . No interest which could be subserved by so rigid an application of *stare decisis,* is superior to that of a system of justice based on a considered and consistent application of the Constitution of the United States.[40]

[38] Group *#1 Oil Corp.* v. *Bass,* 283 U.S. 279 (1931).

[39] The proceeds from the leasing of the lands were devoted by the state to the support of the University of Texas. Nevertheless, Mr. Justice Stone was able to say for an undivided Court: "Property which has thus passed from either the national or a state government to private ownership becomes a part of the common mass of property and subject to its common burdens. Denial to either government of the power to tax it, or income derived from it, in order to insure some remote and indirect antecedent benefit to the other, would be an encroachment on the sovereign power to tax, not justified by the implied constitutional restriction." 283 U.S. 279, 283 (1931).

[40] In his separate dissenting opinion in the BURNET case, Justice Brandeis, after reviewing some leading reversals by the Court, proceeded to indicate the motivation behind overruling decisions: "The Court bows to

6. *Emergence of New Doctrines*

By 1938, Mr. Justice Stone had already made a significant contribution to the development of the doctrine of tax immunity. That contribution was represented by his effort to bring to the process of adjudication criteria based on economic realities. The immunity from intergovernmental taxation was not to be supported by merely theoretical conceptions of interference with the functions of government. "Actual," "substantial," or "undue" burdens on the activity alleged to be affected had to be proved if the immunity were to be granted. The presumption of constitutionality was in favor of the tax and the burden of establishing its unconstitutionality was on him who claimed exemption from it.

In the cases so far cited and up to the GERHARDT case,[41] this test of "actual effects" was being applied by the Court to but one of the two principal types of situations growing out of the immunity doctrine. Its application was limited to those cases in which private persons or corporations were seeking tax exemption for income derived from their business relations with a governmental agency or enterprise. With respect to them, Mr. Justice Stone had secured general acceptance of his method, although not with uniform success, at least as judged by the results reached by some of his colleagues. All this time

the lessons of experience and the force of better reasoning, recognizing that the process of trial and error, so fruitful in the physical sciences, is appropriate also in the judicial function." And again: "The judgment of the Court in the earlier decision may have been influenced by prevailing views as to economic or social policy which have since been abandoned. In cases involving constitutional issues . . . this Court must, in order to reach sound conclusions, feel free to bring its opinions into agreement with experience and with facts newly ascertained, . . ." 285 U.S. 393 (1932), at pp. 407, 412.

In 1938 in an opinion by Chief Justice Hughes, the Supreme Court reversed *Gillespie* v. *Oklahoma* and *Burnet* v. *Coronado Oil and Gas Co.* as "out of harmony with correct principle." *Helvering* v. *Mountain Producers Corp.*, 303 U.S. 376.

[41] *Helvering* v. *Gerhardt*, 304 U.S. 405, 427 (1938).

he himself was adhering to prevailing theory in the second class of cases. Prior to 1938 taxes directly imposed by one government on the agencies, officers, employees or property of the other were deemed to be invalid interferences with the functions of that government. Mr. Justice Stone did not challenge the view that those agencies through which either government "immediately and directly exercises its sovereign powers" were governmental instrumentalities immune from taxation by the other. They and their income were to remain free from intergovernmental taxation, regardless of the degree or burden of the tax. In this second category of cases the immunity has depended on the nature of the governmental function said to be burdened.[42]

Despite his acquiescence in the distinction between these two classes of cases, there was enough in Mr. Justice Stone's basic approach to indicate that the distinction was for the most part verbal and logically insupportable. Implicit in this approach, as in that of Justice Holmes, was the possibility that even taxes bearing directly on the government itself—its agencies, officers or employees—could be weighed by the burden actually imposed. The inference appears even stronger when

[42] Thus as long ago as 1905, the Supreme Court had held valid a federal license tax on the sale of liquor by state operated dispensaries. *South Carolina* v. *United States,* 199 U.S. 437. The Court classified as "proprietary" the business engaged in by the state, to differentiate it from those "governmental" functions on the exercise of which the continued existence of the state depended. The principle of *South Carolina* v. *United States* has been applied in such recent cases as *Ohio* v. *Helvering,* 292 U.S. 360 (1934) [income from the operation of state liquor stores subject to federal tax]; and *Helvering* v. *Powers,* 293 U.S. 214 (1934) [salary of the trustee of a state-operated street railway taxable by the federal government]. But little over a year before the GERHARDT case was decided, the Court had held the operation of its water supply system by New York City to be a governmental function. Hence the salary of the Chief Engineer was deemed to be immune from federal taxation. Justices Stone and Cardozo concurred in the result on the purely technical ground that the exemption was embraced by Treasury regulations and that those regulations had not been challenged at the bar. *Brush* v. *Commissioner,* 300 U.S. 352, 374 (1937).

viewed in the light of the rationale attributed by Mr. Justice Stone to the concept of tax immunity. The developments since 1938 make it abundantly clear that he for one was not unaware of the need for a single standard of constitutionality applicable to both classes of cases. He made his initial tilt in behalf of the more consistent law in May, 1938, when he wrote the majority opinion in the GERHARDT case.

This case arose as a result of the action of the federal government in taxing the salaries of three employees of the Port of New York Authority.[43] One was a construction engineer and the other two were assistant general managers, but all had taken oaths of office. Asserting that they were employees of an agency performing governmental functions for the States of New York and New Jersey, they claimed the immunity extended to the instrumentalities of government and characterized the tax as in effect an assessment against the Port Authority. The question thus presented to the Court was "whether the imposition of a federal income tax . . . on salaries received by respondents, as employees of the Port of New York Authority, places an unconstitutional burden on the States of New York and New Jersey."

The opinion of Mr. Justice Stone is much more than a mere answer to the question raised by the litigation. It is an elaborate résumé of the Supreme Court's application of the im-

---

[43] The Port of New York Authority is a government corporation which was established in 1921 by a compact entered into by New York and New Jersey. The laws of the two states relating to the Port Authority stipulated that it "shall be regarded as performing a governmental function" in its work of developing the terminal and transportation facilities for use by the people of both states.

"The Port Authority collects tolls for the use of the bridges and tunnels, and derives income from the operation of the bus line and terminal building; but it has no stock and no stockholders, and is owned by no private persons or corporations. Its projects are all said to be operated in behalf of the two states and in the interest of the public and none of its profits inure to the benefit of private persons." (Quoted from Mr. Justice Stone's opinion in *Helvering* v. *Gerhardt*.)

munity doctrine. As a recapitulation of past events it is historically significant for its exposition of those events, and above all, for its novel interpretation of *McCulloch* v. *Maryland*. In a sense, therefore, it represents a break with past theory and adumbrates the shape of constitutional doctrines to come.

The principle of tax immunity is not required by any express language of the Constitution; it is a product of judicial inference. Heretofore, the Supreme Court had construed Marshall's opinion in *McCulloch* v. *Maryland* as having accorded the principle the status of a constitutional law doctrine, in the sense that the immunity of federal instrumentalities was made necessary by the dual system of government created by the Constitution. No one can doubt that Marshall was deeply concerned with establishing the superiority of federal over state action, but the decision in *McCulloch* v. *Maryland* was not based solely on the principle of national supremacy. What he termed the "just theory" of the "total failure" of power in the states to tax the operations of federal instrumentalities must be regarded as Marshall's chief justification for the invalidation of the Maryland tax. He rested his opinion squarely on the mandate of the Constitution.

Mr. Justice Stone, on the other hand, has advanced a view opposite to this century-old one. In his opinion in the GERHARDT case he speaks of the immunity—inferred by Marshall from the nature of our federal system—as though it had resulted from the Court's recognition of the supremacy of an Act of Congress. According to him, *McCulloch* v. *Maryland*

. . . held that Congress, having power to establish a bank by laws which, when enacted under the Constitution, are supreme, also had power to protect the bank by striking down state action impeding its operations; and it was thought that the state tax in question was so inconsistent with Congress's constitutional action in establishing the bank as to compel the conclusion that Congress intended to forbid application of the tax to the federal bank notes.

Since the agency involved in the GERHARDT case was the creature of states and not of the federal government, so new an interpretation of an old case, it may be assumed, was no mere statement of momentary judicial strategy. That he regarded his view of *McCulloch* v. *Maryland* as the correct one is clear from Mr. Justice Stone's remarks on its significance, although he relegated them to a footnote:

It follows that in considering the immunity of federal instrumentalities from state taxation two factors may be of importance which are lacking in the case of a claimed immunity of state instrumentalities from federal taxation. Since the acts of Congress within its constitutional power are supreme, the validity of state taxation of federal instrumentalities must depend (a) on the power of Congress to create the instrumentality and (b) its intent to protect it from state taxation. Congress may curtail an immunity which might otherwise be implied, . . . or enlarge it beyond the point where, Congress being silent, the Court would set its limits.

So interpreted, intergovernmental immunity may yet lose its former constitutional status. Whether or not such will be its fate, enough has happened since 1938 to suggest that the new approach is significant in at least two important respects. In the future, the immunity of federal instrumentalities may depend exclusively on the intent of Congress.[44] Congress itself

---

[44] The tax immunity to be extended to federal instrumentalities would thus be governed by the same principle which the Court applied in 1935 in answering the question whether public corporations created by the federal government were immune from state judicial process. *Federal Land Bank* v. *Priddy,* 295 U.S. 229 (1935). After pointing out that the Court had held in several previous cases that federal land banks were "instrumentalities of the federal government, engaged in the performance of important governmental functions," Mr. Justice Stone went on to say for a unanimous Court:

"So far as they [federal land banks] partake of the sovereign character of the United States, Congress has full power to determine the extent to

would be in a position to determine whether the immunity should be extended or diminished. In that event, the second and possibly the more significant result will appear. For then the United States Supreme Court will have relinquished one of the chief constitutional weapons with which it has been adjusting federal-state relations.[45] These repercussions will be examined more fully later, as the Court's pronouncements since 1938 are analyzed.

In the GERHARDT case itself, Mr. Justice Stone placed special emphasis on the much neglected distinction drawn by Marshall, the distinction between state taxation of federal instrumentalities and national taxation of institutions created by the states.[46] Paraphrasing Marshall, he wrote:

. . . in laying a federal tax on state instrumentalities the people of the states, acting through their representatives, are laying a tax on their own institutions and consequently are subject to political restraints which can be counted on to prevent abuse. State taxation of national instrumentalities is subject to no such restraint, for the people outside the state have no representatives who participate in the legislation; and in a real sense, as to them, the taxation is without representation. The exercise of the national taxing power is thus subject to a safeguard which does not operate when a state undertakes to tax a national instrumentality.

It was true that the Supreme Court had repudiated the distinction by its decision in *Collector* v. *Day*. But the more significant fact was that *Collector* v. *Day* had confined the reciprocal immunity to a state official (a probate judge) who was exercising a function in which the states engaged at the

which they may be subjected to suit and judicial process. . . . Whether federal agencies are subjected to suit and, if so, the extent to which they are amenable to judicial process, is thus a question of Congressional intent." P. 231.

[45] For a discussion of similar trends in the Court's disposition of state action affecting interstate commerce, see below, pp. 82-91, 94n., 96-97.

[46] See above, pp. 9-10.

time the Federal Constitution was launched.[47] Today, even more than before, there are compelling reasons for narrowly limiting the implied restrictions on the power of Congress to tax. When Congress taxes, the people of all the states, through their representatives, are in a position to shape federal tax policies. They are thus taxing themselves, and that fact in itself may be enough to prevent tax abuses. Access to these "processes of political action" affords the people in the states "a readier and more adaptable means than any which courts can afford, for securing accommodation of the competing demands for national revenue on the one hand, and for reasonable scope for the independence of state action on the other."

In recent decades, the states have assumed new functions which were nowhere performed by government at the time the Republic was established. Many businesses formerly operated as private enterprises, subject to federal taxation, have come to be managed by state governments. These businesses and those employed by them have demanded in the name of the states immunity from federal taxation. Mr. Justice Stone admitted that the tax burdens on those having dealings with the states may be shifted economically to the government itself, but added that the degree of the burden on the government is not "capable of precise measurement." Granting full exemption to these new forms of state activity would only result in the crippling of the national taxing power by diminishing the taxable resources available to the federal government.[48] And this condition would be so much the more deplorable, for the reason

[47] Mr. Justice Stone recalled also that in its own terms the opinion in *Collector* v. *Day* meant to protect against the taxing power of Congress only those institutions without which no state "could long preserve its existence." (The quoted words are from the opinion by Justice Nelson.)

[48] In his opinion for the majority of five in *South Carolina* v. *United States,* Justice White also relied heavily on the argument that should state-operated businesses (previously conducted privately) be relieved from the liability for federal taxation, the taxable resources of the federal government might some day be seriously curtailed.

that "the burden of the immunity is thrown upon the national government with benefit only to a privileged class of taxpayers." Mr. Justice Stone emphasized that any tax immunity extended for the protection of a state is at the expense of the national taxing power. This fact makes it important that the immunity allowed should not go "beyond the necessity of protecting the state." [49]

Mr. Justice Stone has been frank to concede that the Supreme Court's decisions regarding state immunity do not "present a completely logical pattern." Nevertheless, he found two "guiding principles" for limiting the tax immunity of state instrumentalities. One is that when a state enters a business previously conducted by private persons, it surrenders its immunity and brings itself within the scope of the federal taxing power.[50] And this is so even though the federal taxes are paid

[49] Something Mr. Justice Stone said with respect to the manner of overcoming excessive state immunity is further proof of his high regard for the adequacy of the normal political processes as channels for corrective action: "Once impaired by the recognition of a state immunity found to be excessive, restoration of that power [national taxing power] is not likely to be secured through the action of state legislatures; for they are without the inducements to act which have often persuaded Congress to waive immunities thought to be excessive." Presumably, Congress would respond to the pressures from the states which regarded the immunity as too restrictive of their taxing power. There would be no similar political pressure on the state legislatures to reduce the effect of the immunity on the taxing power of Congress.

[50] The analysis is similar in the regulatory field. Thus in 1936, the Supreme Court in an opinion by Mr. Justice Stone unanimously upheld the contention of the federal government that a state-operated railroad was fully subject to the Federal Safety Appliance Act. The State of California had fought the fine imposed on it for violating the act on the ground that the act could not be applied to it because it was engaged "in performing a public function in its sovereign capacity." Mr. Justice Stone thought that it was unimportant whether in operating its railways the state was engaged in a "sovereign" or "private" capacity, and agreed that the state was "acting within a power reserved to the states." Nevertheless the Court held that: "California, by engaging in interstate commerce by rail, has subjected itself to the commerce power, and is liable for a violation of the Safety Appliance Act, as are other carriers, . . ." *United States* v. *California,* 297 U.S. 175, 185 (1936).

out of the money in the state treasury. Behind this principle has stood the argument that the function so taxed was not indispensable to the continued existence of the state. The enterprise might be conducted privately. The second principle of limitation has not extended the immunity to persons having business relations with the states, unless the tax were shown to burden or actually interfere with the functioning of the state government. The immunity has been denied in the latter type of case for two reasons. The first is that the alleged burden to the state was "so speculative and uncertain" that if the immunity were granted it would only curtail the taxing power of Congress without "affording any corresponding tangible protection to the state government." The immunity is denied for the additional reason that the tax complained of will be "substantially or entirely absorbed" by the taxpayer himself.

Although both of these principles were impliedly raised by the litigation in the GERHARDT case, Mr. Justice Stone addressed himself to only one of them. The activity of the New York Port Authority is essentially not different from the activity involved in *South Carolina* v. *United States* or the more recent cases of *Ohio* v. *Helvering* and *Helvering* v. *Powers*. Mr. Justice Stone referred to them throughout his opinion, but only for purposes of illustration. He did not answer the question posed by their similarity, namely, whether the Port Authority was performing a proprietary function.[51] Instead, he based his opinion wholly on the second principle he had outlined:

[51] On the same day that the GERHARDT case was decided, the Court upheld a federal tax on the receipts from inter-collegiate football games staged by the University of Georgia. The income from the admissions to the games made possible the university's program of physical education. Mr. Justice Roberts acknowledged that the activity being taxed was part of an essential governmental function, but said for the Court that when a state undertakes for gain an activity which might be conducted by private persons, the activity remains subject to non-discriminatory federal taxation. *Allen* v. *Regents of University System,* 304 U.S. 439 (1938).

The challenged taxes . . . are upon the net income of respondents, derived from their employment in common occupations not shown to be different in their methods or duties from those of similar employees in private industry. . . . A nondiscriminatory tax laid on their net income, in common with that of all other members of the community, could by no reasonable probability be considered to preclude the performance of the function which New York and New Jersey have undertaken, or to obstruct it more than like private enterprises are obstructed by our taxing system.

It was conceivable that in the absence of federal income taxes New York and New Jersey might be able to staff the Port Authority with personnel paid less than the prevailing rates in private industry. Indirectly, therefore, such taxes might add to the operating expenses incurred by the two states. Mr. Justice Stone noted this possibility but rejected its implication as unsound. As he had said before, the incidence of income taxes defies precise measurement even by economists. Their effect on the price of labor and materials used by the states is "conjectural." If the tax were disallowed, the Port Authority employees would be freed of their obligation as citizens to help defray the cost of administering the federal government.[52] The relief would thus be made to depend on nothing more substantial than the speculation that some benefit would accrue to the state. The advantage to the state was "theoretical" and "insubstantial." And should the economic burden of the tax be passed on in part to the states, the risk was unavoidable in a political system under which two governments are able to tax the same individual.

Aside from its implications for future decisions, the basis

[52] Mr. Justice Bradley had voiced a similar view in his lone dissent in *Collector* v. *Day:* "The general government has the same power of taxing the income of officers of the state governments as it has of taxing that of its own officers. It is the common government of all alike; and every citizen is presumed to trust his own government in the matter of taxation. No man ceases to be a citizen of the United States by being an officer under the state government." 11 Wall. 113, 128 (1870).

of the opinion in the GERHARDT case was not at all startling. It was just one more application of the economic approach to tax immunity questions. Reduced to its essence, the opinion by Mr. Justice Stone simply held that payment by the Port Authority employees of a non-discriminatory federal income tax would in no way impede New York and New Jersey in the performance of functions essential to their existence. In this view Mr. Justice Stone had the support of Chief Justice Hughes and Justices Brandeis, Roberts, and Black.[53]

Mr. Justice Black was pleased more with the result than with the reasoning by which it had been reached. In his separate concurring opinion he let it be known that he was unable to reconcile the Stone opinion with *Collector* v. *Day* and related cases. He urged the Court to undertake a revision of the doctrine of tax immunity in the light of the Sixteenth Amendment.[54] He objected to the Court's classification of state activities into "essential" and "non-essential," and said that the classification had been responsible for conflicting opinions. The contradictory results in such cases as *Helvering* v. *Powers* and *Brush* v. *Commissioner* had led to a situation where some public employees were paying federal income taxes and others were not. Such a condition is destructive of uniformity in

[53] In his dissenting opinion, Mr. Justice Butler argued that the Port Authority employees were indistinguishable from other state officers and employees. The exemption of their salaries from federal income tax was settled by such decisions as *Collector* v. *Day* and *Brush* v. *Commissioner.* Mr. Justice McReynolds concurred in this dissent.

[54] Made necessary by the Supreme Court's decision in *Pollock* v. *Farmers' Loan and Trust Co.,* 157 U.S. 429 (1895), the Sixteenth Amendment authorized Congress to "lay and collect taxes on incomes, from whatever source derived." Three years after its adoption, the Supreme Court declared that the sole effect of the Amendment was "to relieve all income taxes when imposed from apportionment and from a consideration of the source whence the income was derived." *Brushaber* v. *Union Pacific R.R. Co.,* 240 U.S. 1, 18 (1916). Despite the clear language of the Amendment, the Court has held that it does not authorize Congress to tax subjects which were beyond the reach of the federal taxing power prior to its adoption. *Evans* v. *Gore,* 253 U.S. 245 (1920).

taxation. There was only one way to overcome such discrimination, and that was to give the Sixteenth Amendment "its most obvious meaning."

To this day the Supreme Court has not responded to Mr. Justice Black's appeal. The sweeping language of the Sixteenth Amendment has not been invoked as a basis for setting aside any of the implied tax immunities. But the salutary purpose set forth by Mr. Justice Black has for the most part been realized, although by a different course of action. The Court has swept aside some of the landmarks.

The first precedents to go were the cases which had established the tax immunity of official salaries. Less than a year after the GERHARDT case was decided, the Supreme Court overruled *Dobbins* v. *Erie County, Collector* v. *Day, New York* ex rel. *Rogers* v. *Graves* [55] and *Brush* v. *Commissioner.*[56] The action was taken by a 6 to 2 vote and climaxed Mr. Justice Stone's opinion for the Court in *Graves* v. *New York* ex rel. *O'Keefe.*[57]

The New York Tax Commission had ventured to tax the salary of O'Keefe, an examining attorney for the Home Owners' Loan Corporation and a resident of the state. O'Keefe first included his salary in his tax return, but later asked for a refund on the ground that as an employee of a federal instrumentality his compensation was not taxable by a state.

[55] *New York* ex rel. *Rogers* v. *Graves* was decided in January 1937. 299 U.S. 401. The Court held that the salary received by the General Counsel of the Panama Railroad, in his capacity as an officer or employee of the railroad, was immune from state taxation. The railroad, as an auxiliary to the Panama Canal, was judged to be an instrumentality of the federal government. The opinion was by Mr. Justice Sutherland and was unanimous. Mr. Justice Stone took no part in the case on account of illness.

[56] Although the Court overruled only *Collector* v. *Day* and *New York* ex rel. *Rogers* v. *Graves,* in view of the result all four cases must be assumed to have been set aside. Mr. Justice Frankfurter concurring, and Justices Butler and McReynolds dissenting, all agreed that such was the effect of the decision.

[57] 306 U.S. 466, 492 (1939).

This was the position taken by counsel for O'Keefe. The federal government was not a party to the suit, but entered the case as *amicus curiae* to support the state's claim to the tax. In their brief, Solicitor General Jackson and his assistants asked the Court to set aside the immunity of official salaries. They argued that *Collector* v. *Day* had been based on erroneous doctrine and that it was no longer true that a tax on income was a tax on its source.[58]

In his brief for New York, Solicitor General Epstein made it clear that he resented the government's intervention and referred to its challenge to the immunity doctrine as "wholly impertinent." He rested the state's claim to the tax on the theory that the employees of the Home Owners' Loan Corporation were not employees of the United States and implied that the Home Owners' Loan Corporation was performing a proprietary function. "The Home Owners' Loan Corporation has all the earmarks of a regular private business corporation," he told the Court.

This argument was rejected by the Supreme Court, which held that the distinction between proprietary and governmental functions did not apply to the activities of the federal government. The federal government is a government of delegated powers, whose "every action within its constitutional power is governmental action, and since Congress is made the sole judge of what powers within the constitutional grant are to be exercised, all activities of government constitutionally authorized by Congress must stand on a parity with respect to their constitutional immunity from taxation." So far as the

[58] Mr. Jackson has since revealed the motive behind the government's intervention in the case. It appeared to the officials in the Justice Department that the chances for bringing the Court to repudiate the immunity doctrine would be greater in a case in which they would be "conceding to the state a power to tax rather than asserting a broader scope to federal power . . ." Robert H. Jackson, *The Struggle for Judicial Supremacy* (New York: Alfred Knopf, 1941), p. 243.

Court was concerned, the case raised but one question: "Whether the tax laid by the state upon the salary of respondent, employed by a corporate instrumentality of the federal government, imposes an unconstitutional burden upon that government." Mr. Justice Stone emphasized that although the reciprocal tax immunities were intended to obviate interference by one government with the exercise of its powers by the other, the two classes of immunity have not had equal force. Some distinction between the two has been recognized ever since *McCulloch* v. *Maryland.* It has been held that Congress by virtue of its implied powers and the supremacy of federal legislation could grant to or withhold from federal agencies immunity from taxation by the states.[59] But if it is part of the implied authority of Congress to protect its agencies from taxation by the states, does it follow that Congress may enlarge the immunity implied by the Supreme Court? In other words, is it within the power of Congress to confer upon agencies of the federal government an immunity from state taxation which is broader and more extensive than the implied constitutional immunity? Mr. Justice Stone raised but left unanswered this important question.

His silence may have been motivated by a desire to repudiate completely the constitutional ground on which tax exemption of official salaries had been rested. Congress had given no indication in the act creating the Home Owners' Loan Corporation whether the salaries of the officers and employees of that agency were to be free from state taxation.[60] Did Con-

[59] As authority for this principle, Mr. Justice Stone cited cases in which the Court had sustained the right of Congress to determine the extent to which agencies employed by it in the execution of its powers were subject to or free from state taxation. The Supreme Court has sustained a state tax on the property of the Reconstruction Finance Corporation on the basis of the permission granted by Congress for such taxes. *Baltimore National Bank* v. *State Tax Commission,* 297 U.S. 209 (1936).

[60] The Home Owners' Loan Act of 1933 declared the corporation to be an instrumentality of the United States and exempted its bonds, capital,

gress by its silence signify its expectation that immunity would be extended only for the purpose of keeping one government from interfering with the functions of the other? [61] If so, the Court was left free to inquire into the effect on the federal government of state taxes on federal salaries:

. . . there is no basis for implying a purpose of Congress to exempt the federal government or its agencies from tax burdens which are unsubstantial or which courts are unable to discern. Silence of Congress implies immunity no more than does the silence of the Constitution. It follows that when exemption from state taxation is claimed on the ground that the federal government is burdened by the tax, and Congress has disclosed no intention with respect to the claimed immunity, it is in order to consider the nature and effect of the alleged burden, and if it appears that there is no ground for implying a constitutional immunity, there is equally a want of any purpose on the part of Congress to create an immunity.

Once having disposed of these side issues, Mr. Justice Stone took up the challenge to the immunity doctrine itself. As applied to salaries, the doctrine was based on contentions which were unreal. He admitted that in the four leading cases dealing with the subject, the Court had extended the immunity of the government or agency in question to the salary of its employees and officers. He also admitted that the Home Owners' Loan Corporation was an instrumentality of the United

reserves, loans, and income from federal and state taxation. The exemption did not apply to its real estate.

[61] The implications to be drawn from the failure of Congress to act with respect to tax immunity are quite different from the implications drawn from the failure of Congress to regulate interstate commerce. As first set forth in *Cooley* v. *Board of Port Wardens,* 12 How. 299 (1851), the scope of state regulation of interstate commerce, Congress being silent, depended on the nature of the subject matter sought to be regulated. See below, pp. 51-52. For a discussion of Mr. Justice Stone's views on the implications of congressional silence in the field of state taxation of interstate commerce, see below, pp. 87, 89-90.

States and as such was fully clothed with the tax immunity enjoyed by the government which created it. But he denied that its immunity extended to the salaries of those employed by it. The earlier rule associated official salaries with the employer and so assumed an identity of interests which in reality did not exist. Said Mr. Justice Stone: "The theory . . . that a tax on income is legally or economically a tax on its source is no longer tenable." [62]

The rest of Mr. Justice Stone's analysis was a restatement of his views in the GERHARDT case and sought to ascertain the nature and effect of the New York tax. The tax was a nondiscriminatory levy on income in the form of salaries, and was not "in form or substance" a tax on the Home Owners' Loan Corporation or its assets. As such, it was a tax on earnings which, once received by the taxpayer, became his property. It was thus paid to the state out of his own funds and not "directly or indirectly" with funds belonging to the federal government. The economic burden of the tax was therefore on the taxpayer and not on the government which employed him. Under the circumstances, the employee was seeking to take advantage of a principle which was intended, not for the benefit of private taxpayers but for the protection of one government against the obstruction of its operations by the other.

Congress, in the exercise of its delegated powers, might have undertaken to protect the salaries of the Home Owners' Loan Corporation employees from state taxation. No such purpose can be gathered from the act creating the agency, so that the Court was concerned only with the effect of the tax. Mr. Jus-

[62] Mr. Justice Stone has taken a similar stand in the cases dealing with the problem of the jurisdiction to tax as it has arisen under the Fourteenth Amendment. Thus he has upheld the right of a state to tax the income earned by its residents from land situated in other states. The tax, he said, was not on the property outside the state but on the resident as his contribution to the financial support of the state whose protection he enjoyed. "Income is not necessarily clothed with the tax immunity enjoyed by its source." *New York* ex rel. *Cohn* v. *Graves*, 300 U.S. 308, 313 (1937).

tice Stone made it clear that in the absence of any express claim to immunity on the part of the federal government, the Court's inquiry would be the same, whether the challenged tax is a federal levy on the salaries of state employees or a state levy on the salaries of federal employees. Actual burden on the government alleged to be taxed must be the sole constitutional ground for allowing immunity from taxation. When viewed in the light of this test, *Collector* v. *Day* and *New York ex rel. Rogers* v. *Graves*, by assuming that the taxpayer shared the immunity of the government which employed him, were erroneously decided. The assumption on which the decision in those cases rested is inconsistent with the "reasoning" and "conclusions" of the more recent cases.[63] Accordingly, *"Collector* v. *Day* and *New York* ex rel. *Rogers* v. *Graves* are overruled so far as they recognize an implied constitutional immunity from income taxation of the salaries of officers or employees of the national or a state government or their instrumentalities." Any slight increase in the cost of operating the taxed government which the new doctrine might entail was not a prohibitive burden. It was a risk which the existence of the concurrent power to tax made inevitable, and was therefore "one which the Constitution presupposes." [64]

7. *Significance of Recent Trends*

The Supreme Court's reexamination of the immunity doctrine is too recent to sanction any final appraisal of its long range significance. It is clear, however, that its full import is

[63] *Helvering* v. *Gerhardt,* 304 U.S. 405 (1938), *Metcalf and Eddy* v. *Mitchell,* 269 U. S. 514 (1926), *Group #1 Oil Corporation* v. *Bass,* 283 U.S. 279 (1931), *James* v. *Dravo Contracting Co.,* 302 U.S. 134 (1937), *Helvering* v. *Mountain Producers Corporation,* 303 U.S. 376 (1938).

[64] On the authority of the decision in the O'KEEFE case, the Supreme Court has held valid a tax imposed by Utah on the salary of an attorney for the Home Owners' Loan Corporation and the Regional Agricultural Credit Corporation. *State Tax Commission* v. *Van Cott,* 306 U.S. 511 (1939).

not to be gleaned from the results so far announced. Their spectacular character is unimportant when compared with the permanent value of the route by which they were reached. The attitudes and trends they reveal are sufficiently significant in themselves to warrant at least a tentative estimate of their probable effects. It must be borne in mind that the doctrine of tax immunity had its origin in political necessity. In Marshall's day, the states and the nation were still looked upon as mutually hostile entities whose antagonisms might disrupt the Union. In particular there was the apprehension that a militant state sovereignty—the vital defect to which the Federalists had attributed the failure of the Articles of Confederation—might continue to threaten the "more perfect Union." In a real sense, Marshall's formulation of the immunity doctrine was part of his larger struggle against states' rights. It is little wonder, then, that he should have sought legal formulas which would permanently protect the federal government from encroachment on its authority and institutions by the states. The resulting doctrine of tax immunity was a product of this period of anxiety. Its character as a rule of absolute prohibition is but a clue to the all important purpose it was to fulfill.

With all his faith in legal conceptions, the great Chief Justice was too much of a realist to ascribe to them powers of self-enforcement. In the last analysis, they were devised to facilitate judicial intervention in behalf of the federal equilibrium in general and national supremacy in particular. The United States Supreme Court was to remain the impartial but active umpire in disputes between the nation and the states.

What was thus intended to arm the federal government with a constitutional weapon against hostile acts by the states was gradually enlarged far beyond the needs which it was originally designed to serve. So it came in time to be applied in its reciprocal form as a limitation on the national taxing power for the benefit of state governments. Moreover, whether the immunities were invoked for the theoretical advantage of the federal or a state government, in practice they proved to be of sole benefit to private taxpayers who happened to have dealings with the government.[65] For over a century the Supreme Court continued to ignore the actual effects of immunity from governmental taxation. As construed, the doctrine long ago lost its value for our constitutional system, but the Court persisted in applying it as though the occasion which had given rise to it was still a reality.

During the past twenty years several of the Court's members frequently protested against so rigid an application of an old formula. More than once, Justices Holmes, Brandeis, and Stone pleaded eloquently for the repudiation of the distinctions which were no longer serving any useful purpose. At first their views were expressed mostly in dissents, but they have since come to be embodied in majority opinions. Leadership in this sustained effort to secure realistic application of the principles of intergovernmental immunity has fallen preeminently to Mr. Justice Stone.

The principles of constitutional construction championed by Mr. Justice Stone represent a significant departure from the twin tradition of legal formalism and judicial primacy initiated by Marshall. Although not unmindful of the great historic purpose behind the immunity doctrine, Mr. Justice Stone has

[65] It may be of interest to note that the use of the immunity doctrine for the benefit of private wealth did not go unchallenged by Marshall's own colleagues. Objecting to the constitutional implication that the states were without power to tax income earned by private persons from their investments in federal bonds, Mr. Justice Johnson said:

"Why should not the stock of the United States, when it becomes mixed up with the capital of its citizens, become subject to taxation in common with other capital? Or why should one who enjoys all the advantages of a society purchased at a heavy expense, and lives in affluence upon an income derived exclusively from interest on government stock, be exempted from taxation?

"No one imagines that it is to be singled out and marked as an object of persecution, and that a law professing to tax, will be permitted to destroy; . . ." *Weston* v. *Charleston*, 2 Pet. 449, 472 (1829).

refused to adhere to the legal abstractions which have been infused into its century-old interpretation. He has vigorously opposed every effort to extend immunity beyond the need of protecting the government alleged to be burdened. When too rigidly applied, it has benefited private taxpayers to the detriment of the taxing government.

Mr. Justice Stone's analysis of the immunity doctrine has not consisted of merely negative criticism of past judicial utterance. He has tried to apply it in the light of the actual needs and problems of present-day government. To this end he has developed positive criteria for its realistic use.

From the outset of his judicial career, Mr. Justice Stone has been emphatic in urging his colleagues to give a practical construction to the questions raised by the doctrine of tax immunity. He has weighed the advantage to be derived from the exemption against the detriment to the taxing government in order to ascertain the actual effects the challenged tax would produce. In this search for concrete results, he has not infrequently found the alleged burden on the taxed government to be hypothetical and illusory. Implicit in such an economic analysis was, of course, the denial of the traditional view which associated the taxpayer with the government that employed him or was the source of his income. Mr. Justice Stone's statement in the O'KEEFE case, "the theory, that a tax on income is legally or economically a tax on its source, is no longer tenable," thus only made explicit the "major premise" of his approach to the doctrine of tax immunity.[66]

Two other features of Mr. Justice Stone's views on inter-

[66] The recent trend of judicial decisions has encouraged the Treasury Department to hope that the Supreme Court will construe state and municipal bonds to be a constitutional source of federal revenue. On January 19, 1939, President Roosevelt asked Congress to authorize the taxation of future issues of state and municipal bonds. *84 Cong. Rec. 467-68.* So far, Congress has remained silent. Nevertheless, the Bureau of Internal Revenue has set in motion litigation which will bring the question before the Supreme Court. It has sent deficiency notices to bondholders of the Port

governmental immunity may prove to be of the greatest significance for the future. The theory of congressional consent and the distinction between the immunity of federal and state instrumentalities may hold important consequences for judicial supervision of federal-state relations in the United States. Their ultimate impact on judicial review itself is but one of the important questions posed by the recent line of decisions.

Whatever its justification, the distinction between the two classes of immunity does leave the states less secure. Assuming that our constitutional system depends for its survival on the maintenance of "an indestructible Union, composed of indestructible states," [67] it may be dangerous to speak of one government as possessing greater authority to protect its institutions than is allowed to the other. To be sure, Mr. Justice Stone does not think that the distinction he draws will threaten the states with oppressive federal taxation. The representation of the states in Congress is regarded by him as a sufficiently adequate safeguard for their interests. Too much cannot be said for the recognition by the Supreme Court that it is not the sole protector of the rights of the states. From that standpoint, emphasis on the fact that the interests of the states are represented in the national legislative process should be welcomed as a healthy manifestation of judicial humility. The doctrine that the immunity of the two governments rests on a different basis is reinforced by the principle of congressional consent.

Although the Supreme Court has not yet defined the limits of the power of Congress to determine the degree of immunity to be extended to federal instrumentalities, enough has been said to suggest that the federal government is to enjoy greater protection than the states. This inference could become un-

of New York Authority and the Triborough Bridge Authority. New York *Times* (July 20, 1941), p. 9.

[67] The quoted words are from the opinion of Chief Justice Chase in *Texas* v. *White,* 7 Wall. 700, 725 (1869).

tenable should the Court some day hold that the states too might confer on their agencies immunity from federal taxation. Such a development seems unlikely, in view of the fact that the power of Congress to endow federal instrumentalities with immunity from state taxation has been evolved as a corollary to the supremacy of federal legislation.

Whether or not immunity is to be extended to a federal agency will thus be a question of congressional intent.[68] In the absence of a congressional declaration of immunity, the Court's function will be to discover the actual effects of the tax. Thus the only occasion when the Court will actively intervene will be to prevent one government from discriminating against or substantially interfering with the activities of the other.

This emphasis on congressional intent may profoundly affect the Supreme Court's function in applying the doctrine of tax

---

[68] The Supreme Court has applied this principle since its decision in the O'KEEFE case. A Maryland tax on mortgages was held invalid as applied to a mortgage offered for record by the Home Owners' Loan Corporation. The Court based its decision squarely on the provision of the Home Owners' Loan Act of 1933 which made the corporation's loans immune from state taxation. The state had argued that since the tax neither discriminated against nor imposed any substantial burden on the operations of the Home Owners' Loan Corporation, it met the pragmatic test of constitutionality currently used by the Court. Consequently, any act of Congress which conferred a greater immunity on the agency was "unconstitutional and void," since Congress was without power to "grant an immunity of greater extent than the constitutional immunity." Chief Justice Hughes rejected this contention for a unanimous Court. Congress, in the exercise of its implied power to protect the activities of the agencies it lawfully creates, might exempt them from taxation by the states. *Pittman* v. *Home Owners' Loan Corporation,* 308 U.S. 21 (1939).

A comparable result was reached in *Alabama* v. *King and Boozer,* 312 U.S. 1 (1941). In an opinion by Mr. Justice Stone, the Court upheld a state sales tax as applied to a purchase of building materials for use in constructing an army camp for the United States under a "cost-plus" contract. Although admitting that the economic burden of the Alabama tax would be passed on to the national government, Mr. Justice Stone pointed out that Congress had not undertaken to free "cost-plus" contractors from state taxation, even where its economic burden would be passed on to the United States. The Court in this case overruled *Panhandle Oil Co.* v. *Mississippi.*

immunity. For in the future, whether or not a particular federal instrumentality or activity shall be deemed immune from state taxation will be a legislative and not a judicial question. In this respect, Mr. Justice Butler's indictment of the current trend of judicial decision as making immunity or liability "depend on legislative discretion not subject to judicial revision" [69] may prove to be an accurate, even if somewhat alarmist view of the present position of the Supreme Court.[70] While it is too early to say that the function of the Supreme Court under the immunity doctrine has been liquidated, it is apparent that it has been greatly curtailed.

The Butler prognosis is nevertheless alarmist because its inference that the new doctrine will expose one government to destructive taxation by the other is insupportable.[71] Granted even that the entire doctrine of reciprocal immunity is abolished, it does not follow that the Supreme Court would condone any palpable interference by the federal government with the lawful activities of a state, or vice versa. Barring cataclysmic change or a drastic transformation of our constitutional system by legal means, it is difficult to imagine that the Supreme Court would tolerate federal action which threatens the continued existence of the states. The reassurance implicit in the words of Mr. Justice Holmes, "the power to tax is not the power to destroy while this Court sits," should serve to allay such fears.

[69] Dissenting in the O'KEEFE case.

[70] Justices Butler and McReynolds thought that in view of the implications of the opinion in the O'KEEFE case the whole doctrine of reciprocal immunity was "marked for destruction." Their fear may have been engendered by the experience of Australia and Canada, which is recounted by Mr. Justice Frankfurter in his concurring opinion in the same case. The Supreme Court of Canada and the High Court of Australia have repudiated the doctrine of intergovernmental immunity.

[71] As Justice Butler said in the O'KEEFE case: "Futile indeed are the vague intimations that this Court may protect against excessive or destructive taxation. Where the power to tax exists, legislatures may exert it to destroy, to discourage, to protect or exclusively for the purpose of raising revenue." 306 U.S. 466, 493 (1939).

CHAPTER II

THE COMMERCE CLAUSE AND STATE POWER

1. *Nature of the Problem*

EVER SINCE the decision in *Gibbons* v. *Ogden*,[1] the vital constitutional question as to the precise effect of the commerce clause upon the powers of the states has continued to engage the attention of the Supreme Court. Although not at all times explicitly so stated, this is the fundamental problem confronting the Court whenever it has before it a statute, enacted in the exercise of a state's regulatory or taxing powers, and attacked as creating or permitting an unconstitutional interference with interstate or foreign commerce.

This was the general question posed by the arguments of counsel in *Gibbons* v. *Ogden*. The assailants of the New York law sanctioning a monopoly in the operation of steamboats urged upon the Court that the mere grant to Congress of the power to regulate commerce among the states invested it with full authority over such commerce and deprived the states of any power over it.[2] During the course of his lengthy opinion in

---

[1] 9 Wheat. 1 (1824).

[2] Webster denied the existence of a general concurrent power over commerce, although he admitted that all regulations which might affect commerce were not under the exclusive control of the national government. Such laws as those providing for the establishment of ferries, bridges and turnpikes, as well as quarantine regulations were characterized by him as "rather regulations of police than of commerce in the constitutional understanding of that term." The attorneys for the owners of the steamboat monopoly, on the other hand, argued that the power to regulate interstate commerce resides in both the nation and the states and that state regulations affecting interstate commerce, which do not have an "extraterritorial operation," are valid exercises of that power.

48

this case, Marshall noted that counsel defending the New York statute had not refuted this argument, but added that it was unnecessary for the Court to pass upon so broad a question.

The "sole question" which he undertook to answer was: "Can a state regulate commerce with foreign nations and among the states while Congress is regulating it?" His opinion held the New York law invalid, not because it was prohibited by the Constitution itself but because it was in conflict with the Coasting License Law enacted by Congress.

The ground for the decision in *Gibbons* v. *Ogden* thus suggested that the exclusive character of federal control may stem from either of two sources. Exclusiveness of national regulation might be required by the Constitution itself or stem from an act of Congress. It would therefore be possible to defend freedom from state regulation of interstate or foreign commerce, either on the ground that such freedom was to be deduced from the very nature of the specific grant of power to the nation, or on the theory that Congress, by appropriate legislation, has willed that the subject remain free from state control. In *Gibbons* v. *Ogden*, the contention was that the exclusiveness was by direct constitutional mandate. The outcome in the case did not resolve the fundamental issue raised by these conflicting interpretations. The Court refused to say what effect the commerce clause, *per se*, had upon the powers of the states.[3] Still, Marshall's opinion in *Gibbons* v. *Ogden* was clearly in keeping with his policy of expanding the scope of national control by construing liberally the powers of Congress. By holding the New York statute to be in conflict with an act of Congress, the Court was announcing a principle

[3] It has been pointed out that although *Gibbons* v. *Ogden* and *Brown* v. *Maryland* rest on a "finding of conflict between Congressional and state statutes," it was clearly Marshall's intention that these opinions should develop a "doctrine of limitations upon state authority implied from the commerce clause." Felix Frankfurter, "Taney and the Commerce Clause," *XLIX Harv. L. Rev. 1286, 1288,* n. 6 (June, 1936).

which could be utilized by Congress as a basis for excluding the states from any field within its province. For, presumably, Congress by virtue of the "supremacy" clause could make its laws exclusive.

Three years following the decision in *Gibbons* v. *Ogden*, when called upon to determine the constitutionality of a state tax upon importers of foreign goods, the Court ruled that the power over foreign commerce resided exclusively in Congress and that there was a total want of power in the states to tax such commerce.[4] *Brown* v. *Maryland* was decided upon the same principle employed by Marshall in striking down the state tax involved in *McCulloch* v. *Maryland*, to wit, the doctrine of total immunity. Just as in the latter case operations of federal instrumentalities were made totally immune from taxation by the states, so in *Brown* v. *Maryland* foreign commerce was declared to be beyond the reach of the taxing power of the states.[5]

The suggestion in *Gibbons* v. *Ogden* that the "dormant" commerce clause, by its own force, imposed limitations upon state authority was shaped by Marshall into an explicit doctrine in *Brown* v. *Maryland*. It was this interpretation of the commerce clause which, in the words of Felix Frankfurter, "at once challenged and confined the creative efforts" [6] of Marshall's successor to the Chief Justiceship.

Marshall, appointee of the Federalist Party, set himself the task of consolidating by means of the judicial process the gains made in its work of centralization and nationalization while it was still in control of the other branches of the gov-

---

[4] *Brown* v. *Maryland*, 12 Wheat. 419 (1827).

[5] It should perhaps be noted that *Brown* v. *Maryland* also involved a specific prohibition. The Maryland law requiring importers of foreign articles to secure a fifty dollar license violated the provision of the Constitution forbidding the states to tax imports. *Constitution*, Art. I, Sec. 10, par. 2.

[6] Frankfurter, *op. cit.*, 1286.

ernment. Amplification of the national power inevitably became the impelling purpose of Marshall's constructions of the Constitution.

Taney, appointed by a President who was a bitter foe of the great Chief Justice, devoted his energies to the work of weaning the Court away from adherence to his predecessor's central conception. To be sure, the positive influence which conditioned the point of view from which Taney approached his resposibility of interpreting the Constitution was his great concern to preserve intact a maximum of legislative freedom for the states. And so, in his separate concurring opinion in the License Cases,[7] Taney took strong exception to the theory implicit in Marshall's interpretation of the commerce clause, namely, that the mere grant of the commerce power to Congress operated as a limitation on the authority of the states. Taney maintained that exclusiveness of national control over interstate and foreign commerce did not stem from the commerce clause but rather from the will of Congress. The only prohibitions upon the power of the states to regulate such commerce were those prescribed by the Constitution itself. The states could act within their respective jurisdictions so long as their actions did not conflict with any federal regulations on the subject.[8]

Not until the decision in the COOLEY case,[9] however, did a

----

[7] 5 How. 504, 575 (1847).

[8] The "chief difference" between Taney and Marshall in their respective delineations of the commerce clause has been well summarized by Professor Frankfurter in one sentence: "Taney's chief difference with Marshall was in his challenge of the latter's central doctrine that the 'dormant' commerce clause operated to impose restrictions upon state authority which it was the duty of the Court to define and enforce." Frankfurter, *op. cit.,* p. 1288. This is the article in which Professor Frankfurter sought to dispel the oversimplified picture of Taney as a "states-rights doctrinaire." He succeeded in demonstrating that Taney did not bring about "a wholesale reversal of Marshall's doctrines." Pp. 1291, 1288.

[9] *Cooley* v. *The Board of Wardens of the Port of Philadelphia,* 12 How. 299 (1851).

majority of the Court agree that the state, in the statute under attack, was regulating interstate commerce. By the theory developed in this case, the attention was shifted away from an analysis of the commerce power and the subject upon which the power operated was made the central phase of the inquiry. The Court, speaking through Mr. Justice Curtis, declared that the commerce clause did not, *per se*, deprive the states of all power over interstate commerce. Where Congress has failed to take action in regard to certain matters, the first inquiry in a case involving challenged state regulation of them should be directed to determining whether the subject of the legislation was one which demanded a uniform national rule. If such a single system of regulation were found to be necessary, the absence of congressional action was to signify the intention of Congress that no regulation should exist. If, on the other hand, the subject were local in nature and one which did not require uniformity of control, the state might legislate until Congress occupied the field.

The doctrine formulated in the COOLEY case seemingly contemplated two classes of interstate commerce: interstate commerce national in character and interstate commerce local in character. The states were without power to regulate interstate commerce national in its nature. By implying that over some parts of interstate commerce the states might exercise their powers and that over other parts of the same commerce the states were completely divested of power, the decision in the COOLEY case seemed to have struck a compromise. It was a composite of the view that Congress had exclusive power over interstate commerce and the view which regarded this power to be capable of concurrent exercise by the nation and the states.

The rule developed by Marshall in *Brown* v. *Maryland* that a state was powerless to tax foreign commerce continued to be observed. His assertion—"We suppose the principles laid down in this case to apply equally to importations from **a** sister state"—did not prove to be quite as acceptable.

In his opinion for the Court in *Woodruff* v. *Parham*,[10] Justice Miller openly challenged Marshall's dictum. He was willing to accept it as law if it merely meant that a state could not discriminate against goods brought in from some other state and in favor of its own products. There was great economic wisdom, he thought, in not applying the immunity doctrine to articles shipped in interstate commerce. For, the effect of exempting from state taxation articles produced in other states would be to give the sellers of such goods a competitive advantage over those selling similar merchandise made in their own state, for which they were liable for local taxes. He made it clear that a state law which discriminated against interstate commerce, by subjecting the products of another state to a tax from which goods made within its own borders were exempted, would be considered an obstruction to such commerce and would be unconstitutional.

But if Marshall's apparent purpose to make interstate commerce immune from state taxation was frustrated by the decision in *Woodruff* v. *Parham*, neither did Justice Miller's doctrine stand unchallenged for long. Less than twenty years after its decision in the WOODRUFF case, the Court in an opinion by Justice Bradley [11] held invalid a state tax on the ground that it was directly burdening interstate commerce. The Tennessee tax was imposed for the privilege of soliciting orders for manufacturers or merchants of other states. In stating the rules that had up to that time been developed regarding the powers of the states to "affect" interstate and foreign commerce,[12] Bradley treated Marshall's dictum in

[10] 8 Wall. 123 (1869).

[11] *Robbins* v. *Shelby County Taxing District*, 120 U.S. 489 (1887).

[12] These rules were summarized by Bradley as follows: (1) Whenever the commercial matter sought to be controlled is national in nature or requires uniform regulations, the power over it is "necessarily" exclusive;

Brown v. *Maryland* as if it were a binding principle. The states might regulate matters which lend themselves to local control, but could not impose tax restrictions upon or discriminate against interstate commerce. And when it was argued that the Tennessee license tax did not discriminate against interstate commerce inasmuch as local drummers were required to secure a similar license, Justice Bradley replied that the contention was immaterial. The absence of discrimination was not a "material point" in the case, since, as the Court clearly ruled, "interstate commerce cannot be taxed at all." The decision in this case surrounded interstate commerce with the same constitutional immunity from state taxation with which Marshall succeeded in protecting foreign commerce. In later years, however, this sweeping restriction upon the states' taxing power was rejected by the Court.

At the same time that it was thus limiting the states' taxing power, the Supreme Court began to develop doctrines intended to relieve them from some of the strictures on their regulatory power. The new jurisprudence was the Court's response to the constitutional obstacles which stood in the way of the effective enforcement of state prohibition laws. Efforts of the states to prohibit local traffic in intoxicating liquor were everywhere set at naught by importations from outside the state. Up to 1891, the Supreme Court had uniformly held invalid state laws seeking to prohibit the importation of intoxicants or their sale by the importer.[13]

---

(2) The failure of Congress to act with respect to matters demanding a single system of regulation indicates that it is the will of Congress that these subjects remain free from state control; and (3) "The only way in which commerce between the states can be legitimately affected by state laws" is when the states, in the exercise of their police power, regulate matters of local concern, as they do when they regulate highways, canals, railroads, wharves, ferries, etc. Such "police" regulations are lawful even though they "incidentally affect commerce." 120 U.S. 489, 492-93 (1887).

[13] *Bowman* v. *Chicago & N.W. Ry Co.*, 125 U.S. 465 (1888), *Leisy* v. *Hardin*, 135 U.S. 100 (1890).

An idea put forth by Chief Justice Fuller in *Leisy* v. *Hardin* paved the way for the next development. He repeated that the silence of Congress in matters requiring uniform national treatment indicated its will that such commerce remain "free and untrammelled" and added: "A subject matter which has been confided exclusively to Congress by the Constitution is not within the jurisdiction of the police power of the states unless placed there by Congressional action." *Leisy* v. *Hardin* was decided on April 28, 1890. Acting on the suggestion implicit in Fuller's pronouncement, Congress in August of the same year passed the Wilson Act, which subjected all intoxicating liquors brought into any state to the operation of its regulatory power. The Wilson Act was unanimously upheld by the Supreme Court a year later in an opinion by Fuller himself.[14]

In 1917 the Court expanded this new doctrine of congressional consent when it upheld the Webb-Kenyon Act. That act prohibited the shipment of intoxicating liquors into any state whose laws made such shipment illegal.[15] More recently, these principles have made possible federal legislation sanctioning state action directed against the entry within a state of prison-made goods.[16]

This cursory glance at a few of the principal commerce clause decisions may perhaps suggest the extent to which the adjustment of the conflicting national and state claims in the field of commerce has been placed in the keeping of the Justices of the United States Supreme Court. "Clauses are not truly censors; the men who apply them are."[17] The present Chief Justice has been aware of this truth, and not a little of

---

[14] In re *Rahrer,* 140 U.S. 545 (1891).

[15] *Clark Distilling Co.* v. *Western Maryland Co.,* 242 U.S. 311 (1917).

[16] *Whitfield* v. *Ohio,* 297 U.S. 431 (1936), *Kentucky Whip and Collar Co.* v. *Illinois Central R.R. Co.,* 299 U.S. 334 (1937).

[17] Frankfurter, *The Commerce Clause Under Marshall, Taney and Waite* (Chapel Hill: Univ. of North Carolina Press, 1937), p. 47.

his effort has been directed to diminish the scope of judicial control in this area of conflict.

2. *State Regulations "Affecting" Foreign and Interstate Commerce*

The effect of the commerce clause on state power as a problem for our federal equilibrium seems to hold particular interest for Mr. Justice Stone. In his practical approach to this issue, which continues to perplex the Court, he has stressed the need for considering all pertinent facts before reaching any conclusions. He would examine the record to discover whether the national interest in commerce demands that the state be inhibited in its control of situations which are in some way related to foreign or interstate commerce. Before he is willing to restrain the state, he must be satisfied that the challenged state action actually discriminates against or impedes in other ways the mobility of such commerce. All of this he made abundantly clear early in his work on the Court. In registering his forceful dissent against the majority opinion in *DiSanto* v. *Pennsylvania*,[18] he described the method which he thought should be followed in the determination of the issues raised in commerce clause cases.

By a six-to-three decision, the Court, speaking through Mr. Justice Butler, invalidated a Pennsylvania statute of 1921. Under that law persons or corporations (other than railroad or steamship companies) selling steamship tickets and orders for passage between the United States and Europe were required to secure licenses. The legislation was assailed as a violation of the commerce clause on the ground that the selling of tickets and orders was a part of foreign commerce and that the regulation of it by Pennsylvania constituted a "direct burden upon that commerce." It was defended as a proper

[18] 273 U.S. 34, 43 (1927).

exercise of the police power reserved to the states. Readily agreeing that the states could place no direct burden on inter-state or foreign commerce, the state's attorneys insisted that in the exercise of a state's police power such commerce might be "indirectly and incidentally or remotely affected." They argued that Pennsylvania was seeking to remedy a real evil, that of fraud and misrepresentation, and pointed to the known fact that the business of selling steamship tickets and orders was done with immigrants who, because of their ignorance of the language, were easily victimized by dishonest agents or persons who posed as agents. The majority of the Court held that the soliciting of passengers and the sale of steamship tickets were a recognized part of foreign commerce and that the requirements of the statute constituted a direct burden on that commerce. The dissenting Justices contended that the transaction regulated (sale of the tickets or orders) was intra-state in character, and that foreign commerce was not bur-dened by the provisions of the Pennsylvania law. Mr. Justice Brandeis agreed with the defenders of the statute that it was intended to prevent fraud and misrepresentation and that it was a valid exertion of the state's police power.

After agreeing with all that Mr. Justice Brandeis had said, Mr. Justice Stone in his separate dissenting opinion protested against the language of "directness" and "indirectness" used by the spokesman for the majority, and proceeded to expound the factual analysis by which he would test state action af-fecting foreign or interstate commerce.[19] Conceding at the outset that the Pennsylvania statute was regulating an instru-mentality of foreign commerce, he noted that the Court had many times decided that "the purpose of the commerce clause was not to preclude all state regulation of commerce crossing state lines, but to prevent discrimination and the erection of barriers or obstacles to the free flow of commerce, interstate

[19] Justices Brandeis and Holmes concurred in Mr. Justice Stone's dissent.

or foreign." Next came his direct criticism of the conventional test used in prior adjudications:

> In this case the traditional test of the limit of state action by inquiring whether the interference with commerce is direct or indirect seems to me too mechanical, too uncertain in its application, and too remote from actualities, to be of value. In thus making use of the expressions, "direct" and "indirect interference" with commerce, we are doing little more than using labels to describe a result rather than any trustworthy formula by which it is reached.

Mr. Justice Stone considered the use of the expressions "direct" and "indirect" to be prejudicial to a realistic determination of the constitutional issues raised by the challenge to the Pennsylvania law. For that reason, he urged the discontinuance of the use of these adjectives in the discussion of commerce clause cases. He regarded them as terms of legal conclusion, inasmuch as a declaration that state legislation constituted a "direct" or "indirect interference" with commerce was tantamount to holding it unconstitutional or constitutional.[20]

Once freed from the weight of these labels, the Court's chief concern should be to discover the "actual effect on the flow of commerce" of the local regulation under attack. For that purpose, Mr. Justice Stone would subject the legislation to a searching factual analysis. The constitutionality of such regulations should not depend on whether their effect on commerce

---

[20] Professor Ribble has pointed out that the practical consequence of the adoption by the Court of the "language of burdens" is that state legislation seeking to control an activity traditionally designated as a subject of interstate or foreign commerce will always have less chance of being upheld than state regulation of an activity not so classified. In his treatment of the DI SANTO case, he asserts that there was nothing to show why the Pennsylvania statute was considered a burden, other than the "purely formal argument" that it was regulating a transaction which had been characterized "in prior adjudications" as foreign commerce. F.D.G. Ribble, *State and National Power Over Commerce* (New York: Columbia Univer. Press, 1937), pp. 222, 228-29.

was "nominally indirect." If the Court would learn whether
the matter sought to be controlled was local in character and
did not interfere with the "national interest" in preserving the
freedom of interstate commerce, it must be guided by all the
knowledge available regarding the particular situation. The
Court should come to its decision only after "a consideration
of all the facts and circumstances, such as the nature of the
regulation, its function, the character of the business involved
and the actual effect on the flow of commerce." If by means
of such analysis it could not be demonstrated that the practical
effect of the state regulation was to impede the free flow of
commerce, Mr. Justice Stone would allow it to be enforced.

Pennsylvania was seeking to cope with a local situation, the
dishonest dealing found to be practiced in transactions affecting foreign commerce. The requirements of the challenged
statute were designed to stamp out this evil. Until such time
as Congress would undertake to protect the people of Pennsylvania against this deception, Mr. Justice Stone would tolerate
the necessary protective action taken by the state.[21]

Mr. Justice Stone weighed the state interest in the regulation of commerce (foreign or interstate) against the "national
interest" in maintaining for commerce freedom from state

21 Mr. Justice Stone's insistence that the commerce clause was not intended to prevent a state from putting an end to fraudulent activities
seems to echo a strikingly similar thesis advanced by Mr. Justice Harlan
in *Plumley* v. *Mass.,* 155 U.S. 461 (1894). In that case the Court held that
the commerce clause was not designed to keep the states from protecting
their inhabitants against deceptive practices by persons from outside the
state. Harlan wrote:

"If there be any subject over which it would seem the States ought to
have plenary control, and the power to legislate in respect to which, it
ought not to be supposed, was intended to be surrendered to the general
government, it is the protection of the people against fraud and deception
in the sale of food products. Such legislation may, indeed, indirectly or incidentally affect trade in such products transported from one State to another state. But that circumstance does not show that the laws of the
character alluded to are inconsistent with the power of Congress to regulate commerce among the States." P. 472.

regulation. After considering all the relevant facts and circumstances, he found that the local interest sought to be promoted by the state—the protection of its unwary inhabitants against frauds in the sale of steamship tickets—in no way interfered with the national interest in keeping commerce free from obstructions. If Pennsylvania were to wait until the federal authorities stepped in to fight the frauds, the failure of Congress to act nationally would render the state helpless to remedy the local evil. The situation was peculiar to Pennsylvania, and the implied limitations of the commerce clause should not be invoked to prevent a state from controlling conditions which could be most adequately dealt with locally.

On April 28, 1933, the General Assembly of the State of South Carolina adopted a law prohibiting the use on the state highways of motor trucks and "semi-trailer motor trucks" whose widths exceeded 90 inches and whose weight including load exceeded 20,000 pounds. The issues raised by the legal onslaught on this statute were utilized by Mr. Justice Stone to expound more fully the views he had articulated rather sketchily in his dissent in the DiSanto case. On this occasion, however, he was speaking for a majority of his colleagues, so that the views he expressed may be regarded, at least in a technical sense, as those of the Court.

"The principal question for decision," he wrote in *South Carolina State Highway Department* v. *Barnwell Brothers, Inc.*,[22] "is whether these prohibitions [width and weight limitations] imposed an unconstitutional burden upon interstate commerce." Before proceeding to answer the question as stated by himself, Mr. Justice Stone reviewed in detail the conditions which had led the South Carolina legislature to enact the 1933 statute as well as the findings of the lower courts. He noted that South Carolina had built its highways and owned

[22] 303 U.S. 177 (1938).

and maintained them. It had received from the federal government money grants in aid of its highway improvements. The weight and width limitations were adopted for the purpose of protecting those highways from injury and in order to insure their "safe and economical use." Although the federal funds had been employed in improving the highways of the state, Congress had not undertaken to regulate the weight and size of vehicles in interstate motor traffic.

Mr. Justice Stone thought that Congress had left undisturbed the power which the states had "retained under the Constitution" to protect their highways. The mere grant to Congress of the power to regulate interstate commerce did not make unconstitutional all state regulations affecting such commerce. Nevertheless, certain state actions are ruled out by the commerce clause of the Constitution. That clause "by its own force" prohibits all forms of discrimination against interstate commerce. Mr. Justice Stone would not permit the states to resort to measures whose purpose or result was to achieve "a local benefit by throwing the attendant burden on those without the state." Such state regulations infringed the commerce clause "even though Congress has not acted." According to Mr. Justice Stone, judicial nullification of these barriers to interstate commerce is made necessary by the inability of those without the state to combat discrimination by the offending state. "When the regulation is of such a character that its burden falls principally upon those without the state," he wrote, "legislative action is not likely to be subjected to those political restraints which are normally exerted on legislation where it affects adversely some interests within the state."

The South Carolina legislation was not such a forbidden burden. Mr. Justice Stone implied that the weight and width limitations were among those permissible state regulations embraced by the rule of the COOLEY case. Control of the use of the highways was likened by him to local regulations of rivers, harbors, piers, docks, and quarantine laws. In the absence of congressional action such measures have been sustained, even though they incidentally interfere with interstate commerce. Unlike the railroads, local highways are built, owned and maintained by the states or their political subdivisions. Their competence to take steps to insure the safety and conservation of the highways cannot be questioned. Such restrictions are bound to have a substantial effect upon interstate commerce. Mr. Justice Stone recognizes the right of the states to apply their regulations of the highways to traffic moving interstate, so long as they do not discriminate against such traffic. Their burden on interstate commerce, he said, is "one which the Constitution permits because it is an inseparable incident of the exercise of a legislative authority, which under the Constitution has been left to the states."

Mr. Justice Stone's opinion in the BARNWELL case is notable for its discussion of the role of the judiciary in reviewing challenged legislation. Implicit in this analysis of the judicial process is his objection to the use by the Court of its authority to make of itself an arbiter of public policy. Of special interest is his treatment of the technique and scope of judicial review in commerce clause cases.

He began by pointing out that in order to protect the "national interest" in commerce, Congress could by appropriate legislation forestall or remove state restrictions upon interstate commerce which, in its judgment, were too onerous. The determination of how the national interest in commerce is best to be preserved is a "legislative not a judicial function, to be performed in the light of the Congressional judgment of what is appropriate regulation of interstate commerce, and the extent to which, in that field, state power and local interests should be required to yield to the national authority and interest." If the Court must intervene, especially where Congress has not formulated its policy, Mr. Justice Stone would limit the scope of the Court's use of the commerce clause as a censor of state action by confining its attention to the inquiry whether the means adopted by the state were reasonably related to a lawful legislative purpose. And so we find him saying:

In the absence of such legislation [Congressional] the judicial function, under the commerce clause as well as the Fourteenth Amendment, stops with the inquiry whether the state legislature in adopting regulations such as the present has acted within its province and whether the means of regulation chosen are reasonably adapted to the end sought.

It appeared from the record that much of the controversy surrounding the enactment of the South Carolina law centered on the relative merits of "gross weight limitation" as against an "axle or wheel weight limitation." The legislature had chosen the gross weight formula. Those resisting enforcement of this provision were successful in producing evidence showing that the stresses on the roads were determined by wheel rather than gross load weight. This testimony was introduced for the purpose of convincing the Court that the legislature of South Carolina had made an arbitrary choice. "South Carolina's own experience is not to be ignored," remarked Mr. Justice Stone, and it was clear from that experience that it was easier for those who load trucks to make certain that they have complied with a gross load limitation than with an axle or wheel weight limitation. He added:

When the action of a legislature is within the scope of its power fairly debatable questions as to its reasonableness, wisdom, and propriety are not for the determination of courts, but for the legislative body on which rests the duty and responsibility of decision. This is equally the case when the legislative power is one which may legitimately place an incidental burden on interstate commerce. It is not any the less a legislative power committed to the states because it affects interstate commerce and courts are not any the more entitled, because interstate commerce is affected to substitute their own for the legislative judgment. Since the adoption of one weight or width regulation rather than another is a legislative not a judicial choice, its constitutionality is not to be determined by weighing in the judicial scales the merits of the legislative choice and rejecting it if the weight of evidence presented in court appears to favor a different standard.

Mr. Justice Stone would decide questions of reasonableness raised in connection with state regulations affecting interstate commerce in the same way as he would settle similar problems pressed for solution in due process inquiries. In both fields, he would resolve the doubts in favor of the legislative judgment. He drew the analogy even closer when he explicitly stated that the presumption of constitutionality was in favor of the choice made by the legislature.[23] What interested Mr. Justice Stone was whether there was "rational basis" for the legislative choice, and he was satisfied that the record showed affirmatively that there was "adequate support" for the legislation. The burden of proving that the method selected by the legislature was unreasonable was on those alleging the unreasonableness. He dismissed the charge of unreasonableness by declaring that the choice of the weight limitation, based as it was "on convenience of application and consequent lack of need for rigid supervisory enforcement," was for the legislature to make. It was not for the courts to determine that the state's preference

[23] Justice Brandeis has taken a position opposite to that of Mr. Justice Stone on the question of presumption. Justice Brandeis would require the state to show affirmatively that its action does not burden interstate commerce in certain important respects: "It must appear that it is imposed solely on account of the intrastate business; that the amount exacted is not increased because of the interstate business done; that one engaged exclusively in interstate commerce would not be subject to the imposition; and that the person taxed could discontinue the intrastate business without withdrawing also from the interstate business." *Sprout* v. *City of South Bend,* 277 U.S. 163, 171 (1928).

for the one over the other standard was "in any sense arbitrary or unreasonable." [24]

It will be seen that in his opinion upholding the South Carolina statute, Mr. Justice Stone was extending to the states the same freedom to regulate matters of local concern affecting interstate commerce for which he had pleaded in his dissent in the DiSanto case with respect to foreign commerce. In the latter case he defended the right of a state to safeguard its people against deception practiced locally, notwithstanding that the transactions being regulated were a part of foreign commerce. By his opinion in the Barnwell case, he sought to preserve the power of the states to conserve the use of their facilities and to protect their people against dangers due to the use of these facilities by persons engaged in interstate commerce. Implicit in both opinions is his solicitude for the people within a state who would suffer if the state were kept from protecting them against the conduct of those who are engaged in activities related to interstate or foreign commerce. Where Congress has failed to enact the necessary meliorative legislation, Mr. Justice Stone would permit the states to exert their regulatory power, provided they did not discriminate against or actually impede the mobility of such commerce.

Mr. Justice Stone would thus expand the scope of the states' regulatory power in order not to render them helpless to cope with those of their local affairs which Congress could control if it chose to do so. In his interpretations of the relation of the commerce clause to the states' taxing power, he continues to exhibit the same sympathy for the needs of the states.

3. *Fees for the Use of State Facilities and Services*

Fortunately for our state governments, the doctrine developed by Bradley in *Robbins* v. *Shelby County* did not prevail

[24] The width limitations of the South Carolina statute were upheld in the same terms and for the same reasons.

for long. The implications of his theory that the states were without power to tax interstate commerce, had they been rigidly accepted, might have seriously curtailed the taxable resources of the states.[25] But they were not; and it came to be recognized that the states could, under certain circumstances, tax interstate commerce. When such commerce may be taxed, however, still remains the point at issue.

One of the first cases in which Mr. Justice Stone was confronted with this difficult question was *Helson* v. *Kentucky*.[26] This case involved the validity of a Kentucky tax upon gasoline used in making interstate journeys. The Court set aside the Kentucky tax on the ground that it directly burdened an instrumentality of interstate commerce. Out of deference to earlier decisions of the Court, Mr. Justice Stone acquiesced in the result as announced by Mr. Justice Sutherland, but he refused to accept the reasoning by which it was reached. He was unable to find

any practical justification . . . for an interpretation of the commerce clause which would relieve those engaged in interstate commerce from their fair share of the expense of government of the states in which they operate by exempting them from the payment of a tax of general application which is neither aimed at nor discriminates against interstate commerce.

This apologetic concurrence in the result presaged Mr. Justice Stone's attempts to win from his colleagues a greater measure of tolerance for state taxes aimed to compel those engaged in interstate commerce to contribute to the upkeep of the state in which they operate. His efforts in this direction

---

[25] To be sure, Bradley himself denied that this would be the effect of his theory and argued that the states would still be able to exert their "just power of taxation" when goods brought in from other states became part of the "general mass of property" within the state. 120 U.S. 489, 497 (1887).

[26] 279 U.S. 245, 252 (1929).

seem to have produced the desired result, at least as judged
from his opinions for the Court in two cases decided in 1933.
Both dealt with the question whether a state may lawfully tax
an article used in the operation of an interstate business. In
the first of these cases,[27] the Court sustained a Tennessee tax
of two cents per gallon imposed on all gasoline stored within
the state, as applied to the gasoline bought by the railway
outside the state and stored within its tanks. A similar result
was reached in *Edelman* v. *Boeing Air Transport, Inc.*,[28] with
Mr. Justice Stone again speaking for an undivided Court. A
Wyoming tax on the "use" of gasoline in the state was there
held valid as applied to gasoline stored in the state by the
transport company and subsequently used by it for the fueling
of interstate planes.

The tax involved in these two cases was levied on the storage
and withdrawal from storage of gasoline, irrespective of the
use to which the gasoline was to be put. In neither case was the
Court confronted with a situation where interstate commerce
had been singled out for special taxation; the element of discrimination was absent. But the test Mr. Justice Stone would
have employed to ascertain the effect of such taxation on interstate commerce he had already set down five years earlier
in *Interstate Buses Corporation* v. *Blodgett*.[29]

The Court's decision in that case upheld the right of a state
to make a reasonable charge for the use of its highways by
interstate motor vehicles. Specifically, the subject of litigation
here was a Connecticut tax of one cent for each mile of highway traversed in the state by any motor bus used in interstate
commerce, the proceeds of which were to be applied to the
maintenance of the state's public highways. No such mileage

[27] *Nashville, Chattanooga, and St. Louis Railway Co.* v. *Wallace*, 288
U.S. 249 (1933).
[28] 289 U.S. 249 (1933).
[29] 276 U.S. 245 (1928).

tax was imposed on those using motor vehicles in intrastate commerce. Instead, the same Connecticut act subjected all companies operating motor buses in intrastate commerce to a three per cent gross receipts tax.

In their brief attacking the Connecticut tax as contravening the commerce clause, counsel for the bus corporation attempted to prove that interstate transportation by motor vehicle had been singled out by the Connecticut statute for the imposition of the tax. They argued further that in granting federal aid to the states for the construction of highways, Congress meant that such highways shall be open to interstate commerce. Moreover, the mileage tax was a greater burden on interstate transportation by motor bus than was the gross receipts tax on intrastate transportation by the same means. Replying to these allegations, the attorneys for the state contended that the corporation had failed to prove the charge that as enforced the act actually operated to discriminate against interstate commerce. The tax was a charge for the privilege of using the roads of the state, and when imposed on those using the roads in interstate commerce did not thereby offend the commerce clause.

Speaking for a unanimous Court, Mr. Justice Stone agreed that the bus corporation did not establish the fact of discrimination by showing that the two taxing schemes were different in form. He made it clear that it was insufficient to point to substantial differences in statutory forms as evidence of discrimination. To satisfy the Court of the essential fact of discrimination, the complaining party must demonstrate that "in actual practice the tax of which it complains falls with disproportionate economic weight on it."

As in the case of state regulatory actions affecting foreign and interstate commerce, so in the case of state taxation of interstate commerce, it is the actual effect of the legislation that is significant for Mr. Justice Stone. His opinions in cases involving fees exacted by the state for the use of its highways by interstate commerce have been predicated on the accepted principle that the states do not exceed their constitutional powers when they impose taxes as a charge for the use of their facilities in such commerce. When such state taxes are objected to on the ground of discrimination, the responsibility for showing that the fees exacted were subjecting interstate commerce to a greater burden than the one borne by comparable intrastate commerce is on those alleging the discrimination. And Mr. Justice Stone would require those seeking relief to prove the discrimination by a factual reference to the concrete results of the tax.

This striking similarity between Mr. Justice Stone's approach in this case and the method of the factual inquiry in due process cases was thrown into even sharper relief by the language he used in replying to the complaint that the mileage tax was unreasonable. When the tax in itself is reasonable, Mr. Justice Stone pointed out, it is not to be deemed excessive because other taxes were imposed by the state on the same taxpayer for the use of its highways. The taxpayer must show that the aggregate charge "bears no reasonable relation to the privilege granted."

In two cases decided in 1935 and 1936 respectively, Mr. Justice Stone continued to apply the rule that a state could impose on those engaged in interstate commerce within its borders charges for actual services rendered. The first of these cases, *Clyde Mallory Lines* v. *Alabama*,[30] was concerned with the validity of a "harbor fee" of $7.50 imposed by the Alabama Docks Commission on vessels of "500 tons and over" entering the harbor at the port of Mobile. The revenue to be derived from this fee was to reimburse the state for the cost of policing the harbor. The steamship company, which operated vessels of more than 500 tons between New York and Mobile, attacked

[30] *296 U.S. 261* (1935).

the harbor fee as being a tonnage duty and a burden on interstate commerce.

In delivering the opinion for a unanimous Court, Mr. Justice Stone met the first objection by showing that a charge such as the Alabama harbor fee was not within the "historic meaning" of the phrase "duty of tonnage" and that the constitutional prohibition [31] did not apply to it. While the constitutional prohibition against tonnage duties precludes taxes whose effect is to exact a charge for the privilege of using a port, it does not apply to charges—even though measured by tonnage—for services and facilities extended to vessels. He found that the record supported the conclusion of the Alabama Supreme Court that the contested fee was a charge made for the policing of the harbor. The harbor fee was not a charge for the privilege of using the harbor but a reasonable levy to cover the cost incident to the enforcement of the regulations which were intended to promote the safety of vessels using the harbor facilities. It was immaterial that certain vessels made less use of the services than did others, since vigorous enforcement of harbor regulations would inure to the benefit of all who entered it.

Neither was the Alabama harbor fee a burden on interstate or foreign commerce forbidden by the commerce clause. The avowed purpose and demonstrated use of the tax was to defray the cost of a "purely local regulation of harbor traffic." Although they might "incidentally affect" interstate or foreign commerce, such state regulations, so long as they did not conflict with federal legislation, were not to be deemed an unconstitutional burden on such commerce.

In the closing remarks of his opinion, Mr. Justice Stone pointed out that the latest manifestation of charges imposed by a state to defray the cost of enforcing regulations in aid of

---

[31] "No State shall, without the consent of the Congress, lay any duty of Tonnage, . . ." *Constitution,* Art. I, Sec. 10, cl. 3.

interstate commerce were exactions for the use of state highways by interstate automobile traffic. *Clyde Mallory Lines* v.
Alabama was decided in December, 1935, and in May of the
following year, in *Morf* v. *Bingaman*,[32] the Court was confronted with the claim that this form of state taxation was an
unconstitutional burden on interstate commerce. In the latter
case, it sustained a New Mexico law of 1935 exacting a fee for
the privilege of transporting motor vehicles (on their own
wheels) over the highways of the state for the purpose of
sale.[33]

Again writing for a unanimous Court, Mr. Justice Stone accepted the trial court's interpretation of the legislation and
held the permit fee to have been an essentially reasonable charge
for the use of the state's highways.[34] He likened the manner of

---

[32] 298 U.S. 407 (1936).

[33] Chapter 56 of New Mexico Laws, 1935, forbids the use of the state's
highways for the transportation of motor vehicles, on their own wheels,
for the purpose of sale, unless the vehicles are licensed by the state, or
are owned by a licensed automobile dealer and operated under a "dealer's
license," or are operated under a special permit issued by the Commissioner
of Revenue, for which a fee is charged. The permit fee is $7.50 if the ve-
hicle is moved by its own power and $5 if it is drawn by another vehicle.
Chapter 136 of the acts of the same session of the New Mexico legislature
provides that there shall be set up on the main highways of the state regis-
tration stations or "ports of entry" to issue the necessary permits and
collect the fees. No permit was ‘to be issued until the vehicle was inspected
and found to be "in safe and roadworthy condition, properly equipped
with all lights, brakes and other appliances" required by the laws of the
state. Morf was engaged in the business of buying new and used automobiles in eastern and southern states and transporting them, on their
own wheels (usually in processions or "caravans"), over the highways of
New Mexico for the purpose of offering them for sale in California.

[34] In construing the statute, the trial court found that its provisions
were made necessary by the business of transporting automobiles over the
highways of the state in caravans for sale, and that the transportation of
motor vehicles in this manner was a business of considerable magnitude in
the state. It found further that this class of automobile traffic causes "increased wear and tear of the highways and interferes with their safe and
convenient use by others." The trial court concluded that these circumstances justified the state in separately classifying this traffic for the
purpose of police regulations and in exacting a fee or tax for the privilege
of using the state highways for such traffic.

collecting the permit fee to that followed in the collection of a toll for the privilege of entering and using the highways, and concluded that its manner of collection established its character as such a charge. Such a levy, if non-discriminatory, may be imposed by a state on interstate automobiles passing over its highways.

However, one objection to the permit fee was that it discriminated in favor of intrastate and against interstate commerce. It was said that its effect was to exempt from the fee cars operated under a dealer's license when transported for sale. Mr. Justice Stone pointed out that the transportation of motor vehicles across the state in caravans for purpose of sale was a "distinct class of business." The hazards and inconveniences shown to be due to this traffic, as well as the added expense to the state involved in the road repairs made necessary by it, justified the state in adopting special licensing and taxing provisions.

To sustain their charge that the New Mexico tax was a forbidden burden on interstate commerce, the attorneys for Morf pointed also to the fact that it was a "levy of a flat fee" and not a tax graduated according to the number of miles traversed in the state. This assertion of counsel elicited from the spokesman for the Court a useful distinction between a state tax "on" the use of the highways and one for the "privilege" of using the highways. Evidently, the reason why Mr. Justice Stone considered the challenged permit fee to be a tax, not on the use of the highways but one imposed for the grant of the privilege of using them, was that no limit had been set to the number of miles that might be traversed. If the fee exacted for the privilege were reasonable, it need not be based on mileage.

Finally, the constitutionality of the New Mexico statute was called into question on the ground that a part of the revenue yielded by it was not used directly for highway maintenance.

Mr. Justice Stone denied that the validity of a state tax for the privilege of using its roads in interstate commerce depends upon the use of all the proceeds of the tax to pay the cost of maintaining them. The only time it is necessary to prove that the fees collected have been definitely earmarked for highway maintenance is when it is not clear that the tax is for the privilege of using the highways.

This final unavailing ground on which Morf rested his case against the New Mexico law was substantially identical with that on the basis of which he prevailed upon the Court a year later to invalidate similar legislation adopted by California.[35] A considerable difference in the amount of the tax as well as significant differences in the method of allocating it account for these seemingly conflicting decisions. California required the payment of a permit fee for the movement over its highways of motor vehicles intended for sale.[36] As in the earlier case, the lawyers for Morf assailed the exaction of the $15 permit fee as an unconstitutional burden on Morf's interstate business and as discriminating against him. More specifically, they contended that the tax had to fall since it was excessive or unreasonable in amount and bore no reasonable relation to the increased cost of policing the traffic involved.[37] The fee was defended as a "charge for the privilege of using the public highways for a distinctive commercial use" and as a "police power license fee."

Citing the decision in *Clyde Mallory Lines* v. *Alabama* as controlling, Mr. Justice Stone repeated that the states are free

---

[35] *Ingels* v. *Morf*, 300 U.S. 290 (1937).

[36] California's "caravan" act of 1935 exacted a special permit fee of fifteen dollars for each automobile. It directed that the fee collected be paid into the general fund in the state treasury.

[37] Their brief presented evidence to show that 15,000 cars were brought into the state annually for sale under the conditions defined in the "Caravan Act," so that permit fees would yield an annual return of $225,000. The additional expense of policing the highways would be only $24,000, and the expense involved in issuing permits was about $5 per car.

to tax interstate commerce if the exaction "is demanded as re-
imbursement for the expense of providing facilities or of enforcing regulations of the commerce." Either purpose might be
gathered from one of two possible sources. The purpose of the
burdening exaction, which is indispensable to its constitutionality, may appear from the statute itself, as in *Morf* v. *Bingaman,* or from the use of the fees collected to cover the cost
incurred by the state, as in *Interstate Buses Corporation* v.
Blodgett. Ingels, Director of the California Department of
Motor Vehicles, had not shown that the money collected was
used to defray the expense of the construction or maintenance
of the highways. Neither did he point to any statute appro-
priating a part of the general fund of the state treasury for
such highway purposes.

In the absence of testimony showing that the fees collected
were employed for the construction or maintenance of the highways, the Court must "look to the statute itself to ascertain the
purpose for which the permit fees are collected." The challenged legislation clearly provided that the fees were intended
to defray the cost to the state of administering and enforcing
the caravan act and policing the caravaning traffic. This
explicit language, Mr. Justice Stone thought, belied the contention of the state that the permit fee was exacted as a charge
for the use of the highways. The statutory declaration of the
purpose of the levy was not in itself an appropriation and did
not foreclose the use of the moneys collected for highway
maintenance. But "until such appropriation is made, the
statute itself states the legislative purpose, and precludes
state officials from asserting that the fees are collected for
any other." [38]

[38] A New Mexico statute of 1933 imposed a tax of five cents per gallon
on all gasoline used or sold in the state. Basing its decision on the State
Supreme Court's construction of the tax as an excise tax, the United States
Supreme Court held that a state excise tax on the use of gasoline by interstate buses was a "direct burden." The Court suggested, however, that had

To the question of excessiveness, Mr. Justice Stone replied that the burden of proving that a fee exacted by a state is excessive rested on the party claiming that it unconstitutionally burdened interstate commerce. The trial court's finding that the California permit fee was unreasonable in amount was "amply supported by evidence." The "arithmetical gap" between the cost of administering the act and policing the traffic and the actual fee charged established the fact that the permit fee bore no reasonable relation to the expense incurred by the state.[39]

Mr. Justice Stone recognizes that the cost to the states in providing services and facilities used by business is great; and he would impose upon those making use of them, even though engaged in an interstate business, the responsibility of sharing that cost. He would therefore reserve to the states the right to tax such business for the use of these accommodations. But to protect persons and corporations doing business in more than one state against the abuse of this power, he would limit its exercise in two important respects. The fee exacted must be levied to defray the expense actually incurred in making available these conveniences. Moreover, the burden on interstate commerce represented by such a charge must not be greater than the one borne by comparable local business.

4. *Privilege or Occupation Taxes*

Corporations carrying on interstate activities may not be required by a state to obtain a license for the purpose of engaging in such commerce, nor are they liable for state taxation

the taxes been expressly levied for road maintenance they might have been upheld. Thus it was the "declared purpose" of the tax which again determined whether it was a forbidden burden on interstate commerce. *Bingaman* v. *Golden Eagle Western Lines,* 297 U.S. 626 (1936).

[39] California modified its legislation to meet the objection to the 1935 law. The California Caravan Act of 1937, the substitute for the invalidated statute, was upheld by the Supreme Court in an opinion by Mr. Justice Stone. *Clarke* v. *Paul Gray, Inc.,* 306 U.S. 583 (1939).

measured by their interstate business. However, for the privilege of doing local business, it is permissible for the states to tax interstate commerce, whether engaged in by domestic or "foreign" corporations. The taxes exacted as a condition of doing local business must, nevertheless, meet certain constitutional requirements.[40]

The power of a state to make the right to engage in intrastate commerce conditional upon the payment of a fee does not authorize the state to tax in ways which burden or discriminate against interstate commerce. That is, such state taxation may not, either by actual provision or by its necessary operation, make the amount of the tax depend upon the volume of interstate business done or the property used in conducting such business. Neither may a state discriminate between the property of concerns engaged in interstate commerce and the property of those doing a purely local business. Thus the basis of the tax or its practical effect on interstate commerce would determine whether the state is exceeding its constitutional power to tax for the grant of the privilege to engage in intrastate commerce.

During his tenure on the Bench, Mr. Justice Stone has been the Court's spokesman in several important cases in which state franchise or occupation taxes had been challenged as violating the commerce clause. Two of the most significant of these cases are *Fisher's Blend Station* v. *State Tax Commission* [41] and *Western Livestock* v. *Bureau of Revenue*.[42] In the earlier

[40] Mr. Justice Holmes, dissenting in *Western Union Telegraph Co.* v. *Kansas,* 216 U.S. 1, 52 (1910), insisted that since a state had the absolute power under the Constitution to deny to or confer upon a foreign corporation the right to enter the state for the purpose of engaging in local business, it must be allowed to tax for the privilege it grants to the foreign corporation upon any basis it might choose. "As to foreign corporations seeking to do business wholly within a State, that State is the master, and may prohibit or tax such business at will." P. 52.

[41] 297 U.S. 650 (1936).

[42] 303 U.S. 250 (1938).

case an occupation tax of the State of Washington, measured
by the entire gross receipts from radio broadcasting within the
state, was held to be an unconstitutional burden on interstate
commerce. The later case decided that New Mexico did not
infringe the commerce clause when it imposed on all engaged in
the business of publishing newspapers or magazines a privilege
tax on the gross receipts from the sale of advertising.

A 1933 statute of the State of Washington subjected the
owners of radio stations to a tax measured by the gross receipts
of their business. The owners of Fisher's Blend Station conducted two radio stations in the state, one broadcasting
throughout the "fifth zone" and the other throughout the
United States.[43] The stations transmit advertising programs
for customers to listeners in the areas for which they are
licensed. The Washington tax on the income derived from the
sale of these programs was assailed as burdening interstate
commerce.

In presenting the opinion of the Court, which reversed the
judgment of the Supreme Court of the State of Washington
upholding the tax, Mr. Justice Stone admitted that the sounds
making up the performances or programs broadcast are produced by those who pay for the programs. He nevertheless
pointed out that the "broadcasting of radio emanations, as
distinguished from the production of the sounds broadcast,"
was effected by the radio station and not by its customers. The
defenders of the tax had conceded that the radio station pro-
duces the radio emanations which actuate the receiving mechanism located in other states. Accordingly, Mr. Justice Stone
could find no more reason for viewing the stations' customers
as doing the broadcasting "than for saying that a patron of
a railroad or telephone company alone conducts the commerce
involved in his railroad journey or telephone conversation."

[43] The fifth zone comprises eleven western and northwestern states, and
Alaska and Hawaii.

The business of the radio company was clearly that of transmitting advertising programs from the stations in Washington to the listeners in other states. In "all essentials" its mode of operation did not "differ from that employed in sending telegraph or telephone messages across state lines, which is interstate commerce." The transmission interstate of information, whether by wires or through the "ether," is a "form of intercourse" which is commerce. Since the earnings of the company operating the stations in Washington are derived from interstate commerce, the Washington tax, computed on the basis of the company's gross income, was an unconstitutional burden on interstate commerce.

An opposite result was reached in *Western Livestock* v. *Bureau of Revenue.* A New Mexico tax on the gross receipts from the sale of advertising by newspapers or magazines was held valid as applied to a journal published within the state, the circulation of which was partly interstate. The appellants in this case were the owners of a monthly livestock journal, *Western Livestock*, which they prepared, edited and published wholly within the State of New Mexico. The journal circulated in New Mexico and other states. Some of the advertisements appearing in the journal were paid for by advertisers in other states, so that the gross income of the owners of *Western Livestock* was derived in part from contracts with advertisers from other states. Under these contracts, the necessary advertising materials were to be supplied by the advertisers themselves. It was conceded that the transmission of these materials, as well as the remittance of the payment for their printing by the journal, were effected by interstate facilities.

The publishers contended that the New Mexico tax as applied to their business infringed the commerce clause of the Federal Constitution, and rested this contention on two grounds. They insisted, first, that their income derived under the advertising contracts was not taxable by the state for the reason that they were consummated by transactions across state lines. These contracts provided for the shipment of the advertising materials from advertiser to publisher through the channels of interstate commerce. In substance, their argument was that a contract entered into by persons in different states is protected by the commerce clause. They alleged, further, that the "performance" of the contracts depended upon the interstate circulation of the livestock journal. The tax, they argued, violated the commerce clause because it was measured by gross receipts derived in part from the interstate circulation of their magazine. Remittance of the payment for the advertising was not to be made until the advertisements had been printed in the journal and the journal had been distributed to the paid subscribers through the mails or other means of transportation.

"The question for decision," Mr. Justice Stone wrote for a majority of the Court, "is whether the tax . . . on appellants, who sell without the state to advertisers their space in a journal which they publish in New Mexico and circulate to subscribers within and without the state imposes an unconstitutional burden on interstate commerce." To resolve this inquiry, he analyzed at length the second ground on which the New Mexico taxing statute was challenged. He dismissed the first objection by invoking the settled doctrine that in the absence of congressional action, "the mere formation of a contract between persons in different states is not within the protection of the commerce clause . . . unless the performance is within its protection." The business of publishing the livestock journal was distinctly local and the interstate contractual transactions preceding publication did not give the business an interstate character.

The effect of the tax upon the performance of the advertising contract was the only issue to be decided. More precisely, the question raised by the "impact" of the tax upon the execution of the advertising contracts was, as stated by Mr. Justice

Stone, "whether the tax is invalid because the performance of the contract, for which the compensation is paid, involves to some extent the distribution, interstate, of some copies of the magazine containing the advertisements." Before answering this question, he discussed in some detail the effect of the commerce clause on the taxing powers of the states. The commerce clause does not prevent a state from taxing the local property of those engaged in interstate commerce, nor do the states infringe that clause when they measure an occupation tax by the amount of intrastate business done by a corporation engaged in interstate commerce. Such state taxes, merely because they "burden" interstate commerce in the sense that they increase the cost of conducting it, are not forbidden. Yet state taxes measured by the gross income from interstate commerce have been held invalid.

In distinguishing local tax burdens upon interstate commerce deemed constitutional and those "pronounced" unconstitutional, Mr. Justice Stone revealed the basis for the Court's validation of the New Mexico statute.

The vice characteristic of those which have been held invalid is that they have placed on the commerce burdens of such nature as to be capable, in point of substance, of being imposed or added to with equal right by every state which the commerce touches, merely because interstate commerce is being done, so that without the protection of the commerce clause, it would bear cumulative burdens not imposed on local commerce.

If the states were allowed to utilize the gross receipts from an interstate business as a basis for taxation, the same earnings could be made the measure of a tax in every state where that business was carried on. The purpose in holding invalid local taxes measured by the gross receipts from interstate commerce is to protect such commerce from "multiple taxation not borne by local commerce."

Mr. Justice Stone went on to say that the New Mexico tax

finds support in reason and in the practical needs of a taxing system which, under constitutional limitations must accommodate itself to the double demand that interstate business shall pay its way, and that at the same time it shall not be burdened with cumulative exactions which are not similarly laid on local business.

The analogy drawn between this tax and those measured by gross receipts derived directly from interstate communication or the interstate transportation of goods was unfounded.[44] The danger inherent in the latter type of taxes is that they can be repeated by other states. This "vice" was not present in the New Mexico statute.

The New Mexico tax, as applied to the business of preparing, printing and publishing magazine advertising, was neither in form nor in substance a tax which could be duplicated elsewhere so as to impose additional burdens on the interstate circulation of the magazine. That portion of the gross earnings of the publishers of *Western Livestock* attributable to the interstate distribution of the journal and taxed by New Mexico could not be reached by the taxing power of any other state.

By his opinions in the cases just examined, Mr. Justice Stone continued to uphold the right of the states to tax interstate business for privileges granted by them. So long as such taxes are measured by the amount of commerce done within the state, he does not consider them to be forbidden by the commerce clause. But should the nature of the levy be such that its counterpart could be imposed by other states on the same in-

[44] The owners of *Western Livestock* relied on *Fisher's Blend Station* v. *State Tax Commission.* In distinguishing, Mr. Justice Stone argued that had the Court in that case validated the excise measured by the gross receipts from radio broadcasting, reception too would have been made taxable by the states. If reception could be taxed, a "cumulative tax burden would be imposed on interstate communication such as might ensue if gross receipts from interstate transportation could be taxed."

come from the same interstate business, he would not allow it to stand.

5. *Challenge to the "Multiple Taxation" Theory*

As the basis for invalidating nondiscriminatory state franchise or occupation taxes measured by gross receipts from interstate commerce, the ban on "multiple taxation" was first set forth in 1936 by Mr. Justice Stone in his opinion in *Fisher's Blend Station* v. *State Tax Commission*. Then he spoke for a unanimous Court, and the minority in the WESTERN LIVESTOCK case disagreed only with the result reached. Evidently, Justices Butler and McReynolds were dissenting from the failure of the Court to apply the multiple burden theory against the New Mexico statute.

Western Livestock v. *Bureau of Revenue* was decided February 28, 1938. On May 16, when the majority did invoke the new formula to strike down a state tax said to threaten interstate commerce with multi-state burdens, the theory of multiple taxation itself was challenged by the Court's junior member. Satisfied with the outcome, Mr. Justice Black voted with the majority in the WESTERN LIVESTOCK case and did not question the basis for the decision. But in May he proceeded to make a frontal attack on the theory so recently developed by Mr. Justice Stone. This he did while dissenting from the opinion by Mr. Justice Roberts in *Adams Manufacturing Co.* v. *Storen*.[45]

This case was concerned with the validity of the Indiana Gross Income Tax Act of 1933. For the privilege of engaging in business and receiving income within the state, the act levied a tax on "the receipt of gross income." The *Adams Manufacturing Co.* makes road machinery, 80 per cent of which it ships abroad and to other states. It objected to paying the Indiana

[45] 304 U.S. 307, 316 (1938).

tax on the ground that the state was taxing income from its sales in interstate and foreign commerce.

Mr. Justice Roberts agreed that as applied to the Adams Manufacturing Co. the Indiana act infringed the commerce clause and cited the WESTERN LIVESTOCK case as precedent. Since the company sells to customers in other states and foreign countries, the tax was in effect on the gross receipts from interstate and foreign commerce. The tax was, moreover, one which, if upheld, other states might adopt to reach the same income.

The possibility that the Indiana tax might be duplicated by other states was thus made the sole ground for the decision by the majority. Against this theoretical basis for invalidating state taxes on gross receipts from interstate commerce Mr. Justice Black registered a vigorous dissent. He questioned the competence and jurisdiction of the Supreme Court to formulate and apply the ban against multiple taxation. He began by asking the question whether

. . . in the absence of regulatory legislation by Congress condemning state taxes on gross receipts from interstate commerce—the commerce clause, of itself, prohibits all such state taxes, as "regulations" of interstate commerce, even though general, uniform and nondiscriminatory.

The very way in which Mr. Justice Black phrased the question revealed his attitude toward the constitutional problem precipitated by the attempts of the states to reach the gross income from interstate commerce. That problem, he argued at length, was one which only Congress was authorized by the Constitution and equipped with the necessary machinery to resolve. The Indiana tax did not discriminate against interstate commerce. If state gross receipts taxes should be found to constitute too great a burden on interstate commerce, Congress might prohibit such taxes by way of effectuating its authority to regulate and protect interstate commerce. No such national action had been taken, and the question was therefore whether all state taxes on gross receipts from interstate commerce were forbidden by the Constitution itself.

Whether the states shall be free to impose uniform taxes on the gross income derived from interstate commerce was not the concern of any one state. The problem had become national in scope; and according to Mr. Justice Black, "the only repository of a power touching complex and national aspects of interstate commerce is . . . not the Judiciary but the National Congress." Until such time as the Congress adopted a contrary policy, he would allow the states to impose "uniform and nondiscriminatory taxes" on interstate and intrastate business alike. Otherwise, intrastate business would be subjected to "unjust and unequal" burdens, since interstate commerce would be relieved of the obligation to contribute to the maintenance of the government of the states in which it was carried on.

Mr. Justice Black protested that use of the multiple taxation theory had led the Court to decide cases on the basis of sheer speculation and hypothesis. He agreed that it was within the province of the Court to safeguard interstate commerce from "unfair and unjust" burdens imposed by a state. But there was no evidence that the Indiana tax actually discriminated against or unduly burdened the interstate sales of the Adams Manufacturing Co. The Court was therefore invalidating the tax merely on the supposition that it might lead to a situation where interstate commerce would be weighed down with cumulative tax burdens. Congress and not the courts, he insisted, possessed the necessary machinery to study the problem and prescribe a uniform policy for the future.

Indiana was taxing the receipt of income within the state. "The receipt of income is a taxable event and need not necessarily enjoy the immunity of the income's source. . . ." In other words, since all remittances were made to the home office of the Adams Manufacturing Company located in Indiana, only Indiana could tax receipts of the company's gross income. Mr. Justice Black admitted that in his view a state to which the road equipment was shipped might impose a nondiscriminatory sales tax on the distributors of the product in that state. So long as such sales taxes did not discriminate against the interstate article he would allow them to stand. The Indiana tax as well as those possibly to be imposed on distributors in other states were the price for the protection afforded to interstate commerce by the states in which it is conducted.

Mr. Justice Black renewed his direct criticism of the theory of multiple tax burdens when he again dissented from its application eight months later. This time he was debating the issue with Mr. Justice Stone, who once more relied on the theory. The opinion by Mr. Justice Stone held invalid the right which the State of Washington asserted to tax gross receipts derived from interstate transactions.[46] Washington's "business activities" tax was the legislation involved.

For the "act or privilege" of engaging in business activities within the state, Washington imposed a tax of one-half of one per cent on the "gross income of the business." As applied to the earnings of Gwin, White and Prince, the levy was objected to as a violation of the commerce clause of the federal Constitution. The firm is marketing agent for fruit growers and growers' cooperatives in Washington and Oregon.[47] Its business is to negotiate sales and arrange for the transportation of fruit to other states and abroad, and its income depends upon the number of boxes of fruit it succeeds in selling. These activities were said by Washington to be a local business.

Mr. Justice Stone began his analysis of the "constitutional effect" of the tax by denying that the "interstate commerce service" rendered by the marketing agent was performed solely

[46] *Gwin, White and Prince* v. *Henneford,* 305 U.S. 434, 442 (1939).
[47] During trial in the lower courts, the Tax Commission of Washington agreed that the state was not entitled to the tax on the Oregon business of the concern.

in the state of Washington. All the important transactions incident to marketing—negotiation of the sales, execution of the contracts of sale, deliveries and collection—were effected outside that state. The compensation for these services was determined by the volume of business yielded, and this was also the measure of the tax demanded by Washington. On the basis of this information Mr. Justice Stone concluded that although the gross income tax was nominally imposed on activities going on in Washington, the amount of the tax was in effect measured by the "entire interstate service" rendered both within and without the state. Consequently, the business of Gwin, White and Prince was burdened "in direct proportion to its volume."

As applied to the marketing concern, the Washington business activities tax thus was stricken down as reaching receipts from interstate commerce. Yet not every such state tax has been held unconstitutional. These conflicting results, Mr. Justice Stone stated again, are fully reconciled by the logic of the multiple taxation rule. Those engaged in interstate commerce may be taxed for the privilege of carrying on activities within a state, but the tax must be measured by the income yielded by these local activities. When a state measures such a tax by the entire income from interstate business, it is in effect charging for the privilege of engaging in interstate commerce. In the absence of action by Congress, interstate commerce may not be subjected to such burdens or discrimination by the states. If state taxes on gross receipts from interstate business were allowed, the very conditions would ensue which it was the purpose of the commerce clause to preclude. The same income could be reached by each state in which the business is conducted, with the result that interstate commerce would be exposed to multiple tax burdens. Such burdens would amount to actual discrimination against interstate commerce, since the earnings from intrastate commerce would be subject to the taxation of but one state. They would, said Mr. Justice Stone, "reestablish the barriers to interstate trade which it was the object of the commerce clause to remove."

At the time *Gwin, White and Prince* v. *Henneford* was decided, Mr. Justice Stone's view of state gross receipt taxes was shared by all the members of the Court except Mr. Justice Black. The two Justices differed sharply over the role of the judiciary in controlling barriers to interstate commerce. Mr. Justice Stone construed the silence of Congress in the matter of gross receipt taxes to mean that it was the responsibility of the Court to remove the obstructions.[48] In the absence of congressional action the commerce clause itself prohibits such exactions.

With this position Mr. Justice Black disagreed, and argued for an interpretation which would prohibit only two types of state laws. Those that actually discriminated against interstate commerce and in favor of local commerce and those in conflict with an act of Congress should be stricken down. He reiterated his assertion that the Court was judging state taxes by purely hypothetical burdens which were not shown to have been caused by the legislation in question. The Washington tax was general and non-discriminatory, demanded alike of those engaged in intrastate and interstate activities. "Equality" was its essence and application of the multiple tax formula will only result in "unequality."

It was not the Court's function to invalidate a state taxing statute on the mere "conjecture" that other states might utilize the same income as the measure of taxation. If the

---

[48] The Supreme Court has been enforcing the ban against state privilege taxes measured by the entire volume of interstate commerce ever since its decision more than fifty years ago in *Philadelphia and S. M. Steamship Co.* v. *Pennsylvania*, 122 U.S. 326 (1887). Mr. Justice Stone thought it significant that since then Congress has made no effort to modify the rules developed by the Court. As he said, "Congress has accommodated its legislation, as have the states, to these rules as an established feature of our constitutional system." 305 U.S. 434, 441 (1939).

cumulative effect of otherwise lawful state taxes constitutes a potential threat to the free flow of interstate trade, only Congress is equipped to study its extent and to adopt regulations for the protection of the nation's economic system. Mr. Justice Black stressed the need for preventing the states from imposing "discriminatory and retaliatory" burdens on interstate and foreign commerce, but he thought that it was equally important that the judiciary should "scrupulously observe its constitutional limitations." Both of these desirable conditions, he argued, would be realized if the Court would resurrect the rule first announced by Mr. Justice Field in 1876. That is to say, Mr. Justice Black would have the Court return to the principle that, aside from state laws actually directed against interstate commerce, only Congress shall "determine how far [interstate commerce] . . . shall be free and untrammeled, how far it shall be burdened by duties and imposts, and how far it shall be prohibited." [49]

It is only necessary to read their opinions in the ADAMS MANUFACTURING COMPANY and HENNEFORD cases to appreciate the fundamental difference in outlook which at that time separated Mr. Justice Stone from Mr. Justice Black in their interpretations of the commerce clause. In view of the substantial difference in their approach to the question, Mr. Justice Stone's next opinion involving the validity of local taxation of interstate commerce came as an unexpected development.[50] Not only is his opinion in the BERWIND-WHITE case at variance with his earlier views, but in it he comes close to adopting views like those set forth by Mr. Justice Black in his dissenting opinions.

Mr. Justice Stone held for a majority of five [51] that the

[49] The quoted words are from Justice Field's opinion for the Court in *Welton* v. *Missouri,* 91 U.S. 275, 280 (1876).

[50] *McGoldrick* v. *Berwind-White Coal Mining Co.,* 309 U.S. 33, 59 (1940).

[51] In addition to Mr. Justice Stone, Justices Black, Douglas, Reed and Frankfurter constituted the majority. Mr. Justice Murphy, who had been

New York City sales tax did not infringe the commerce clause as applied to the Berwind-White Coal Mining Co.[52] The Berwind-White Co., a Pennsylvania corporation, sells more than 80 per cent of the coal produced in its mines in that state to public utility and steamship companies in New York City. The coal is shipped by rail to the dock in Jersey City and from there by barge to the point of delivery. The company has a sales office in New York City where the sales contracts with its New York customers were made.

Although nominally laid on the local purchaser of the coal, the New York City sales tax, as applied to the sales of coal by Berwind-White to its New York customers, was resisted as an unconstitutional burden on the interstate business of the coal mining concern. Mr. Justice Stone rejected this view of the ultimate effect of the tax. His preliminary description of the tax as being "conditioned upon events occurring within the state" foreshadowed the outcome in the case. For he thereby implied his acceptance of the version of the tax scheme which had been advanced by the City's Corporation Counsel.

Mr. Justice Stone found that the "taxable event" was the transfer to the New York purchasers of products the interstate movement of which had come to an end. So conditioned, New York City's sales tax could be likened to a tax on the "use" of property which had been transported in interstate commerce. The levy was similar to the many sales taxes which the Court has sustained beginning with its decision in *Wood-*

appointed to the place left vacant by the death of Mr. Justice Butler, had not yet ascended the Bench.

[52] Defining "sales" as "any transfer of title or possession or both," New York City, beginning in 1934, has imposed annually a 2 per cent tax on the receipts from every sale in the City. The tax, levied on the purchaser of personal tangible property (with certain exceptions), is to be paid by the purchaser to the seller "for and on account of the City of New York." Thus although the vendor is to collect the tax it is the consumer or purchaser who pays it. Local Law No. 24 of 1934, p. 164. The rate was changed to one percent in October 1941.

ruff v. *Parham.* Mr. Justice Stone defended these sales tax decisions as having the "support of reason and of a due regard for the just balance between national and state power."

The purpose of the commerce clause, we were again told, was to protect interstate commerce from "discriminatory or destructive" action by the states. The concern of the states, on the other hand, was so to exercise their taxing power as to exact from interstate commerce its share of tax burdens. Mr. Justice Stone admitted that it was the function of the judiciary to reconcile these "competing demands." But he could find "no adequate ground" for holding that the New York City sales tax was the kind of local regulation "which, in the absence of Congressional action the commerce clause forbids." The tax was neither directed against nor did it in its practical operation discriminate against interstate commerce. It was imposed on all purchasers of goods for consumption, regardless of whether the merchandise had been moved in interstate commerce.

Mr. Justice Stone stressed the absence of discrimination under the New York tax as between intrastate and interstate commerce. This emphasis on the "equality" of the tax made it easier, of course, to dispose of the objection based on the cumulative burden theory. As demanded of Berwind-White, the New York City sales tax was said to constitute a levy on the gross income from interstate commerce. If New York could exact such "tribute," the other states through which the commerce passed might subject it to similar tax burdens not borne by local business. Rejecting the basis for the decision in the ADAMS MANUFACTURING Co. case as inapplicable, Mr. Justice Stone replied that the sales tax was "conditioned upon a local activity, delivery of goods within the state upon their purchase for consumption." The tax, he repeated, neither discriminated against nor obstructed interstate commerce.

But the fact that the tax was nondiscriminatory impressed

the minority as unimportant and irrelevant. Chief Justice Hughes, speaking for himself and Justices McReynolds and Roberts, bluntly chided the majority for ignoring the danger of multiple taxation. He denied that the delivery of the coal was a taxable event. It was an integral part of the entire inter-state transaction involved in the sale of the coal by Berwind-White to its New York customers. New York could no more tax the delivery of the coal than its transportation interstate. If New York could tax the delivery, Pennsylvania might tax its shipment and New Jersey the trans-shipment. Such serious threats to the uninterrupted flow of interstate business are not made any the less objectionable merely because the challenged taxes also apply to local or domestic trade. The Chief Justice insisted that the purpose of the commerce clause was to provide a "free national market" by preventing the erection of barriers to intercourse between the people of the different states. He reminded his colleagues that the Supreme Court has a duty to help maintain this national market.

6. *Summary and Conclusions*

The chief value of judicial scrutiny of the facts is that it enables the judge to clarify the issues involved in the controversy. For Mr. Justice Stone, it is not enough to show that the state is seeking to regulate a matter which in the past was deemed to be outside its province. The only question which is important for him is whether the state by its legislation is placing real obstacles in the way of the movement of commerce. He is anxious to have a realistic basis for his answer to this question; and to that end, he would ask for all available information relating to the actual effect of the assailed regulation. He is particularly wary of legal formulas which tend to becloud these issues.

As one who recognizes the limitations of legal terminology, he is too well acquainted with the treacherous way in which the same technical rules can be utilized for contradictory purposes not to be on guard against their use to justify findings having no basis in reason or in real needs. For Mr. Justice Stone, logical consistency need not depend on the use of "labels" about which all that can be said is that they were once used by the Court in solving related problems. To make certain that sound conclusions are reached, he would have the judge familiarize himself with the "actualities" of the situation. He would say with his fellow dissenter in the DiSanto case, "the logic of words should yield to the logic of realities." [53]

If the realities of the situation are such that in the absence of federal regulation a state would be unable to discharge its duty to its people to protect them against fraud and misrepresentation, Mr. Justice Stone would allow the state to take the necessary action. He does not think that the commerce clause was intended to lead to a condition where, because of inaction by Congress, the unscrupulous in local communities could go their evil way unmolested by organized society. If the actualities are such that without the help of Congress a state would be unable to conserve the use of its facilities or to protect its inhabitants against hazards resulting from the use of the facilities by those engaged in interstate commerce, Mr. Justice Stone would have the state control the situation. In either case, the legislative purpose of the state being legitimate, his only other concern is that the means selected by the state bear a reasonable relation to the conditions sought to be regulated. The inquiry he pursues in deciding commerce

[53] Mr. Justice Brandeis, dissenting in *DiSanto* v. *Pennsylvania,* 273 U.S. 24, 43 (1927). The DiSanto case has since been overruled. *California* v. *Thompson,* 313 U.S. 109 (1941). In an opinion by Mr. Justice Stone, the Court upheld unanimously a California law requiring "transportation agents" to secure a license assuring fitness and to file a bond. These agents are persons who sell or offer to sell or negotiate for transportation on the public highways of the state.

clause cases is thus an essentially due process inquiry. And as in questions of due process, so in commerce clause determinations, he places the burden of proving the invalidity of the governmental action on those attacking it. He presumes the legislation to be valid unless the contrary can be established. His sympathy is all on the side of the practical needs of the state.

Mr. Justice Stone exhibits the same attitude in cases involving the relation of the commerce clause to the states' taxing power. He agrees with Mr. Justice Holmes that "taxes are what we pay for civilized society;" [54] and he would not let the mere circumstance that the political system by which the American people are governed happens to be federal in nature to free business from this obligation to society. He is aware that American corporate enterprise is constantly expanding its activities on a nation-wide scale. Such business enjoys privileges in more than one state. Mr. Justice Stone would permit each state to tax business of this character for the protection or services it affords. "Even interstate business must pay its way." [55]

Interstate motor traffic traverses highways built and maintained by the states or their political subdivisions. Pending appropriate action by Congress, Mr. Justice Stone would not impede the power of the state to regulate the use of their highways by this class of business. He realizes that interstate motor carriers cause added wear and tear to these roads and would sanction state taxes imposed to cover the cost of constructing and maintaining the facilities furnished at state expense.

The coming of the automobile, the airplane and the radio has brought new issues to the Court involving the scope of the

---

[54] *Compania General de Tabacos de Filipinas* v. *Collector of Internal Revenue*, 275 U.S. 87, 100 (1927).

[55] Mr. Justice Clarke in *Postal Telegraph-Cable Co.* v. *Richmond*, 249 U.S. 252, 259 (1919).

states' powers of regulation and taxation "to affect" these new forms of interstate commerce. What should be the attitude of the Court to these issues?

In these fields as in others where interstate commerce is concerned [Mr. Justice Stone told the members of the American Bar Association in 1928] it seems clear that the function of the Court must continue to be, as in the past, to prevent discrimination and the erection of barriers against interstate commerce, but upon the careful scrutiny of every relevant fact and circumstance, to save to the states the regulation and control of all interest in maintaining untrammeled the freedom of commerce across state lines.[56]

Mr. Justice Stone's insistence on the right of the states to compel interstate business to bear its just burden of government is thus no mere unqualified dogma. When he is convinced that the state is resorting to practices which it was the purpose of the commerce clause to forbid, he does not hesitate to protect such commerce by invoking relevant constitutional limitations. He would not tolerate any state tax which in its operation clearly discriminated against an interstate business and in favor of like intrastate enterprise. To satisfy Mr. Justice Stone that the levy is discriminatory, those who make the complaint must establish the fact of discrimination by showing that there is no reasonable basis for it.[57] He would make an

[56] Harlan F. Stone, "Fifty Years Work of the United States Supreme Court," *53 A.B.A. Rep. 259,* 265 (1928).

[57] Since his decision in the BARNWELL case, Mr. Justice Stone seems to have shifted his ground with respect to presumption in commerce clause cases. A majority of the Court held invalid an Arkansas law taxing gasoline in excess of twenty gallons carried in motor vehicles. *McCarroll* v. *Dixie Greyhound Lines,* 309 U.S. 176, 183 (1940). The facts showed that when the buses arrived at the Arkansas lines their tanks contained some seventy-seven gallons of which only sixteen would be consumed within the state.

Concurring, Mr. Justice Stone agreed that the tax "must fall because the statute on its face and in its application discriminates against the commerce by measuring the tax by the consumption of gasoline moving in interstate commerce which occurs outside the state." Two sentences in

exhaustive economic analysis to ascertain the practical effect
of the state law on the particular business being taxed.

One other form of state taxation affecting interstate commerce which Mr. Justice Stone would disallow, as prohibited
by the commerce clause, is that capable of being repeated by
other states. He interprets the commerce clause as restraining
the states from imposing taxes on the gross receipts from
interstate commerce. The "vice" inherent in such levies is that
the same income directly derived from interstate transactions
would be subjected to multiple state taxation. The result
would be that interstate business would be burdened with cumulative exactions "not borne by local business."

Such, at any rate, were Mr. Justice Stone's fears of multiple taxation as he had voiced them prior to the decision in
the Berwind-White case. While his opinion in that case did
not remove the constitutional objection to double taxation,
his failure to stress it may well presage its eventual abandonment. The complaint based on the possibility of cumulative
burdens proved unavailing; and it was rejected, it must be

his opinion convey the impression that he has come over to the view set
forth by Justice Brandeis in *Sprout* v. *City of South Bend* (cited above, n.
23), and this case is in fact cited by him. He said: "Since the subject taxed,
gasoline introduced into the state in the tank of a vehicle, for use solely
in propelling it in interstate commerce, is immune from state taxation
except for a limited state purpose, the exaction of a reasonable charge for
the use of its highways, it is not enough that the tax when collected
is expended upon the state's highways. It must appear on the face of
the statute or be demonstrable that the tax as laid is measured by or
has some relationship to the use of the highways for which the charge
is made." P. 181.

In a joint dissenting opinion, Justices Black, Frankfurter and Douglas
renewed their argument that the responsibility for "striking a fair balance" between state taxing power and the national interest in commerce
was a legislative one. Since the need for revenue was on the increase for
both governments, they insisted, it was "important that potential conflicts between state and national powers should not be found where Congress has not found them, unless conflict is established by demonstrable
concreteness." They thought that the majority had departed from the rule
in favor of the presumption of constitutionality.

noted, because the Justices were unable to say that the New York sales tax discriminated against interstate commerce.

In the last analysis, there is but one fundamental problem implicit in the divergent judicial views of the commerce clause. And that problem, as yet unresolved, is this: Precisely what does the commerce clause by its own force enjoin the states from doing? As stated, the question may seem highly technical and perhaps academic. But the answer to it may prove to be of great practical moment for the role of the Supreme Court in maintaining a free national market and, therefore, for the future of the American economy itself. For involved in this seemingly theoretical issue is the relative competence of the legislative and judicial processes to cope with the Balkanization of our national market. There is unanimity of judicial opinion that the commerce clause forbids outright discrimination against interstate and foreign commerce.[58] But undiguised hostility has not been the main peril. The years of the depression saw how manifold and ingenious are the ways of discriminating against interstate business and in favor of local interests.[59] Which branch of the government is most competent to deal with these state and local barriers to the free flow of trade? [60] A majority of the Court seems to have been won over to Mr. Justice Black's view that Congress, and not

[58] *Baldwin* v. *Seelig,* 294 U.S. 511 (1935), *Hale* v. *Bimco Trading Co.,* 306 U.S. 375 (1939).

[59] See Eugene F. Melder, *State and Local Barriers to Interstate Commerce in the United States* (Orono, Me.: Univ. of Maine Press, 1937).

[60] For a discussion of this problem, see Noel T. Dowling, "Interstate Commerce and State Power," *27 Va. L. Rev. 19* (Nov. 1940). Although Professor Dowling treats his proposal at some length, advancing five reasons for its adoption, its essence can be gathered from the following paragraph:

". . . in the absence of affirmative consent a Congressional negative will be presumed in the courts against state action which in its effect upon interstate commerce constitutes an unreasonable interference with national interests, the presumption being rebuttable at the pleasure of Congress. Such a doctrine would free the states from any constitutional disability but at the same time would not give them license to take such action as

the courts, is best able to deal with state actions interfering with interstate commerce.[61]

The commerce clause has been the main source of the Court's pronouncements concerning federalism. Chief Justice Stone would want the Court to be guided in its interpretation of that clause by an awareness of the problems of our society. Its responsibility is to "maintain the national interest and at the same time bring it into an effective harmony with local interests and the principles of local government." [62] If wisely applied, the commerce clause can continue to be a powerful influence for national unity:

> Great as is the practical wisdom exhibited in all the provisions of the Constitution, and important as were the character and influence of those who secured its adoption, it will, I believe, be the judgment of history that the Commerce Clause and a wise interpretation of it, perhaps more than any other contributing element, have united to bind the several states into a nation.[63]

they see fit irrespective of its effect upon interstate commerce. With respect to such commerce, the question whether the States may act upon it would depend upon the will of Congress expressed in such form as it may choose. State action falling short of such interference would prevail unless and until superseded or otherwise nullified by Congressional action." P. 20.

[61] In a case decided subsequent to the period covered by this study, Chief Justice Stone has reaffirmed his belief in the need for the ban on multiple tax burdens. By a bare majority of five, the Supreme Court in an opinion by Mr. Justice Frankfurter sustained a Minnesota tax on the entire fleet of airplanes operated in interstate transportation. *Northwest Airlines* v. *Minnesota,* 322 U.S. 292, 308 (1944). As the state of the company's "home port" and legal domicile, Minnesota was entitled to tax for the protection and benefits afforded. Dissenting, Chief Justice Stone protested that in upholding the tax the Court was exposing air transport to the risk of multiple taxation. Justices Roberts, Reed and Rutledge joined in this dissent.

[62] *53 A.B.A. Rep. 259, 264 (1928).*

[63] *Ibid.,* p. 264.

CHAPTER III

SCOPE OF FEDERAL POWER

1. *Federal Spending and the Constitution*

LONG BEFORE Franklin D. Roosevelt had launched his ill-starred effort to reform the judiciary by enlarging its membership, Mr. Justice Stone had scored his conservative colleagues and with far greater candor.[1] Probably the Justice's most forthright outcry against judicial censorship of public policy is to be found in his now famous dissenting opinion in the BUTLER case,[2] decided just one year before President Roosevelt submitted his court reorganization plan. And not the least interesting feature of the debate between Mr. Justice Stone and Mr. Justice Roberts in that case is the light it shed on the conflicting conceptions of the role of the Supreme Court in interpreting the Constitution. Revealing as they do sharp differences within the Court itself, the two opinions only help to document the background of the constitutional crisis that culminated in the New Deal's challenge to the judiciary. Yet the irony of that "crisis in power politics," as Robert H. Jackson has termed it,[3] is that the first and undoubtedly most measured criticism of the abuse of judicial power emanated from the Court's own members.

The wonder is, indeed, that in the face of such verbal as-

[1] It will be recalled that President Roosevelt's initial statement in behalf of an enlarged Court was rested primarily on the alleged overcrowded condition of its docket. Message to Congress, *81 Cong. Rec. 877* (Feb. 5, 1937).

[2] *United States* v. *Butler,* 297 U.S. 1, 78 (1936).

[3] The quoted phrase is the subtitle of Mr. Jackson's book, *The Struggle For Judicial Supremacy.*

saults as those by Mr. Justice Stone and others,[4] the President should nevertheless have remained silent concerning the need for constitutional reform during his appeal for reelection in the 1936 campaign. Whatever considerations may have dictated this strategy of official silence, it was clear even then that the New Deal experiments had precipitated some very serious questions of constitutional power. That the United States Supreme Court was deeply divided in its attitude toward these questions was obvious. Equally obvious was the refusal of the majority on the Bench to find in the Constitution authority for much of the federal action and control to which the administration had pledged itself.

By its decision in the BUTLER case, furthermore, the Court was apparently ignoring its own prior adjudications. For in striking down the second of the two major New Deal weapons for economic reconstruction,[5] the Court seemed to abandon the doctrine that it will not review the constitutionality of federal appropriations.[6] The purposes to which federal expenditures are to be put present no justiciable issue, Justice Sutherland had written for a unanimous Court in 1923.[7]

[4] See also Mr. Justice Stone's dissenting opinion in *Morehead* v. *New York* ex rel *Tipaldo*, 298 U.S. 587, 631 (1936), Chief Justice Hughes, dissenting in *Railroad Retirement Board* v. *Alton R.R. Co.*, 295 U.S. 330, 374 (1935), Mr. Justice Cardozo, dissenting in *United States* v. *Constantine*, 296 U.S. 287, 297 (1935).

[5] Six months earlier the Court had unanimously set aside the program for industrial reconstruction as embodied in Title I of the National Industrial Recovery Act. *Schechter Brothers Poultry Corp.* v. *United States*, 295 U.S. 495 (1935).

[6] *Massachusetts* v. *Mellon*, 262 U.S. 447 (1923).

[7] Thus in dismissing for want of jurisdiction the taxpayer's complaint to the grants of money under the Federal Maternity Act of 1921, Justice Sutherland said: "His [the taxpayer's] interest in the moneys of the treasury . . . is shared with millions of others; is comparatively minute and indeterminable, and the effect upon future taxation, of any payment out of the funds, so remote, fluctuating and uncertain, that no basis is afforded for an appeal to the preventive powers of a court of equity." And in dismissing the suit brought by the State of Massachusetts seeking to restrain the enforcement of the act, the Justice used this sweeping language: "In the last analysis, the complaint of the plaintiff State is brought

To the architects of the New Deal's program of recovery, this limitation on judicial interference with the power of the purse must have appeared like the "open sesame." It made less hopeless the task of overcoming the constitutional obstacles in the way of direct federal action. It suggested interesting possibilities for emergency economics and even for the administration's plan for more permanent social reconstruction. The Agricultural Adjustment Act of 1933 was the first major experiment with these possibilities.

One of the gravest problems inherited by the Roosevelt Administration was the agricultural decline of the post-war years. It was generally agreed that the economic distress of the American farmer was due to low prices and overproduction. To diminish the farm surplus at its source and thereby raise farm prices was the purpose of the Agricultural Adjustment Act. It was designed, according to its preamble, "to relieve the existing national economic emergency by increasing agricultural purchasing power." The Secretary of Agriculture was authorized to enter into contracts with farmers under which they were to reduce their output by taking part of their land out of cultivation. In return the farmers were to receive rental or benefit payments. These cash payments were to come out of the funds raised by the processing tax imposed by the act.[8] It was expected that these devices would raise the prices of agricultural products to the relative levels that prevailed between August, 1909 and July, 1914.[9]

to the naked contention that Congress has usurped the reserved powers of the several states by the mere enactment of the statute, though nothing has been done and nothing is to be done without their consent; and it is plain that the question, as it is thus presented, is political not judicial in character and, therefore, is not a matter which admits of the exercise of judicial power." 262 U.S. 447, 483 (1923).

[8] The so-called processing taxes were to be collected from the first domestic processor of the products covered by the act.

[9] 1909-1914 was the base period for wheat, corn, rice, hogs, dairy products and cotton. In the case of tobacco the intention was to raise prices to the level prevailing between 1919-1929.

This elaborate scheme for crop reduction and price raising was challenged in more than seventeen hundred separate
suits in the lower federal courts before it was finally set aside
by the United States Supreme Court on January 6, 1936.[10]
To the extent that the opinion by Mr. Justice Roberts sought
to show that there were no sanctions in the Constitution for
the Agricultural Adjustment Act, it must be regarded as one
of the most self-contradictory utterances ever to emanate from
the Court. Not only did the majority of six depart from
precedent in passing judgment on the validity of congressional appropriations, but it exposed itself to serious criticism
because of the logical inadequacies of its own reasoning. Its
decision can be reduced to three main propositions.

The first is that a federal tax is unenforceable if it is an
integral part of a system of regulation which the Congress
lacks the constitutional authority to undertake. The government had contended that the receivers of the Hoosac Mills
Corporation had no standing to challenge the collection of the
processing tax on cotton. Its position was that the tax was a
revenue-raising measure, enacted to raise funds for the Treasury, and that no taxpayer could question the legality of such
exactions. In distinguishing *Massachusetts* v. *Mellon*, Mr. Justice Roberts replied that the government was in effect request-
ing the Court to divide the Agricultural Adjustment Act into
two separate statutes, the provisions imposing the tax and
those disbursing the funds in the form of cash payments to
the farmers. He denied that the present suit was similar to
the assault on the Maternity Act of 1921. *Massachusetts* v.
Mellon laid down the principle that taxpayers may not question federal expenditures on the ground that such illegal di-
versions from the Treasury will enhance the burden of future

---

[10] "1600 injunctions had been granted by district judges to restrain
collection of the processing tax under the Agricultural Adjustment Act,
and denied in only 166 cases." Jackson, *op. cit.*, p. 140.

taxation. In the BUTLER case, on the other hand, the objection to the tax was that it formed an "indispensable" part of a scheme for controlling agricultural production, an activity over which Congress had no legislative warrant.

It may be said that the distinction drawn by Mr. Justice Roberts begs the question.[11] His exact language was:

> It was there [*Massachusetts* v. *Mellon*] held that a taxpayer of the United States may not question expenditures from its treasury on the ground that the alleged unlawful diversion will deplete the public funds and thus increase the burden of future taxation. . . . But here the respondents who are called upon to pay moneys as taxes, resist the exaction as a step in an unauthorized plan. This circumstance clearly distinguishes the case.

But this distinction is verbal and ignores the fact that the Federal Maternity Act was resisted because of the alleged unlawful purposes to which the federal funds were to be put. The program of aid to the states in promoting infant and maternal hygiene was fought in the courts on the ground that the federal government was tempting the states to surrender part of their sovereignty by the offer to them of financial assistance.

Mr. Justice Roberts declared that the only type of tax involving the "expropriation of money from one group for the benefit of another" deemed constitutional is one "imposed to effectuate regulation of a matter in which both groups are interested and in respect of which there is a power of legisla-

11 As a purely formal matter the problem involved in *Massachusetts* v. *Mellon* can be differentiated from the issue in the BUTLER case by the fact that the processing taxes were earmarked for a definite purpose. Seen in this technical light, it is possible to argue that while the interest of the federal taxpayer in the general funds of the Treasury is too indefinite for him to be able to question the constitutionality of a particular expenditure, the interest of those subject to an "earmarked" tax was sufficiently definite to give them standing to question the expenditure for a purpose said to be forbidden by the Constitution.

tive regulation." Even if this were a sound principle of construction, it still was true that in *Massachusetts* v. *Mellon* a unanimous Court declined to inquire into the legality of the policy embodied in the challenged act. The ultimate constitutionality of the legislative objectives was deemed to raise "political" questions lying outside the Court's jurisdiction. Yet despite this earlier rule on which the government relied as precedent, the majority in the BUTLER case proceeded to invalidate the processing taxes solely on the ground of the alleged unlawful purposes to which the funds raised by them were to be devoted. That this was the basis for the Court's decision was vigorously maintained by Mr. Justice Stone in his opinion for the minority.[12] As he said:

> The constitutional power of Congress to levy an excise tax upon the processing of agricultural products is not questioned. The present levy is held invalid, not for any want of power in Congress to lay such a tax to defray public expenditures, including those for the general welfare, but because the use to which its proceeds are put is disapproved.

More astounding, however, than even its reason for taking jurisdiction was the Court's approach to what Mr. Justice Roberts called "the great and controlling question in the case." This was the question whether the expenditures contemplated by the Agricultural Adjustment Act were authorized by the general welfare clause of the Constitution.[13]

Solicitor General Reed had argued that since the economic dislocations in agriculture were nationwide in their extent and effects, the expenditure of federal funds in aid of farmers was within the power of Congress to impose taxes "to provide for

---

[12] Justices Cardozo and Brandeis joined in Mr. Justice Stone's dissent.
[13] "The Congress shall have the power (1) to lay and collect taxes, duties, imposts, and excises, to pay the debts, and provide for the common defense and general welfare of the United States; . . ." *Constitution,* Art. I, Sec. 8, Par. 1.

the . . . general welfare." He also contended that the clause ought to be liberally construed to apply to any activity conducive to national welfare. It was for Congress to determine what would promote the welfare of the United States; courts are powerless to pass on the legality of such legislative decisions.

These contentions led the Court to examine the recurring historic controversy over the intent and scope of the general welfare clause. Mr. Justice Roberts noted that three separate views have been held as to the meaning of the phrase in dispute. According to the first, the clause conferred on Congress power to provide for the general welfare, independently of or by means other than the taxing-spending power.[14] In this view, Congress possesses a separate substantive power to promote the general welfare of the nation. Mr. Justice Roberts observed that this interpretation has never been "authoritatively accepted." [15] Also unsatisfactory was the view advocated by James Madison. According to Madison, the clause in question meant no more than that Congress was obliged to limit the spending of the funds raised by taxation to the purposes represented by the specific powers conferred on it by the Constitution. The grant of power to tax and spend for the general welfare, in other words, could not reach fields to which the regulatory powers did not extend.[16] In rejecting the Madisonian theory, Mr. Justice Roberts pointed out that its adop-

[14] Mr. Justice Roberts conceded that "the power to appropriate is as broad as the power to tax."

[15] Mr. Justice Story had long ago said that if the first view were ever adopted, then "under color of the generality of the words to 'provide for the common defense and the general welfare' the government of the United States [would] in reality, [be] a government of general and unlimited powers, notwithstanding the subsequent enumeration of specific powers." (Quoted by Mr. Justice Roberts.)

[16] These views were set forth by Madison in a letter to Andrew Stevenson, Nov. 27, 1830, to be found in *Writings of James Madison*, ed. Gaillard Hunt (New York: G. P. Putnam's Sons, 1910), IX, 1819-36.

tion would render the general welfare clause superfluous, since "taxation and appropriation are or may be necessary incidents of the exercise of any of the enumerated legislative powers."

Alexander Hamilton has lent his name to the third view as to the meaning of the general welfare clause. In his famous Report on Manufactures, Hamilton had maintained that the Constitution confers on Congress a separate and distinct power to tax and appropriate and that the sole limitation to which it was subject was that it be exercised to provide for the national or general welfare.[17] It is obvious that the import of the Hamiltonian doctrine was that the spending power of the federal government extended to purposes beyond those represented by the specific enumerated powers and that, therefore, the spending power was much broader than was the power to regulate.

Mr. Justice Roberts, as spokesman for the majority in the BUTLER case, accepted Hamilton's view as the true construction of the general welfare clause. He said:

Study of all these [the three interpretations] leads us to conclude that the reading advocated by Mr. Justice Story is the correct one. While, therefore, the power to tax is not unlimited, its confines are set in the clause which confers it, and not in those of Section 8 which bestow and define the legislative powers of the Congress. It results that the power of Congress to authorize expenditure of public moneys for public purposes is not limited by the direct grants of legislative power found in the Constitution.[18]

17 "The only qualification of the generality of the phrase in question [the general welfare clause], which seems to be admissible, is this: that the object to which an appropriation of money is to be made be general, and not local; its operation extending in fact or by possibility throughout the Union, and not being confined to a particular spot. Alexander Hamilton, *Papers on Public Credit, Commerce and Finance*, ed. Samuel McKee, Jr. (New York: Columbia Univ. Press, 1934), pp. 239-40.

18 Mr. Justice Story in his *Commentaries* also treated the Hamiltonian thesis as the correct one.

If on January 6, 1936, one had read the excerpt just quoted and nothing else from the majority opinion, it would have looked as though the Government had won its case. For the Government too had claimed that the phrase "to provide for the . . . general welfare" qualifies the power "to lay and collect taxes" and that the grant of power to tax and spend was not to be confined to the enumerated legislative fields committed to Congress. Yet after adopting unequivocally the Hamilton-Story version as the Court's own position, the majority proceeded to apply it to the case in hand in a form which not only seems wholly contrary to that view but was more in keeping with Madison's conception of the general welfare clause.

Under that conception, it may be asked, what exactly was the constitutional barrier to federal expenditures for the relief of farm distress? Presumably, Madison might have objected that among the enumerated powers of Congress was not to be found the authority to control agricultural production. Strangely enough, that also was one of the grounds advanced by Mr. Justice Roberts. Though he had espoused the Hamiltonian theory, he refused to discuss the scope of the general welfare clause. That inquiry was unnecessary, he said, because the Agricultural Adjustment Act must fall as constituting an unconstitutional encroachment upon the reserved powers of the states. He wrote:

The Act invades the reserved rights of the states. It is a statutory plan to regulate agriculture and control agricultural production, a matter beyond the powers delegated to the federal government. The tax, the appropriation of the funds raised, and the direction for their disbursement, are but parts of the plan. They are a means to an unconstitutional end.

. . . powers not granted [to the federal government] are prohibited. None to regulate agricultural production is given, and therefore legislation by Congress for that purpose is forbidden.[19]

[19] Mr. Justice Roberts likened the processing taxes to the tax involved in the the CHILD LABOR TAX case, *Bailey* v. *Drexel Furniture Co.*, 259 U.S. 20

There are two obvious weaknesses in this argument based on the alleged restrictions of the Tenth Amendment. In the first place, if it is true that the power of Congress to spend funds raised by taxation is not confined to the specific delegated powers—and the Court so assumed—then it is something less than logical to point to the absence of the power to regulate agricultural production as the chief ground for declaring the Agricultural Adjustment Act unconstitutional. The Court was really saying that the taxing-spending power does not extend to the regulation of agriculture because the power over interstate commerce does not encompass the control of agricultural production. The Court was thus ignoring the only legal question that should have been raised: Were the cash benefits for the general welfare of the United States?

The conclusion to which the Court came, moreover, was notable for a second major fallacy. Assuming that Congress can appropriate money in promotion of the general welfare, it is immaterial that the scheme implementing the purpose of Congress has an effect on the internal economy of the states. The supremacy clause of the Constitution, it must be remembered in this connection, declares acts of Congress to be the supreme law of the land.[20] Furthermore, to say that the re-

(1922). But as Mr. Justice Stone pointed out in his dissent, the tax involved in the CHILD LABOR TAX case was itself the means or instrument for effecting the regulation sought by Congress. The regulatory effect of the Agricultural Adjustment Act, that is, curtailment of acreage, on the other hand, was to follow not from the imposition of the tax on the processors but only by means of the cash benefits made to the farmers. The regulation contemplated by the Agricultural Adjustment Act, Mr. Justice Stone declared, was to be "accomplished not by the tax but by the method by which its proceeds are expended and would equally be accomplished by any like use of public funds, regardless of their source."

20 "This Constitution, and the laws of the United States which shall be made in pursuance thereof; and all treaties made, or which shall be made, under the authority of the United States, shall be the supreme law of the land; and the Judges in every State shall be bound thereby, anything in the Constitution or laws of any State to the contrary notwithstanding." *Constitution,* Art. VI, cl. 2.

Writing in 1936, Professor Corwin remarked that the "test" by which

served powers of the states limit the spending power of Congress is to assume that the reserved powers are specifically enumerated in the Constitution.

But the third and final ground on which the majority rested its decision was perhaps the weakest of all, as it was also the most vulnerable.

> If the taxing power may not be used as the instrument to enforce a regulation of matters of state concern with respect to which the Congress has no authority to interfere, may it as in the present case, be employed to raise the money necessary to purchase a compliance which the Congress is powerless to command?

With this question Mr. Justice Roberts introduced the Court's repudiation of the government's contention that because the acreage reduction program depended on the voluntary cooperation of the farmers, the Agricultural Adjustment Act should not be viewed as coercive federal control of local matters. He denied that the scheme embodied in the Agricultural Adjustment Act was voluntary and insisted that it was compulsory. Admitting that the farmers might refuse to accept the terms of agreement offered by the Secretary of Agriculture, he stated that the "price of such refusal is the loss of benefits." In other words, the majority in this case, turning psychoanalysts, allowed themselves to discuss an important constitutional issue in terms of concealed motives.[21] The temptation

---

Justice Roberts concluded that the Agricultural Adjustment Act invaded the reserved power of the states to regulate agricultural production was "to all appearances applied in a form that would totally repeal the supremacy clause so far as the spending power is concerned, . . ." Edward, S. Corwin, *The Commerce Power* v. *States Rights* (Princeton: Princeton Univ. Press, 1936), p. 242.

[21] As Justice Cardozo said in speaking of the prevailing opinion in *United States* v. *Constantine,* "The judgment of the Court rests upon the ruling that another purpose, not professed may be read beneath the surface, and the purpose so imputed the statute is destroyed. Thus the process of psychoanalysis has spread to unaccustomed fields." 296 U.S. 297, 299 (1935).

held out by the cash benefits was too great, they said, for the individual farmer to be able not to yield to it. Paraphrasing Marshall's dictum with respect to the power to tax, Mr. Justice Roberts asserted that the "power to confer or withhold unlimited benefits is the power to coerce or destroy," and added that rather than leaving the farmers any genuine power of choice the Agricultural Adjustment Act involved "coercion by economic pressure."

Nor did the Court stop there. It went on to hold that even if the agricultural program were one for voluntary cooperation, the federal government would still lack the authority to undertake it. The whole plan was designed to "purchase" compliance with a system of regulation for which there was no constitutional sanction. It was "a scheme for purchasing with federal funds submission to federal regulation of a subject reserved to the states." While funds appropriated by Congress may be expended under contracts between the government and private persons, such contracts are illegal when the federal government lacks the authority to undertake the activities they seek to promote. Accordingly, the contracts for the reduction of acreage entered into by the Secretary of Agriculture and individual farmers "offend" the Constitution, because the expenditures they contemplated were intended to induce action in a field over which the federal government had no power. "The Congress cannot invade state jurisdiction to compel individual action," said Mr. Justice Roberts, "no more can it purchase such action."

To all of these arguments, three of the Court's justices entered a most emphatic dissent. Seldom has the position taken by a majority of the Court been subjected to so withering an assault as is contained in the forthright rebuke administered by Mr. Justice Stone in the BUTLER case. Not only did he uproot the foundation from under every one of the grounds advanced by the majority, but in Holmes-like language he challenged the majority's conception of the Court's function under the Constitution.

After setting down "guiding principles of decision which ought never to be absent from judicial consciousness," Mr. Justice Stone began his sharply worded refutation. He came at once to what he called the "pivot" of the decision: "The present levy is held invalid, not for want of any power in Congress to lay such a tax to defray public expenditures, including those of the general welfare but because of the use to which its proceeds are put is disapproved." He was assuming that the majority agreed with him that the regulation was not effected by the processing tax imposed under the Agricultural Adjustment Act. He also assumed that expenditures in promotion of the general welfare are as valid as expenditures for any other governmental purpose.

With these uncontroverted matters in mind, Mr. Justice Stone proceeded to analyze what he regarded as the indefensible basis for the majority's opinion, that the disbursements to the farmers were an indirect invasion of state power. He pointed out that every federal tax could be found to have some effect upon the internal economy of the states, and argued that that collateral result is not to be assigned as ground for upsetting the tax if it is one authorized by the Constitution. The tax on processors was typical of innumerable other federal excise levies. If such were the case, then why did the majority of the Court object to the collection of the tax?

In answering this question, Mr. Justice Stone made it plain that he regarded the outcome in the case as a "contradiction in terms," particularly when seen in the light of the majority's acceptance of the Hamilton-Story view of the federal spending power. According to that theory, the federal government's power of the purse was in addition to and independent of any of the delegated powers. Yet Mr. Justice Roberts justified the

Court's nullification of the Agricultural Adjustment Act by arguing in the main that among the delegated powers there was not to be found any to control agricultural production. The minority, on the other hand, was able to find the necessary constitutional authority in the specifically granted power to expend federal funds in promotion of the general welfare. Mr. Justice Stone maintained that the assertions of the majority were completely contradicted by two salient facts implicit in its own discussion. The first was the recognition that the agricultural depression was nationwide in its extent and effects, so that he could see "no basis for saying" that federal expenditures for relief of the farm problem were not within the power of Congress to impose taxes to provide for the general welfare. The second was the obvious truth that the sole means for making certain that the constitutional requirement concerning the expenditure of public funds is met is for Congress to attach conditions to such expenditures.[22] Conditional payments and grants are made necessary, at least from a constitutional standpoint, simply because many problems sought to be controlled cannot be reached by Congress in any other way.

The Constitution requires [Mr. Justice Stone declared] that public funds shall be spent for a defined purpose, the promotion of the general welfare. Their expenditure usually involves payment

[22] Although Mr. Justice Roberts did not deny that Congress may attach conditions to federal grants, he argued that those seeking the conditional payments may not be required to make contracts under which they agree to undertake activities not subject to federal regulation. "Appropriations and expenditures under contracts for proper governmental purposes cannot justify contracts which are not within federal power. And contracts for the reduction of acreage and the control of production are outside the area of that power." These distinctions ignore the numerous instances in which the Court sanctioned federal action in fields which could not be reached by direct federal regulation.

For an analysis of the "unsatisfactory line of reasoning" followed by Mr. Justice Roberts in discussing the federal government's contractual powers, see Charles S. Collier, "Judicial Bootstraps and the General Welfare Clause," *4 Geo. Wash. L. Rev. 211,* particularly pp. 225-28 (Jan. 1936).

on terms which will insure use by the selected recipients within the limits of the constitutional purpose. Expenditures would fail of their purpose and thus lose their constitutional sanction if the terms of payment were not such that by their influence on the action of the recipients the permitted end would be attained. The power of Congress to spend is inseparable from persuasion to action over which Congress has no legislative control.[23]

So long as the terms of the contracts entered into between the Secretary of Agriculture and individual farmers were in furtherance of the policy for which the money was appropriated, it made no difference that the power of Congress to tax and spend was being used to cope with an economic condition with which Congress could not deal by direct legislative action. The effects of the promises and conditions contained in these contracts—including any effects on the internal economy of the states—were but incidents of the congressional power to spend public funds to provide for the general welfare.[24] By insisting that this "purchased regulation" of agricultural production constituted an invasion of state power, the majority was allowing itself to apply a test of the limits of the spending power which the Court had rejected in relation to the other powers of Congress. Mr. Justice Stone charged that the majority was in effect reversing the "time-honored principle of con-

[23] Mr. Justice Stone illustrated by reference to the several objects of federal grants-in-aid, such as the appropriations in aid of agricultural education. Thus he wrote: "Congress may not command that the science of agriculture be taught in state universities. But if it would aid the teaching of that science by grants to state institutions, it is appropriate, if not necessary, that the grant be on the condition . . . that it be used for the intended purpose. Similarly it would seem to be compliance with the Constitution, not violation of it, for the government to take and the University to give a contract that the grant be so used."

[24] To the argument that the payments to the farmers were a form of economic coercion, Mr. Justice Stone replied that no such objection had been presented by the taxpayers. His attitude to that contention is best summed up in the terse sentence: "Threat of loss, not hope of gain, is the essence of economic coercion."

stitutional interpretation that the granted power includes all those which are incident to it." [25]

Mr. Justice Stone was particularly disturbed by the possible devitalizing effects of the Roberts opinion upon the general welfare clause itself. The power to tax and spend seemed to be threatened by unworkable restrictions on the uses to which federal funds might be put. He complained that the majority's insistence that the payments to the farmers were infringing state power was setting up a limitation which might render useless the vital power to spend for the public welfare.

Such a limitation is contradictory and destructive of the power to appropriate for the public welfare, and is incapable of practical application. The spending power of Congress is in addition to the legislative power and not subordinate to it. This independent grant of the power of the purse, and its very nature, involving in its exercise the duty to insure expenditure within the granted power, presupposed freedom of selection among divers ends and aims, and the capacity to impose such conditions as will render the choice effective. It is a contradiction in terms to say that there is power to spend for the national welfare, while rejecting any power to impose conditions reasonably adapted to the attainment of the end which alone would justify the expenditure.[26]

[25] Regulation of intrastate rates by the Interstate Commerce Commission in protection of interstate rates was cited by Mr. Justice Stone as one of the evidences of the Court's adherence to this principle. See the SHREVE-PORT RATE case, where Justice Hughes said: "Wherever the interstate and intrastate transactions of carriers are so related that the government of the one involves the control of the other, it is Congress, and not the state, that is entitled to prescribe the final and dominant rule, for otherwise Congress would be denied the exercise of its constitutional authority and the state, and not the Nation, would be supreme within the national field." *Houston E. & W. Ry. Co.* v. *United States,* 234 U.S. 342, 351-52 (1914).

[26] Following this statement, Mr. Justice Stone enumerated some of the "absurd consequences" which might ensue if the Court's conception of the general welfare clause prevailed. For example, the federal government would be allowed to make gifts of money to those out of work but not to require the recipients to work or to contribute to the support of their families.

It is not often that such widely divergent opinions are written in the same case as those read by Justices Stone and Roberts in the Butler case. The differences that separated them, moreover, were more significant than is indicated by their disagreement over the meaning of a vital clause of the Constitution. Their opinions reveal a fundamental conflict with respect to the Court's role under our constitutional system, and the divergence would have been evident even if the Justices had not stopped to engage in explicit discussion regarding the nature of the judicial function. In reading that discussion one senses the drama of the debate that must have taken place in conference. Dignified judicial utterance could not cloak the fact that feeling must have run high before the final vote. And it can also be surmised that the minority's charge of abuse of power against the majority rankled most of all. The charge did not go unanswered; and the response which it elicited from Mr. Justice Roberts is in the best tradition of the Marshallian apologia for the exercise of judicial power.[27]

We are warned against the "misconception" that the United States Supreme Court has assumed a power "to overrule or control the action of the people's representatives." We are reminded that it is the Constitution which is the supreme law of the land "ordained and established by the people," and that "all legislation must conform to the principles it lays down." Then follows a description of the Court's function under the Constitution which is by far the best statement of what Professor Corwin has called "the theory of the automatism of the Court's role in relation to the Constitution." [28] Mr. Justice Roberts wrote:

[27] "Judicial power as contradistinguished from the power of the laws has no existence. Courts are the mere instruments of the law and can will nothing." Chief Justice Marshall, *Osborne* v. *United States Bank,* 9 Wheat 738, 766 (1824).

[28] Edward S. Corwin, *Twilight of the Supreme Court* (New Haven: Yale Univ. Press, 1934), p. XXV.

When an act of Congress is appropriately challenged in the courts as not conforming to the constitutional mandate the judicial branch of the Government has only one duty,—to lay the article of the Constitution which is invoked beside the statute which is challenged and to decide whether the latter squares with the former. All the Court does, or can do, is to announce its considered judgment upon the question. The only power it has, if such it may be called, is the power of judgment. This Court neither approves nor condemns any legislative policy. Its delicate and difficult office is to ascertain and declare whether the legislation is in accordance with, or in contravention of, provisions of the Constitution; and having done that, its duty ends.

This claim that the act of constitutional interpretation is mechanically automatic obviously assumes more than it is possible to prove. Indeed, it is little short of amazing that so informed a jurist as Mr. Justice Roberts has proved himself to be on many occasions should have permitted himself to paint so naïve and simple a picture of the judicial function. His thesis takes for granted contentions to which the entire history of the judicial veto as exercised by the United States Supreme Court has afforded a never-ending series of refutations. Among these refutations, one is tempted to add, must be included the sharp division of the Court in the BUTLER case itself.

Actually, the claim of automatism in the day-to-day operation of the judicial process distorts seriously the nature of our Constitution as well as the nature of constitutional construction in the United States. Such a theory must assume that the provisions of the Constitution are clear, specific and undebatable. Since the days of Marshall, it has been recognized that the vital clauses of the Constitution, because they are anything but unambiguous, depend for their practical application upon the interpretations they have elicited. The simple mechanical approach assumes, in the second place, that constitutional interpretation has remained changeless, unequivocal and indeed fixed. But most unrealistic of all is the implication that the Justices are left no choice in their exercise of judicial power.[29]

In his dissenting opinion, Mr. Justice Stone has unequivocally repudiated the view of constitutional interpretation which pictures judicial decisions as being completely devoid of subjective factors. He rejected the notion that the Supreme Court is without choice in the meanings which it ascribes to the Constitution, and asserted that ultimately self-restraint is the sole check upon the exercise of judicial power. With candor rare in judicial utterance, he commenced his analysis of the Agricultural Adjustment Act with a statement which indicated his awareness of the extent to which the fate of legislative efforts has come to depend upon judicial discretion. He placed first among the propositions to which he assigned "controlling influence in determining the validity of the Act," the unique power of the judiciary to control the actions of the other two branches of government.

The power of courts to declare a statute unconstitutional is subject to two guiding principles of decision which ought never to be absent from judicial consciousness. One is that courts are concerned only with the power to enact statutes, not with their wisdom. The other is that while unconstitutional exercise of power by the

29 It is both ironic and instructive to recall that the highly mechanistic conception of the judicial function voiced by Mr. Justice Roberts in the BUTLER case should have been contradicted by himself when he wrote the opinion upholding the Agricultural Adjustment Act of 1938. *Mulford* v. *Smith*, 307 U.S. 38, 51 (1939). Over the objections of Justices Butler and McReynolds that the 1938 law sought to control farm production in violation of the Tenth Amendment, the majority in an opinion by Mr. Justice Roberts, sustained an act which was considerably more compulsory in its terms than the original experiment with acreage reduction schemes. In the course of denying that the Agricultural Adjustment Act of 1938 was a "statutory plan to control agricultural production and, therefore, beyond the powers delegated to Congress," Mr. Justice Roberts is found saying: "The motive of Congress in exerting the power [to regulate interstate commerce] is irrelevant to the validity of the legislation." P. 48.

executive and legislative branches of the government is subject to judicial restraint, the only check upon our own exercise of power is our own sense of self-restraint. For the removal of unwise laws from the statute books appeal lies not to the Courts but to the ballot and to the processes of democratic government.

This statement of guiding principles was much more than an appeal for judicial self-limitation. It was but the starting point of a plea for a more generous appreciation of the great functions assigned to the executive and legislative departments in the maintenance of practical democracy. Both of these fundamentals of judicial statesmanship were fully elaborated in the closing paragraphs of his dissent. The majority, he emphasized, allowed itself the luxury of upsetting an important statute upon the "groundless speculation" that the power under which it was enacted might be seriously abused.

"If, in lieu of compulsory regulation of subjects within the states' reserved jurisdiction, which is prohibited," Mr. Justice Roberts had remarked, "the Congress could invoke the taxing and spending power as a means to accomplish the same end, clause 1 of Sec. 8 of Article I would become the instrument for total subversion of the governmental powers reserved to the individual states." Starting with this assumption, he set down a long list of possible abuses which might follow if the view of the federal spending power for which the defenders of the Agricultural Adjustment Act had argued were to prevail. He sought to show that an expanded power to spend might be used by the federal government as a lever for pressing producers of raw materials, manufacturers and miners into compliance with schemes regulating essentially local conditions. The result would be, he feared, that "every business group which thought itself underprivileged might demand that a tax be laid on its vendors or vendees the proceeds to be appropriated to the redress of its deficiency of income."

Unimpressed with this "parade of horribles," as Thomas

Reed Powell has characterized this brand of judicial reasoning, Mr. Justice Stone said of the suggestion that unless judicially limited the power of the purse might be used for undesirable and constitutionally prohibited ends, that it "hardly rises to the dignity of argument." His simple retort was: "So may judicial power be abused." Its implication that the judiciary must protect against reckless governmental action irked him much; for it argued for a power in courts to weigh the wisdom of legislation when considering its constitutionality. The judiciary was but one of the guardians of the freedom and well-being of the people; the responsibility of the legislative department was no less great.

A tortured construction of the Constitution is not to be justified by recourse to extreme examples of reckless Congressional spending which might occur if courts could not prevent expenditures which even if they could be thought to effect any national purpose, would be possible only by action of a legislature lost to all sense of public responsibility. Such suppositions are addressed to the mind accustomed to believe that it is the business of courts to sit in judgment on the wisdom of legislative action. Courts are not the only agency of government that must be assumed to have capacity to govern. Congress and the courts both unhappily may falter or be mistaken in the performance of their constitutional duty. But interpretation of our great charter of government which proceeds on any assumption that the responsibility for the preservation of our institutions is the exclusive concern of any one of the three branches of government, or that it alone can save them from destruction is far more likely, in the long run, "to obliterate the constituent members" of "an indestructible union of indestructible states" than the frank recognition that language, even of a constitution, may mean what it says: that the power to tax and spend includes the power to relieve a nationwide economic maladjustment by conditional gifts of money.

Mr. Justice Stone did not wait long for the day when his liberal conception of the spending power came to prevail.

That day came when the Supreme Court, dividing five to four, upheld the Social Security Act of 1935.[30] Although the Court attempted to differentiate the statutory structure of the Agricultural Adjustment Act from the Social Security Act, the constitutional distinction sought to be drawn is rather slender.[31] The outcome in the case may legitimately be considered as in effect reversing the doctrines set down in *United States* v. *Butler*. Justice Cardozo's memorable statement—"It is too late today for the argument to be heard with tolerance that in a crisis so extreme the use of the moneys of the nation to relieve the unemployed and their dependents is a use for any purpose narrower than the promotion of the general welfare"—is but a reassertion of Mr. Justice Stone's view of the general welfare clause in the BUTLER case.

2. *Federal Power over Industrial Conditions*

The history of modern legislation is replete with accounts of resistance to governmental efforts to soften the impact of industrialism. Everywhere, it would seem, every attempt to set limits to the policies of private enterprise has been an uphill climb, along a path strewn with obstacles shaped by inertia, entrenched interests and short-sighted thinking. America has been no exception. On the contrary, efforts to ameliorate the

[30] *Steward Machine Co.* v. *Davis,* 301 U.S. 548 (1937).

[31] Mr. Justice Cardozo compared the two statutes by summarizing the situation presented by the unemployment compensation provisions of the Social Security Act under four headings:

"(a) The proceeds of the tax in controversy are not earmarked for a special group.

"(b) The unemployment compensation law which is a condition of the credit has had the approval of the state and could not be a law without it.

"(c) The condition is not linked to an irrevocable agreement, for the state at its pleasure may repeal its unemployment law, . . . terminate the credit and place itself where it was before the credit was accepted.

"(d) The condition is not directed to the attainment of an unlawful end, but to an end, the relief of unemployment, for which nation and state may lawfully cooperate." 301 U.S. 548, 592-93 (1937).

abuses that had crept into our industrial system have had to overcome an additional hurdle which, at times, effectively blocked those efforts. Enlightened legislators and practical reformers have been faced with the necessity of adapting their proposals to the peculiar requirements of our constitutional structure.

In numerous instances, moreover, endeavors to cope with the "dire consequences of laissez-faire" to borrow a phrase from Mr. Justice Douglas,[32] have been nullified by judicial exposition which was something less than realistic. With the notable exception of its attitude to the problems of railroad regulation, the Supreme Court has failed at times to take into account the economic and social transformations which had necessitated intervention by the national government. As a result, the impression was not infrequently created that the Constitution stood as a barrier to social progress in general and economic stability in particular. Only the persistent dissents by some of the Court's own members helped to detract from that impression, and to dramatize the strategic role of the Court as final interpreter of our fundamental law.

Because the fate of regulation of business was seen as depending ultimately upon judicial attitudes, the Supreme Court often found itself the object of praise and blame by the contending forces in our society. It is not surprising, therefore, that the drastic systems of industrial control instituted by the New Deal administration should have precipitated a challenge to judicial supremacy. Confronted by the country's worst depression, whose ravages affected the entire economy, the Roosevelt administration resorted to remedies that were no less unprecedented.

Having diagnosed the many economic maladjustments as nationwide in their origin and effects, the President and his

---

[32] *Sunshine Anthracite Coal Co.* v. *Adkins,* 310 U.S. 381, 396 (1940).

advisers launched a series of experiments involving untried methods of national action. During the space of one hundred days,[33] the President requested and Congress enacted into law measures for the regulation of the American economy whose implication was the virtual abandonment of laissez-faire economics and prevailing constitutional doctrines.[34] So far as national regulation of industry and agriculture were concerned, probably the most serious obstacle was the formula by which the Supreme Court had erected the Tenth Amendment into a test of the limits of federal power under the commerce and taxing clauses.[35]

Although not with uniform consistency in all cases where the issue was at stake, the Court continued to regard activities and relationships surrounding the productive process—in factory, mine and quarry—as having at most an "indirect" effect on interstate commerce and, therefore, as not being regulable by Congress under its commerce power. The distinction between "interstate commerce" and so-called "production," the classification of production as local or intrastate in character, the use of the Tenth Amendment as a measure of the limits of national authority, all these were part of the larger rationale by which the Court justified in crucial cases its rejection of attempted federal control of the industrial process on

[33] Beginning March 9, 1933, the opening day of the special session of Congress called by President Roosevelt immediately after assuming office.

[34] Professor Corwin's commendable effort of 1934 to anticipate the shape of the constitutional issues about to come before the Court was invaluable then, as it has continued to be, for an understanding of the full significance of these implications. He was examining alternatives in constitutional theory, by way of pointing to those which might have served as a basis for upholding the first innovations of the New Deal. Edward S. Corwin, *Twilight Of The Supreme Court.*

[35] The major exceptions were the country's railroads, *Wilson* v. *New,* 243 U.S. 332 (1917), *Texas & New Orleans R.R. Co.* v. *Brotherhood of Ry. and SS Clerks,* 281 U.S. 548 (1930); stockyards, *Stafford* v. *Wallace,* 258 U.S. 495 (1922); and grain exchanges, *Chicago Board of Trade* v. *Olsen,* 262 U.S. 1 (1923).

the ground that it would result in an invasion of state power.[36] In more concrete terms, it may be said that rates of pay, hours of work and labor relations were among the factors of production which were not subject to regulation by the federal government. It need hardly be added that no single case ever so decided, at least not until the opinion by Chief Justice Hughes in the SCHECHTER case.[37]

Yet dominant Supreme Court thought, beginning with Fuller's opinion in the SUGAR TRUST case, never suggested that regulation under the commerce clause could reach the operations and relationships within the industrial plant itself. Barring its unsuccessful efforts to end the employment of children by prohibiting interstate shipment of products made by them, it was not until 1933 that Congress undertook to regulate labor conditions in industry. The far-reaching provisions of the National Industrial Recovery Act were bound to furnish a crucial test of the Court's conception of the federal commerce power. Would the Court apply to industry in general its broad view of that power as it had applied it, for example, to the railroads?

By its unanimous decision in the SCHECHTER case, the Court made it unmistakably clear that it was not prepared to agree with the Administration that the power of Congress under the commerce clause extended to industry as a whole. In the opinion of the Court, to be sure, the Schechters were operating a strictly local business. The argument of government counsel, based on the possible interstate effects of the practices pursued by the Schechters in their Brooklyn slaughterhouse markets, was characterized by Chief Justice Hughes as "proving too much."

[36] *United States* v. *E. C. Knight Co.,* 150 U.S. 1 (1895), *Hammer* v. *Dagenhart* 247 U.S. 251 (1918), *Bailey* v. *Drexel Furniture Co.* 259 U.S. 20 (1922).

[37] *Schechter Brothers Poultry Corp.* v. *United States,* 295 U.S. 495 (1935).

As to the commerce power feature of the SCHECHTER case, there were some who insisted that the outcome in the case signified nothing more important than that the government had selected a "bad" case with which to test the constitutionality of the N.I.R.A. The Live Poultry Code, particularly as applied to the Schechter Brothers, it was contended, did not involve any of the really basic national industries. This line of reasoning missed the long-range significance of the SCHECHTER opinion. The principle so clearly enunciated by the Chief Justice, that wages and hours were part of local or intrastate activity not to be "governed" by the national authority, should have left no doubt as to its import for the future of regulation of business.[38]

That the more optimistic view of the ruling in the SCHECHTER case was more wish than fact was made even plainer when the Court a year later invalidated the so-called Guffey Coal Act of 1935.[39] On the very face of it, the country's soft coal mines could hardly be considered anything less than a nationwide industry; and yet federal regulation of labor conditions in that industry was thought by six of the Court's Justices not to be authorized by the commerce clause.[40] As Mr. Justice Douglas remarked four years later, when the Court upheld the Bituminous Coal Act of 1937: "If the stra-

---

[38] "The question of chief importance relates to the provisions of the code as to the hours and wages of those employed in defendants' slaughterhouse markets. It is plain that these requirements are imposed in order to govern the details of defendants' management of their local business. The persons employed in slaughtering and selling in local trade are not employed in interstate commerce. Their hours and wages have no direct relation to interstate commerce." 295 U.S. 495, 548 (1935).

[39] *Carter* v. *Carter Coal Co.,* 298 U.S. 238 (1936).

[40] While Chief Justice Hughes agreed with five of his associates that the labor provisions of the Bituminous Coal Conservation Act of 1935 were unconstitutional, he dissented against their refusal to separate those provisions from the price-fixing features of the act. He was of the opinion that the power of Congress under the commerce clause was broad enough to include the fixing of prices for coal shipped interstate. 298 U.S. 238, 317 (1936).

tegic character of this industry [the bituminous coal industry] in our economy and the chaotic conditions which have prevailed in it do not justify legislation, it is difficult to imagine what would." [41]

Clearly, then, the rationale of the SCHECHTER decision, especially as reinforced by Justice Sutherland's even more emphatic pronouncements in the CARTER case,[42] seemed to doom federal efforts at industrial control. If regulation of wages, working conditions and employer-employee relations were matters having "no direct relation to interstate commerce,"[43] the barrier to a uniform national labor policy, even for industries engaged in interstate commerce, seemed well-nigh insurmountable. The SCHECHTER and CARTER opinions viewed attempts by the federal government to reach these conditions as constituting an unlawful regulation of local industry in violation of the Tenth Amendment of the Constitution.

When it is agreed that such was the constitutional status of federal regulation of industry up to April 12, 1937, the result in the first three N.L.R.A. cases,[44] decided that day, must

[41] *Sunshine Anthracite Coal Co.* v. *Adkins,* 310 U.S. 381, 395 (1940). In his dissenting opinion in the CARTER case, Justice Cardozo described the competition among the operators of the bituminous coal mines as having degenerated into anarchy. 298 U.S. 238, 331 (1936).

[42] ". . . The employment of men, the fixing of their wages, hours of labor, and working conditions, the bargaining in respect of these things—whether carried on separately or collectively—each and all constitute intercourse for the purposes of production, not of trade. The latter is a thing apart from the relation of employer and employee, which in all producing occupations is purely local in character. Extraction of coal from the mine is the aim and the completed result of local activities. Commerce in the coal mined is not brought into being by force of these activities, but by negotiations, agreements and circumstances entirely apart from production. Mining brings the subject-matter of commerce into existence. Commerce disposes of it." 298 U.S. 238, 303-4 (1936).

[43] *Schechter Brothers Poultry Corp.* v. *United States,* 295 U.S. 495, 548 (1935).

[44] *National Labor Relations Board* v. *Jones and Laughlin Steel Corp.,* 301 U.S. 1, 76 (1937), *National Labor Relations Board* v. *Fruehauf Trailer Co.,* 301 U.S. 49, 76 (1937), *National Labor Relations Board* v. *Friedman-Harry Marks Clothing Co.,* 301 U.S. 58, 76 (1937). The other two cases

appear as an event approching a "revolution" in the theory of
our federalism. All that the Supreme Court had decided up
to that date, but particularly within the preceding two years,
would have justified a prediction that it would hold labor relations in manufacturing establishments to lie beyond the reach
of the federal commerce power. The National Association of
Manufacturers advised its members to this effect soon after the
N.L.R.A. was placed on the statute books. But "predictability
in the law" was on that day subordinated to the greater
interest.[45]

The firms involved in the three basic N.L.R.A. cases were
all engaged in manufacturing, albeit for an interstate market.
Yet that fact, undisputed by the contending parties, was
treated by the Chief Justice almost as though it were irrelevant.
Disregarding the call to consistency made by the dissenting
Justices,[46] five of the Court's members voted to uphold the

decided that day were *Associated Press* v. *National Labor Relations Board*,
301 U.S. 103 (1937), and *Washington, Virginia and Maryland Coach Co.* v.
National Labor Relations Board, 301 U.S. 142 (1937).

[45] For a discussion of the possible link between the action of the court
in sustaining the N.L.R.A. and the pending battle over the Court reorganization plan, see *National Labor Relations Board Cases*, Charles Aiken,
(ed.) (New York: John Wiley & Sons, 1939), p. 1.

[46] For himself and Justices Van Devanter, Sutherland and Butler, Justice McReynolds insisted that the decision read by the Chief Justice in the
JONES and LAUGHLIN case departed from the "well-established principles"
to which the Court adhered in the SCHECHTER and CARTER cases. They interpreted those decisions as holding that "the power of Congress under
the commerce clause does not extend to relations between employers and
their employees." Exactly two weeks earlier, these same Justices had
joined their colleagues in sustaining an order of the National Mediation
Board directing an interstate railroad to negotiate with the duly certified
representatives of its "back shop" workers. *Virginia Railway Co.* v. *System Federation #40*, 300 U.S. 515 (1937). In the course of his opinion for
a unanimous Court, Mr. Justice Stone had written: "The power of Congress over interstate commerce extends to such regulations of the relations
of rail carriers to their employees as are reasonably calculated to prevent
the interruption of interstate commerce by strikes and their attendant
disorders." P. 553. And again:
"The activities in which these employees are engaged [repairing rolling
stock] have such a relation to the other confessedly interstate activities

Wagner Act as a lawful regulation of conditions "affecting interstate commerce." In the opinion of the majority the source of obstructions to the uninterrupted movement of interstate commerce was not determinative of the federal power to control them. What mattered was whether the conditions sought to be controlled by Congress tended to obstruct the channels of interstate trade. One of the most serious threats to such trade, the Court agreed with the proponents of the Wagner Act, springs from industrial strife resulting from strikes and other impediments to production. The rights guaranteed to labor in the National Labor Relations Act, coupled with the proscription of the unfair labor practices enumerated therein, were intended to remove potential hindrances to the free flow of interstate commerce. In passing the N.L.R.A., therefore, Congress was making use of its power under the commerce clause to protect interstate commerce against those dangers which stem from unsatisfactory relations between employers and their employees. And it was constitutionally irrelevant that the employers ordered by the National Labor Relations Board "to cease and desist" from their unfair labor practices happened to be engaged in manufacturing.

It is possible, at least in a verbal way, to reconcile the

of the petitioner that they are to be regarded as a part of them. . . . The relation of the back shop to transportation is such that a strike of petitioners' employees there, quite apart from the likelihood of its spreading to the operating department, would subject petitioner to danger . . . of interruption of the transportation service. The cause is not remote from the effect." P. 556.

It must be assumed that Justices McReynolds, Sutherland, Van Devanter and Butler agreed with this reasoning. By their dissent against the application of the National Labor Relations Act to the labor relations of concerns admittedly engaged in interstate commerce, they made it clear that they did not regard Mr. Justice Stone's theory as to cause and effect to be applicable to industry as a whole. Their vote for the result in *Washington, Virginia and Maryland Coach Co.* v. *National Labor Relations Board* was apparently a product of their insistence on this distinction. And it must be added that their view as to the reach of the federal commerce power commanded majority support on the Court, at least prior to the adjudications of April 12, 1937.

decisions upholding the validity of the Wagner Labor Relations Act with the result reached in the SCHECHTER case. When the administration decided to salvage Section 7A of the defunct N.I.R.A., greater care was naturally taken in formulating the provisions of the new statute. The Wagner Act does in fact manifest a greater respect for constitutional niceties. For one thing, the act limited in explicit language the application of its provisions to those labor disputes "burdening or obstructing" interstate commerce. It thus imposed a two-fold responsibility upon the agency it created. The Board, that is, was first to establish that the concern against which charges are brought is actually engaged in interstate commerce, and then, that the conduct complained of consists of unfair labor practices outlawed in the statute. The Board, moreover, was an independent agency, armed with the necessary investigatory powers and confined to definite procedures in the discharge of its duties. The Board, its members and its methods had not yet become the storm center of American politics that they came to be soon after the Wagner Act was sustained. And so, it is conceivable that the thoroughness, for example, with which the Board examined the interstate ramifications of the Jones and Laughlin Steel Corporation, the Board's freedom from executive domination, and the elaborate procedures by which the charge of unfair labor practices had to be proved, may have carried some weight with at least some of those who helped to form the majority in the basic N.L.R.A. cases.

Still, even after all these observations are made, the point bears repetition that the import of the decisions in those cases transcends any or all of these distinctions. Their chief significance stems from the fact that the Supreme Court had at last found adequate constitutional authority for a national labor policy in the United States. By conceding that the commerce power of the federal government was broad enough to embrace the regulation of the labor relations of manufacturers producing for interstate and foreign markets, the Court in effect recognized the essential interdependence of the various segments of the American economy. In so doing, it was also stripping the Tenth Amendment of most of its force as a barrier to national action for the solution of national problems.

So viewed, the rulings in the Labor Board cases were an invitation to Congress to reenact the other labor provisions embodied in the N.R.A. codes. Nor was the administration tardy in acting on the possibilities implicit in those decisions. The movement to write a comprehensive federal wage and hour law got under way soon thereafter. But the protracted efforts to secure such a law did not bear fruit until June, 1938, when President Roosevelt approved the Fair Labor Standards Act.

The Fair Labor Standards Act of 1938 sets up an elaborate plan for minimum wages and maximum hours and creates a division in the United States Department of Labor to administer the plan.[47] The act provides for the fixing of minimum wages and maximum hours for workers employed by industries producing or manufacturing for interstate markets. It makes it illegal for such concerns to employ persons in violation of these provisions and to ship in interstate commerce goods made under substandard conditions.[48] The entire law was upheld by the Supreme Court in an opinion for a unanimous Court delivered by Mr. Justice Stone on February 3, 1941.[49]

After a detailed analysis of federal regulation of industrial conditions, Mr. Justice Stone concluded that the Fair Labor Standards Act of 1938 was a logical extension of the power

[47] The Wage and Hour Administration was to be headed by a single administrator who, with the assistance of "industry committees," was empowered to modify some of the terms of the act. For more detailed discussion of the administrative techniques contemplated by the act, see below, pp. 142-143.

[48] The Fair Labor Standards Act also requires employers to keep records in accordance with regulations made by the administrator.

[49] *United States* v. *Darby*, 312 U.S. 100 (1941).

of Congress under the commerce clause to prevent the disruption of the channels of interstate commerce. His statement of the two principal issues presented in the case foreshadowed the removal of some constitutional landmarks, although much homage is also paid to other landmarks, including *Gibbons* v. *Ogden*. The act was being contested by the owner of a Georgia lumber mill which was producing for customers in other states. As applied to his employees, the Wage and Hour Law was alleged to be not a regulation of commerce but an attempt to control conditions in production or manufacturing.

Mr. Justice Stone began his opinion by saying that the several contentions raised two main questions:

. . . first, whether Congress has constitutional power to prohibit the shipment in interstate commerce of lumber manufactured by employees whose wages are less than a prescribed minimum or whose weekly hours of labor at that wage are greater than the prescribed maximum, and, second, whether it has power to prohibit the employment of workmen in the production of goods "for interstate commerce" at other than prescribed wages and hours.

He then pointed out that the reports of the committees which considered the legislation, as well as the policy and findings embodied in the Act itself,[50] make it clear that Congress was seeking to achieve three major objectives. One was to prevent the production of goods under conditions which interfered with the maintenance of national minimum standards essential for

[50] "Sec. 2 (a) The Congress hereby finds that the existence, in industries engaged in commerce or in the production of goods for commerce, of labor conditions detrimental to the maintenance of the minimum standard of living necessary for health, efficiency, and general well-being of workers (1) causes commerce and the channels and instrumentalities of commerce to be used to spread and perpetuate such labor conditions among the workers of the several States; (2) burdens commerce and the free flow of goods in commerce; (3) constitutes an unfair method of competition in commerce; (4) leads to labor disputes burdening and obstructing commerce and the free flow of goods in commerce; and (5) interferes with the orderly and fair marketing of goods in commerce."

health and general well-being. Another was to exclude from the channels of interstate commerce goods made under substandard conditions. And finally, Congress was obviously seeking to foreclose the use of interstate commerce as an instrument of competition and for spreading substandard conditions to workers of other states. Government counsel had likewise argued that employers in whose shops substandard conditions prevail are able to force down labor standards in other states because of their competitive advantage.

The contention that in the guise of regulating commerce Congress was attempting to control local conditions in production naturally led the Court to examine the old issue over the relation between interstate commerce and manufacturing. "While manufacturing is not of itself interstate commerce," Mr. Justice Stone stated, "the shipment of manufactured goods interstate is such commerce and the prohibition of such shipment by Congress is indubitably a regulation of the commerce." He quoted Marshall's assertion in *Gibbons* v. *Ogden* that the power to regulate interstate commerce is the power "to prescribe the rule by which commerce is governed," and recalled that as long ago as 1903 (in the LOTTERY case) the Court had held that regulation of commerce may take the form of a prohibition. Counsel for the lumber company agreed with this construction of *Champion* v. *Ames*, but argued that under the Fair Labor Standards Act Congress was not regulating interstate commerce but was setting down wages and hours within a state which had chosen not to regulate them. This objection moved Mr. Justice Stone to assert that the power of Congress over interstate commerce "can neither be enlarged nor diminished by the exercise or non-exercise of state power." On the positive side, he met the objection by resurrecting the principle so eloquently set forth by Justice Harlan in the Lottery case, a principle eclipsed by the reasoning in *Hammer* v. *Dagenhart*. Mr. Justice Stone said:

Congress, following its own conception of public policy concerning the restrictions which may appropriately be imposed on interstate commerce, is free to exclude from the commerce articles whose use in the state for which they are destined it may conceive to be injurious to the public health, morals or welfare, even though the state has not sought to regulate their use.

Such regulation is not a forbidden invasion of state power merely because either its motive or its consequence is to restrict the use of articles of commerce within the states of destination; and is not prohibited unless by other constitutional provisions. It is no objection to the assertion of the power to regulate interstate commerce that its exercise is attended by the same incidents which attend the exercise of the police power of the states.

Mr. Justice Stone conceded that the "motive and purpose" of Congress in passing the Fair Labor Standards Act were to keep the channels of interstate commerce from being used to ship goods produced under substandard labor conditions. There was no doubt that Congress intended to protect all the states against the competition from those who do not conform to the standards which in its judgment were socially desirable. But the "motive and purpose of the regulation of interstate commerce," he asserted, "are matters for the legislative judgment upon the exercise of which the Constitution places no restriction and over which the courts are given no control." He emphasized that the motives of Congress do not determine the constitutionality of its regulations of interstate commerce, and that the judiciary need not concern itself with legislative motives when passing judgment on the validity of such regulations.

The thesis in the DARBY case obviously clashed with the ruling in *Hammer* v. *Dagenhart*, and Mr. Justice Stone frankly said so. Characterizing the dissent by Justice Holmes in that case as "powerful and now classic," he went on to say that the distinction on which the majority had based its decision was long ago ignored.[51] All the other criteria of *Hammer* v. *Dagenhart* have been limited by subsequent decisions, and since the decision in that case was a "departure" from the principles which have marked the interpretation of the commerce clause, the case was reversed.

Turning next to the validity of the wage and hour requirements themselves, Mr. Justice Stone took up first the meaning of the term "production for interstate commerce" as used in the Fair Labor Standards Act. The act, it will be recalled, provides for the fixing of minimum wages and maximum hours for those industrial establishments only which produce for an interstate market. Accordingly, a controlling definition of such production was an integral part of the more basic issue of the constitutionality of the wage and hour provisions. "Production for interstate commerce," contemplated by the Fair Labor Standards Act, the Court held, "includes at least production of goods, which, at the time of production, the employer, according to the normal course of his business, intends or expects to move in interstate commerce, although through the exigencies of the business, all of the goods may not thereafter actually enter interstate commerce." As to the fundamental question whether the conditions attached by Congress to the production of goods for interstate commerce are a lawful exercise of the federal commerce power, Mr. Justice Stone constructed the Court's answer on a familiar premise. This premise was the principle that the power of Congress to regulate

51 In distinguishing the Lottery Law, the Pure Food and Drug Act and the Mann Act from the Child Labor Law, Justice Day had reasoned that the latter was designed to exclude from interstate commerce articles in themselves harmless and incapable of spreading any evil to the "state of destination." The evil, if any, he stressed, was in the "state of origin," where the children were employed. Mr. Justice Stone reminded us that this distinction was departed from in such cases as *Brooks* v. *United States,* 267 U.S. 432 (1925), *Kentucky Whip and Collar Co.* v. *Illinois Central R.R. Co.,* 299 U.S. 334 (1937), and more recently *Mulford* v. *Smith,* 307 U.S. 38 (1939).

interstate commerce "extends to those activities intrastate which so affect interstate commerce or the exercise of the power of Congress over it as to make regulation of them an appropriate means to the attainment of a legitimate end, the exercise of the granted power of Congress to regulate interstate commerce." Citing the SHREVEPORT case and those that had sustained the Safety Appliance Acts, the Railway Labor Act and the more recent National Labor Relations Act, he construed them as having settled that Congress, in the exercise of its commerce power, may control those local conditions which have a "substantial effect" on interstate commerce or on the power over it.

And what is the function of the courts in passing on the validity of such legislation? "The only function of courts," according to Mr. Justice Stone, "is to determine whether the particular activity regulated or prohibited is within the reach of the federal power." When the power exerted is that over interstate commerce, Congress may choose the method "reasonably" adapted to its policy of excluding from interstate commerce all articles made under conditions which do not conform to the labor standards adopted by it. The congressional policy against the spread of substandard labor conditions via the channels of interstate commerce is enforceable, even though it entails federal control of wholly intrastate activities. Mr. Justice Stone went further and stated that quite independently of the prohibition of shipment or transportation of the condemned goods, the provision for the suppression of their production for interstate commerce is within the commerce power. "The evils aimed at by the Act are the spread of substandard labor conditions through the use of the facilities of interstate commerce," he declared.[52]

52 Mr. Justice Stone compared the Fair Labor Standards Act with the Clayton Anti-Trust Act, pointing out that the 1938 legislation was directed at a species of unfair competition not too dissimilar from the "unfair methods of competition" aimed at by the 1914 statute.

Mr. Justice Stone's clear-cut assertion that the federal commerce power reached local production, when intended for interstate commerce, required examination of the force of the Tenth Amendment. So far as the Court's conclusion in the DARBY case was concerned it was "unaffected" by that amendment. The amendment is not to be construed as a limitation on the authority of the national government to choose all those means for the exercise of its granted powers which are "appropriate and plainly adapted to the permitted end." Mr. Justice Stone wrote:

The Amendment [Tenth Amendment] states but a truism that all is retained which has not been surrendered. There is nothing in the history of its adoption to suggest that it was more than declaratory of the relationship between the national and state governments as it had been established by the Constitution before the Amendment or that its purpose was other than to allay fears that the new national government might seek to exercise powers not granted, and that the states might not be able to exercise fully the reserved powers.

While the language regarding the Tenth Amendment employed by Mr. Justice Stone was not quite as sweeping as that of government counsel in arguing the DARBY case,[53] the version of it adopted by the Court has effectively destroyed the amendment's usefulness as a test of the limits of national power. Henceforth, it would appear, the existence of the states in our Union cannot serve as a basis for diminishing the reach

[53] "The Tenth Amendment merely reserves to the states 'the powers not delegated to the United States.' That is not a limitation upon the exercise of the powers which are delegated to the federal government. . . .

". . . the Court has repeatedly recognized that the Tenth Amendment adds nothing to the Constitution. A few of the relatively recent decisions of this Court suggesting a contrary view cannot be taken to have overruled sub silentio so important a constitutional doctrine." (From the brief for the United States in the DARBY case.)

of the powers delegated by the Constitution to the federal government.[54]

Of more practical moment, however, was the unanimity with which the Court reaffirmed the philosophy of national supremacy in the industrial field which but a bare majority had enunciated in the N.L.R.A. cases.[55] It thereby removed the "no man's land" between the state and federal jurisdictions, and in so doing strengthened the weapons for more effective democratic government. It may also have strengthened, at least so it may be hoped, the faith of the American people in the ability of their government to deal adequately with their peacetime problems.

[54] "Does the existence of the States furnish an independent determinant of, or limitation upon, national power? Of the various questions with which constitutional law and theory have to deal touching the relations of the states and the national government this is the one of greatest practical consequence, as it is also one of the first to have been raised." Corwin, *The Twilight of the Supreme Court* (1936), p. 1.

The theory which treated the Tenth Amendment as a criterion of the scope of the delegated powers of Congress has been labeled by Professor Corwin the doctrine of "dual federalism." *Ibid.* Since then he has coined an apter phrase, to wit, the doctrine of "competitive" federalism. Corwin, *Constitutional Revolution, Ltd.* (Claremont Colleges, 1941), pp. 96-99.

[55] By March, 1941, to be sure, three of the dissenters in the 1937 cases had left the Court and their places were taken by men appointed by President Roosevelt.

CHAPTER IV

RESTRAINING THE ADMINISTRATIVE PROCESS

1. *Relationship of Court and Agency*

"The administrative process," Dean Landis has told us, is essentially "our generation's answer to the inadequacy of the judicial and the legislative processes." [1] But old institutions have a way of resisting the newcomer; and the efficiency of administrative agencies has been seriously impaired at times by the very branches of government whose limitations necessitated the adoption of more effective instruments of public control.[2] Created to deal with the complex problems of an industrial society, their chief responsibility has been to effectuate the legislative policy. They do their work, in the language

[1] James M. Landis, *The Administrative Process* (New Haven: Yale Univ. Press, 1938), p. 46.

[2] The term "administrative agency" or "administrative tribunal" has come to be employed so loosely that it is important to indicate the particular context in which it is being used. For the purposes of the present analysis, the meaning given this term by the Attorney General's Committee on Administrative Procedure is the one intended. The committee declares that the "distinguishing feature" of an administrative agency is "the power to determine, either by rule or by decision, private rights and obligations." *Administrative Procedure in Government Agencies,* Final Report of Attorney General's Committee on Administrative Procedure (1941), p. 7.

This also is the sense in which Dean Landis uses the expression "the administrative process," for, in speaking of the agencies whose functions involve the exercise of the legislative, judicial and executive powers of government he has written: "Rule-making, enforcement, and the disposition of competing claims made by contending parties, were all entrusted to them. . . . These agencies, tribunals, and rule-making boards were for the sake of convenience distinguished from the existing governmental bureaucracies by terming them 'administrative.' The law the courts permitted them to make was named 'administrative law,' so that now the process in all its component parts can be appropriately termed the 'administrative process.'" *Op. cit.,* p. 2.

of President Roosevelt, "with an eye that looks forward to results rather than backward to precedent and to the leading case." [3]

It is this very preoccupation with results that has occasioned collision with the courts. The exigencies of modern administration, requiring as they do the expeditious settlement of numerous controversies arising under particular statutes, hardly lend themselves to treatment by the traditional processes of the courts. This much is today commonplace and is generally recognized to be unavoidable. Disagreement arises when the practical details of the control relationship between court and agency come to be delineated. Always in the background of any such conflict is the fact that under Anglo-American jurisprudence the judiciary has been regarded as the prime instrument for determining private rights.[4] The concept of the "supremacy of law" or "rule of law" thus places administrative tribunals on the defensive, as it were, since so much of their work affects vitally the rights of the contending parties. In the United States, moreover, judicial review of administrative action, embracing as it does interpretation of constitutional provisions, is intrinsically greater in scope than statutory construction alone ever could be. The resulting restrictions on the administrative process can in this country become part of the fundamental law of the land, binding legislators no less than administrators.[5]

Too much, however, of the discussion relating to the extent

[3] Message vetoing the Walter-Logan Bill (H.R. 6324), *86 Cong. Rec. 13942* (1940).

[4] Even so vigorous and frequent a critic of the hostile judicial attitude toward the problems of administrative agencies as Mr. Justice Brandeis has acknowledged this role of the courts in relation to those agencies. "The supremacy of law," he wrote in 1936, "demands that there shall be opportunity to have some court decide whether an erroneous rule of law was applied; and whether the proceeding in which facts were adjudicated was conducted regularly." See his concurring opinion in *St. Joseph Stockyards Co.* v. *United States,* 298 U.S. 38, 84 (1936).

[5] For a brief account, interspersed with much illuminating critical comment, of the unique character of judicial control of administrative action

of judicial review over administrative determinations proceeds on the assumption that it is the practices and techniques of a particular agency which have called forth judicial hostility.[6] Nor is this said to detract in the least from the importance of the contribution to the development of the administrative process represented by the recent investigations of the need for administrative reform. Certainly the work of such groups as the Committee on Ministers' Powers in England and the Attorney-General's Committee on Administrative Procedure in this country is all for the good; and should improvements result, friendlier relations with the courts might follow.[7]

in the United States, see the Presidential address of Professor Charles G. Haines, delivered at the 1939 meeting of the American Political Science Association. It appeared later as *"The Adaptation of Administrative Law and Procedure to Constitutional Theories and Principles"* in *XXXIV Amer. Pol. Sc. Rev. 1* (Feb. 1940).

[6] Much, for example, is made of the fact that today the Interstate Commerce Commission enjoys the respect of the courts. But it still remains to be demonstrated that the cordial relations between that agency and the judiciary are due exclusively to its greatly improved procedures which the courts can recommend to other agencies. In the first twenty years of its existence, the Interstate Commerce Commission was subjected to as much judicial control as the more recently established agencies are today. Writing of the situation prior to the adoption in 1906 of the Hepburn Amendment to the Interstate Commerce Commission Act, the authors of a recent book on administration have said: "It became a common practice for carriers to withhold evidence from the proceeding before the Commission and present it in the first instance in the court when the Commission sought to enforce its order. Reversals of the Commission's orders were rather frequent. The courts were wielding considerable influence on the Commission's activities and were gradually developing the relationships between it and the courts." Chamberlain, Dowling, and Hays, *The Judicial Function in Federal Administrative Agencies* (New York: The Commonwealth Fund, 1942), p. 166.

It is altogether possible, indeed, that the Commission's present enviable relationship with the courts may be due in part to the reconciliation which comes with time. Perhaps even more important may be the fact that the basic industry entrusted to its care has come to depend so much on the protective arm of government. The shift in policy, as reflected by the Transportation Act of 1920, from merely curbing the railroads to one of protecting them as a monopoly on which the entire nation depended, is still another factor not to be overlooked.

[7] The Committee on Ministers' Powers was created by the MacDonald government as a result of the criticism directed at the administrative

It is nevertheless true that not nearly enough consideration is given to the significance of the basic preconceptions with
which the judge approaches the work of administrative agencies. The "inarticulate major premise" may be as decisive in
this phase of the judicial process as it has been found to be
in the review of legislation. The judge's conception of the
need for the modern administrative process, his awareness of
the problems confronting the administrator, perhaps his silent
opposition to the reform which the agency is administering,
his irritation with the challenge to traditional notions of
justice, even his resentment at the way in which administrative
action has invaded fields at one time considered to be the exclusive province of the courts—these and other factors even
more intangible may help shape his attitude in administrative
law cases, at least as much as his dislike for the procedures
of the particular agency. Thus, when the criticism that the
modern administrative machine has led to the rise of a "new
despotism," a "wonderland of bureaucracy" or "administrative
absolutism" is duly analyzed, there is ground for suspecting
that such charges are engendered not only by an exaggerated
fear of excesses but even more by a failure to accept the implications of the emergence of the modern social service state.
There is indeed a remarkably close correlation between the
judge's attitude toward economic regulation generally and his
attitude toward the activities of regulatory agencies.

Of the United States Supreme Court, it may be said that
those Justices who have been tolerant of legislative efforts to
control the American economy have generally been no less
tolerant of the agencies created to administer the reforms. In
this company must be included the present Chief Justice. He
is the author of the widely quoted language suggesting that

process by Lord Chief Justice Hewart and others. In a sense, therefore,
the committee's report is a reply to Hewart's *The New Despotism* (1929).
The committee repudiated most of the objections. *Report of Committee
on Ministers' Powers* (1932), Cmd. 4060.

the relationship of court and agency may be a problem in attitudes. The occasion was his opinion for the Court in the third MORGAN case.[8] In it he set down important principles and sounded a timely warning.

In construing legislation which has created an administrative agency and provided for judicial review of its action, Mr. Justice Stone declared, the courts should be guided by the "cardinal principle" that "courts and agency are not to be regarded as wholly independent and unrelated instrumentalities of justice." Both are but the means which the legislature has chosen for effectuating its policy and the statute should be construed so as to attain the "prescribed end" through "coordinated action." Mr. Justice Stone warned against repeating "in this day the mistake made by the courts of law when equity was struggling for recognition as an ameliorating system of justice." Neither Court nor agency should regard the other "as an alien intruder to be tolerated, if must be, but never to be encouraged or aided by the other in the attainment of the common aim."

2. *Allowable Delegation*

Until 1935, the rule against the "undue" delegation of legislative power remained one of those constitutional doctrines which, while reiterated on appropriate occasions, was never applied.[9] As a corollary to the fundamental doctrine of the separation of the three powers of government, this rule was

8 *United States* v. *Morgan,* 307 U.S. 183, particularly, p. 191 (1939). The saga of the Morgan cases began with *Morgan* v. *United States,* 298 U.S. 468 (1936), and was followed by *Morgan* v. *United States,* 304 U.S. 1 (1937). *United States* v. *Morgan,* 313 U.S. 409 (1941) is the fourth case in the series. All four are discussed by Professors Chamberlain, Dowling and Hays, *op. cit.,* pp. 194-99.

9 On January 1, 1935, the Supreme Court for the first time set aside provisions of a law solely on the ground that they delegated legislative power to the President. *Panama Refining Co.* v. *Ryan,* 293 U.S. 388. This also was one of the chief grounds for the decision in the SCHECHTER case.

never regarded as an insuperable bar to broad grants of authority to the President and administrative officers and agencies to "fill in the details" of congressional legislation. The Supreme Court had uniformly construed the delegation of the rule-making authority as a necessary and proper means for giving practical effect to the powers of Congress generally and in particular as a means for effectuating the immediate legislative policy.[10] In the N.R.A. cases, the Court departed from this liberal attitude and at a time when the need for administrative discretion seemed greatest, at least in the judgment of the other departments of the government.

Fortunately for flexible and therefore effective administration, the newly vitalized doctrine did not stay lusty for long. When in the spring of 1937 the Court began drastically to revamp judicial landmarks, its recent strict application of the separation of powers theory was also abandoned. If prediction on matters of constitutional development were not the hazardous art that it has proved itself to be, one might be tempted to paraphrase Elihu Root and say that the doctrine against the unconstitutional delegation of legislative power has surrendered to the realities and needs of the administrative process, and this time perhaps permanently.[11]

[10] As Chief Justice Hughes himself admitted in the SCHECHTER case: "The Constitution has never been regarded as denying to Congress the necessary resources of flexibility and practicability, which will enable it to perform its function in laying down policies and establishing standards, while leaving to selected instrumentalities the making of subordinate rules within prescribed limits and the determination of facts to which the policy as declared by the Legislature is to apply." 295 U.S. 495, 530 (1935). Nevertheless, the Court was unanimous in holding that the discretion which Congress authorized the President to exercise in approving or prescribing codes was "virtually unfettered" and that the code-making authority conferred by the National Industrial Recovery Act was therefore an unconstitutional delegation of legislative power.

[11] Mr. Root declared in 1916 that because of the tremendous expansion of administrative action "the old doctrine prohibiting the delegation of legislative power has virtually retired from the field and given up the fight." *41 A.B.A. Rep. 355* (1916).

But the role of discretion in modern administration is a vital one; and a judge's attitude toward legislative delegation of discretionary authority is therefore a barometer of his general attitude toward the administrative process itself. Chief Justice Stone has written opinions in some of the recent cases which indicate that the Supreme Court has returned to its erstwhile liberal position with respect to the delegation by Congress of the power to issue necessary rules and regulations.

On the same day that the Supreme Court upheld the constitutionality of the Fair Labor Standards Act of 1938, it also sustained the constitutionality of the delegations of legislative power embodied in the statute.[12] Where in the DARBY case the Court vindicated the general scope of the act in prohibiting the manufacture for and shipment in interstate commerce of goods produced under sub-standard labor conditions, in the OPP COTTON MILLS case it was concerned primarily with the constitutionality of the administrative procedure which Congress set up for establishing the minimum wage in particular industries. The Fair Labor Standards Act declares Congress' policy to be to raise the minimum wage to forty cents an hour "as rapidly as economically feasible without substantially curtailing employment."* It directs that in determining rates the administrator shall give due regard to economic and competitive conditions and that the rates shall not be such as will substantially curtail employment in a particular industry.[13]

[12] *Opp Cotton Mills, Inc.* v. *Administrator of Wage and Hour Division,* 312 U.S. 126 (1941) with Mr. Justice Stone delivering the opinion of the Court.

[13] Wage rates are to be fixed by the administrator in collaboration with "an industry committee" appointed by him for the particular industry. The administrator must appoint an industry committee for each industry engaged in interstate commerce or in the production of goods for such commerce. All industry committees shall have persons representing the public, an equal number representing the employers and an equal number representing the employees. The act further directs that in appointing the persons representing each group, the administrator shall give "due

In establishing classifications within an industry, the administrator and the appropriate industry committee must determine that the wage rate fixed will not substantially curtail employment in the particular class or give a competitive advantage to another group in the industry. The administrator and the committee are required by the act to consider certain "relevant factors" in making these determinations, such as competitive conditions as affected by transportation, living and production costs, and so on. Under the act, no wage is to be fixed which is not first recommended by an industry committee and only after hearing, findings and order by the administrator.

As was to be expected, the complaint that the Fair Labor Standards Act was an unconstitutional delegation of the legislative power of Congress was grounded on the alleged ambiguity of the standards set down by the act. It was claimed that the standards for fixing the minimum wage were so vague and indefinite as to make it impossible for courts to tell whether the orders of the administrator were issued in conformity with the standards adopted by Congress. The authority of the administrator to classify and to determine wage differentials was said to depend upon factors that were so inadequately defined by the act as to afford no standard at all. Opp Cotton Mills argued, that is to say, that the factors which the administrator and industry committee were required to consider in classifying an industry or in allowing wage differentials were described in entirely too general terms to serve as reliable guides for the exercise of administrative discretion. Their general character as well as the silence of the statute as to the weight to be assigned to the various

regard to the geographical regions in which the industry is carried on." Members of these committees are paid on a per diem basis and the committees serve as investigating bodies for the administrator. They investigate conditions and report to the administrator their findings and recommendations for the wage rate.

considerations, it was claimed, left the administrator and an industry committee free to reach any conclusions they chose without regard to congressional intentions.

"The adoption of the declared policy by Congress and its definition of the circumstances in which its command is to be effective," Mr. Justice Stone wrote, "constitute the performance, in the constitutional sense, of the legislative function." Congress cannot be expected to find all the facts which form the basis for the application of general standards to particular instances. Under modern complex conditions, legislatures are compelled to leave that work to administrative agencies. The Constitution is not to be construed as "demanding the impossible or the impracticable," Mr. Justice Stone declared, and added that the essentials of the legislative function "are the determination of the legislative policy and its formulation as a rule of conduct." These requirements, fully satisfied by the provisions of the Fair Labor Standards Act, are met when Congress provides that its policy is to be put into effect only after the "basic conclusions of fact" specified in the statute have been ascertained by the administrative agency.

All Congress could be expected to do was to state the broad legislative objective, in this case the raising of the minimum wage to the forty-cent per hour level. The basic facts justifying the particular rate can be ascertained by the administrator acting in conjunction with industry committees. Theirs was the obligation to determine whether the wage would substantially curtail employment and whether wage differentials would be a means for effectuating the congressional policy. To make these administrative determinations, they were to consider all relevant data which would assist them in arriving at sound conclusions. Mr. Justice Stone compared the action of Congress in authorizing these basic facts to be established administratively with its action in accepting the advice of experts as to social and economic conditions. In neither case do we have anything approaching surrender of the legislative function. Indeed, from the standpoint of practical administration, the only workable procedure is for Congress to authorize the designated administrative agency to determine what weight is to be assigned to the evidence before it rather than attempt the impossible by prescribing in advance the weight to be assigned to various factors.[14]

It is unnecessary to dwell on the delegation question. There is nothing to indicate that the "standards" for administrative action are any more precise or definite today than they were in the brief period when the separation of powers theory became a ground for invalidating delegations of legislative authority. Nor has Chief Justice Stone in his discussion of the problem added anything new to the doctrine or to its application. The point is not that he has not made any contribution to this phase of constitutional law. It is rather that such decisions as his opinion in the OPP COTTON MILLS case only serve to show that what has really happened is that the Supreme Court has reverted to its former pragmatic view. It may once more be said that Congress is free to delegate its powers in ways and to the extent required for their effective exercise.

3. *Some Aspects of Administrative Procedure*

As in other aspects of constitutional law, so in the field of administrative law and practice, agreement on general prin-

[14] Mr. Justice Stone compared the provisions of the Fair Labor Standards Act with the provisions of the Tariff Act of 1922 which authorized the President to raise or lower tariff duties. Under the "flexible" tariff clause, the President was to modify tariff schedules in order to equalize the differences which, with the assistance of the Tariff Commission, he found between the cost of production of articles in this country and in foreign countries. In taking action, the President was to consider certain factors, some being specified by the statute itself and others not; but for neither did the statute prescribe the relative weight to be given to them.

ciples does not always lead to agreement on the decision of the concrete case. Although professing devotion to common ideals and purposes, Supreme Court Justices will often find themselves in sharp disagreement when called upon to apply them. This aspect of the judicial process, so mystifying to the lay mind, is also evident in the Court's relation to administrative agencies. Recognition of the usefulness and special competence of administrative agencies will predispose the judicial mind to a greater appreciation of the needs of modern administration, but does not in itself preclude occasional failures to see a problem in the light of those needs. It is one thing to view court and agency as "collaborative" instruments of justice, as does Chief Justice Stone and probably all of his colleagues; it is quite another matter to put this proposition to the acid test of applying it to the individual controversy.

One recent case in point dealt with the right of the administrator of the Wage and Hour Division to delegate his power to issue subpoenas.[15] The controversy, to be sure, involved a technical question of statutory construction. But the very absence of fundamental disagreement only serves to emphasize the difficulty of predicting the course of constitutional decision even among men who are in essential agreement on fundamentals.

Under section 11 of the Fair Labor Standards Act, the administrator and his designated representatives are authorized to conduct investigations.[16] The act does not define the

[15] *Cudahy Packing Co., Ltd.* v. *Holland,* 315 U.S. 357, 367 (1942).

[16] Section 11 (a): "The Administrator or his designated representatives may investigate and gather data regarding the wages, hours, and the conditions and practices of employment in any industry subject to this act, and may enter and inspect such places and such records (and make such transcriptions thereof), question such employees, and investigate such facts, conditions, practices, or matters as he may deem necessary or appropriate to determine whether any person has violated any provision of this act, or which may aid in the enforcement of the provisions of this act."

subpoena power of the administrator. Nor does it explicitly authorize him to delegate to his subordinates the power to issue subpoenas. The subpoena provisions of the Federal Trade Commission Act are made applicable to such hearings and investigations. In the present case, a regional director of the Wage and Hour Division had signed and issued a subpoena in connection with a pending investigation, but on appeal his authority to do so was questioned.

Strictly speaking, this objection made it necessary for the Supreme Court to decide whether Congress intended to have the administrator share his subpoena power with his subordinates. However, Chief Justice Stone, speaking for a bare majority of five, professed to see a deeper issue. The case raised for him the issue of the abuse of administrative power. The unrestricted authority of an administrative officer to delegate the exercise of the subpoena power "is not to be lightly inferred," he declared. He added that the subpoena power was capable of "oppressive use, especially when it may be indiscriminately delegated and the subpoena is not returnable before a judicial officer." He continued:

The subpoena is in form an official command, and even though improvidently issued it has some coercive tendency, either because of ignorance of their rights on the part of those whom it purports to command or their natural respect for what appears to be an official command, or because of their reluctance to test the subpoena's validity by litigation. All these are cogent reasons for inferring an intention of Congress not to give unrestricted authority to delegate the subpoena power which it has in terms granted only to the responsible head of the agency.

While the authority to gather data and make investigations was made delegable by section 11 of the act, there was no similar express language with respect to the subpoena power. The administrator inferred his authority to delegate the subpoena power to regional directors from the general provisions of the act, particularly section 4-C.[17] In rejecting the administrator's contentions, the Court chose to view the subpoena power as quite distinct from the general investigatory power. It also read the legislative history of the Fair Labor Standards Act as indicating that it was not the intention of Congress to authorize the administrator to delegate to his subordinates the power to issue and sign subpoenas. And yet we have in the present case more than a difference of opinion concerning a narrow question of legislative intent. Viewing the subpoena power as a great instrument of coercion capable of being misused, the Chief Justice and those who with him constituted the majority in the CUDAHY case felt called upon to interpose a judicial check on the indiscriminate use of so powerful a weapon for the exercise of administrative discretion.

The minority, on the other hand, saw no occasion for alarm.[18] With the fervor of an experienced administrator seeing the work of an agency hampered by an unfriendly court, Mr. Justice Douglas dismissed the talk about "oppressive use" of the subpoena as "wholly irrelevant." He not only disagreed with the majority on its view of the legislative history of the Fair Labor Standards Act, but questioned the soundness of the "policy" underlying its position. That policy, he thought was the wish to see "a more restrictive and discriminating use of the subpoena power." If that were the Court's purpose, having the administrator alone exercise the power seemed to him "idle." Calling attention to the numerous and far-flung duties of the administrator under the Fair Labor Standards Act, he pointed out that if the administrator alone were to

---

[17] Section 4 (c) reads: "The principal office of the Administrator shall be in the District of Columbia, but he or his duly authorized representative may exercise any or all of his powers in any place."

[18] Led by Mr. Justice Douglas, Mr. Justice Black, Mr. Justice Byrnes and Mr. Justice Jackson dissented.

issue subpoenas he could hardly be expected to do more than sign them in blank.

Where the Chief Justice expressed real concern lest the subpoena power be abused because indiscriminately exercised by subordinates, Mr. Justice Douglas was no less disturbed by the effect which the restriction set down by the Court might have on the administration of the Wage and Hour Law. He was unable to see how the administrator could be expected to make informed decisions in respect to investigations without relying upon the regional offices.

We have in the present case an interesting example of the way in which difference of opinion as to the values to be subserved will lead judges to different results. For the Chief Justice and the majority of the Court, the controversy before them apparently called for an interdict against the possible abuse of the subpoena power by subordinates. Seeing this as the central issue, they were led to a rather narrow interpretation of a law which could also be construed the way the minority saw it. Mr. Justice Douglas and those in whose name he spoke were primarily concerned with the effect of the Court's decision upon the operations of the Wage and Hour Administration. All that the head of that agency could be required to do in relation to subpoenas was to formulate the general policy to govern the exercise of the power. Unless the administrator's duties were to become merely routine, it was essential that he leave the decision on many matters to the discretion of the regional offices. The determination where hearings shall be held, what documents will be needed, which violations should be investigated, which cases require the use of the subpoena, these and similar questions can be answered not by the administrator but by the officials in the field who are familiar with the nature of the particular controversy. Mr. Justice Douglas insisted that the administrator cannot attend personally to these "minutiae of daily administration" unless, as he said, the "processes of law enforcement are to come to a standstill."

The power to investigate, moreover, is by far the greater of the two powers. In most cases the really significant decision is the decision to conduct an investigation. And yet by section 11(a) of the Fair Labor Standards Act the administrator may delegate that power to his representatives. Accordingly, since the power to conduct investigations can be delegated, the minority concluded that the "lesser but companion power to delegate the issuing of subpoenas should be implied as an incident of the office."

On the subject of the possible abuse of authority, which the Chief Justice implied was inherent in the subpoena power, Mr. Justice Douglas stated that an investigation also exerts a "coercive influence," and so does all law enforcement. "Any power, including the judicial power, may be abused," was his terse answer. The Court was not confronted with an abuse of power. He ended his opinion the way he began, by stressing the importance of effective administration:

We should be alert to prevent sheer technicalities from interposing delay in a law enforcement program. If the subpoena power is abused, Congress and the courts are open to remedy it. Meanwhile the subpoena power should be treated sympathetically and regarded as a necessary legal sanction to obtain compliance with the law by those who, having lost the battle in the legislature, seek a delaying action in the courts.[19]

19 It may be of interest to note that the Attorney-General's Committee on Administrative Procedure agreed with the view taken by Mr. Justice Douglas, that the enforcement personnel in the field are best qualified to make intelligent use of the subpoena power. Speaking of the issuance of subpoenas in the administration of the Fair Labor Standards Act, the committee wrote as follows:

"All requests for subpoenas are directed to the Administrator, and not to the officer presiding at the wage-order hearing. The subpoenas are issued by the Administrator only, after consideration by the review unit and the Administrator. The presiding officer is given no power to issue subpoenas, nor is he called upon to determine whether they should be issued.

The last sentence quoted brings to mind a phase of the opposition to the work of administrative agencies which is not always frankly faced. Mr. Justice Douglas was, after all, appealing to his brethren not to forget that much litigation which on the surface may be directed against the administrative procedure of an agency may actually be motivated by a desire to block enforcement of the legislation which the agency was created to administer. He was asking them not to lend assistance to those "who, having lost the battle in the legislature, seek a delaying action in the courts." In a way, this admonition may be read as something of a canon of construction which Mr. Justice Douglas would like to see the courts use when deciding cases concerned with the activities and procedures of administrative agencies and officers.

Certainly when one thinks back of the days when the National Labor Relations Board was the storm center of American politics, one is compelled to admit that much of the opposition to the work of the Labor Board stemmed from employers who never quite reconciled themselves to the philosophy or purposes of the National Labor Relations Act. This is evident not only in much of the public debate over the alleged maladministration of the act but also in many of the cases which finally reached the courts.[20] The same is also evident in many

Since the presiding officer is best qualified through his knowledge of the progress of the hearings to pass upon the issue, the Committee recommends that he be supplied with subpoenas, signed in blank by the Administrator, which the presiding officer should be empowered to issue in accordance with rules and instructions prescribed by the Administrator." *Administrative Procedure in Government Agencies,* Final Report of Attorney General's Committee on Administrative Procedure (1941), p. 149.

[20] In their article "Politics and Labor Relations," Walter Gellhorn and Seymour L. Linfield examined this problem in some detail. See *XXXIX Columbia L. Rev. 339* (March, 1939). The authors introduce their very careful analysis of the "procedural behavior" of the National Labor Relations Board with these observations:

"While the bitterness of the opposition to the Act [The National Labor Relations Act] has somewhat abated, and while the principle of collective bargaining has been at least verbally accepted by many who formerly

of the cases that reached the Supreme Court, particularly the important cases decided in the early months of 1939. Such decisions as that in the "sit-down strike" case [21] and those in the cases concerned with the nature of the refusal to bargain collectively [22] impelled some critics to suggest that the Court was rewriting the Wagner Act. Others pointed to these decisions as marking the collapse of that liberal trend which first became visible in the spring of 1937 when the Court sustained the Wagner Act and also the Social Security Act.

Individual Justices were castigated for accomplishing by

denounced it, a determined, if covert, resistance continues. Detractors of the NLRB, aided and abetted by many of the leading newspapers and publicists, have branded it as a 'kangaroo court' and 'drum-head court-martial;' charged that 'an employer has as much chance before that board as an aristocrat had before the French tribunes of the Terror,' and suggested that the Act should more appropriately be designated as the 'Strained Relations Act' or even 'An Act to Increase Troubles, to Spread Unemployment, and to Disrupt Industry.'

"The recalcitrants today, however, only infrequently launch direct attacks upon the acknowledged objectives of the Act. . . . Instead they seek to destroy public confidence in the statute by assailing the methods of its administration." Pp. 340-41.

[21] *National Labor Relations Board* v. *Fansteel Metallurgical Corporation,* 306 U.S. 240 (1939).

[22] *National Labor Relations Board* v. *Columbian Enameling and Stamping Co.,* 306 U.S. 292, 300 (1939). *National Labor Relations Board* v. *Sands Manufacturing Co.,* 306 U.S. 332 (1939).

Commenting upon the significance of these three decisions, the editors of *The Nation* wrote:

"In these decisions the court has made four amendments to the Wagner Act as written by Congress. These 'amendments' provide that the courts may review the facts and draw their own inferences from them in Labor Board cases, that strikers forfeit the rights of employees if they are discharged for violence or property damage; that an employer has no obligation under the act if he can show a breach of contract on the part of his employees. These clauses do not appear in the act; provisions embodying them were discussed and rejected by Congress when the law was framed. But the most important 'amendment' made by the court is in regard to the right to strike. The act says that nothing in it 'shall be construed so as to interfere with or impede or diminish in any way the right to strike.' Chief Justice Hughes says, 'But this recognition of "the right to strike" plainly contemplates a lawful strike,' and these three decisions plainly imply that it is the courts which will decide when a strike is lawful." *The Nation,* March 11, 1939, p. 281.

their votes what the foes of the Wagner Act were unable to achieve in the halls of Congress. And among those taken to task was Mr. Justice Stone. He was the author of the opinion for the Court in the COLUMBIAN case and was also with the majority in the other much criticized cases. While the COLUMBIAN and SANDS cases did not evoke as much critical comment as did the more spectacular FANSTEEL decision, the first two seemed in the long run to be no less important. Many felt that in the COLUMBIAN and SANDS cases the Court was destroying the efficacy of the Labor Board's work by diluting its fact-finding authority.[23] In both cases the Court upset a finding that the employer had refused to bargain collectively with the representatives of the employees in violation of section 8 (5) of the Wagner Act.[24]

The Columbian Enameling and Stamping Company had been operated as a non-union shop for more than thirty years. In July, 1934, however, it signed a one-year agreement with the Enameling and Stamping Mill Employees Union, an affiliate of the American Federation of Labor. Relations between the union and the company continued to be strained, and in March of the following year a strike was called involving 90 per cent of the employees. On the initiative of the union, conciliators from the United States Department of Labor entered the case and met with the president of the company on July 23, 1935. The president declared himself to be willing to confer with the conciliators and representatives of the union, but later changed his mind. By September, the strikers were replaced and the company continued to ignore requests of the union for a meeting at which the dispute might be settled. Finally, the union filed charges with the board, complaining that the company had refused to bargain collectively.

[23] Section 10 (e) of the Wagner Act provides: "The findings of the Board as to the facts, if supported by evidence, shall be conclusive."
[24] Section 8. "It shall be an unfair labor practice for an employer (5) to refuse to bargain collectively with the representatives of his employees."

After appropriate investigation and hearing, the board "concluded" that on July 23, 1935, the union represented a majority of the Columbian employees, that the union had sought to bargain with the company and that the company had refused to bargain as requested. It ordered the company to discharge those of its production workers who were not employed by it on July 22, 1935, to reinstate its employees as of that date, and to bargain with the union. These findings were set aside first by the Circuit Court of Appeals and later by the Supreme Court. Mr. Justice Stone spoke for a majority of five:[25]

However desirable may be the exhibition by the employer of a tolerant and conciliatory spirit in the settlement of labor disputes we think it plain that the statute does not compel him to seek out his employees or request their participation in negotiations for purposes of collective bargaining, and that he may ignore or reject proposals for such bargaining which come from third persons not purporting to act with authority of his employees, without violation of law and without suffering the drastic consequences which violation may entail. To put the employer in default here the employees must at least have signified to respondent [the Columbian Company] their desire to negotiate. Measured by this test the Board's conclusion that respondent refused to bargain with the Union is without support, for the reason that there is no evidence that the Union gave to the employer, through the conciliators or otherwise, any indication of its willingness to bargain or that respondent knew that they represented the union.

At the hearing before the trial examiner, the secretary of the union testified that on July 23 he had asked the conciliators to "try and open negotiations." But there was no evidence that the company or its president were informed of that fact or

25 Mr. Justice Black dissented and was joined by Mr. Justice Reed. This case was decided February 27, 1939. Mr. Justice Brandeis had resigned two weeks earlier and Mr. Justice Frankfurter, who had ascended the Bench on January 30, did not participate.

that they were aware that the union was ready to negotiate. Mr. Justice Stone thought that it was rather significant that the conciliators were not called as witnesses and that no attempt was made to corroborate the secretary's testimony. Despite these omissions from the record, the board concluded that the company had declined to enter into negotiations. The Court, on the other hand, drew its own inference.

The testimony is consistent throughout with the inference, and indeed supports it, that the conciliators, so far as known to respondent, appeared in their official role as mediators to compose the long-standing dispute between respondent and its employees; that the employer first consented in advance to attend a meeting, and later withdrew its consent when they had failed for some days to arrange a meeting.

It would thus appear that the entire case was made to turn upon one pivotal point. The Court was not convinced that there was any proof that Columbian's president knew that the conciliators were meeting with him for the purpose of opening negotiations between the company and the union looking toward a collective bargaining agreement. Exactly what happened during the interview between the conciliators and the company president? The Labor Board's answer to this question was that considering all the circumstances, it was inconceivable that during a meeting lasting three or four hours the conciliators had failed to inform the president of the nature of their mission. This version of the meeting was of course the basis for the board's order, but so far as the Supreme Court was concerned that version was not substantiated. As Mr. Justice Black expressed it in his dissenting opinion, "The Court finds only a single link missing in the chain of evidence showing that the Company refused to bargain with the Union, i.e., that there was no evidence to justify the Board's finding that the president of the company was aware the conciliators had approached the company at the request of the Union."

But the Columbian case touched off debate over a far more significant issue than the question regarding the construction to be placed on a meeting between the officials of a struck plant and labor mediators. The majority in this case were applying the substantial evidence test in a way which, if long persisted in, might eventually devitalize the administrative process itself. The power of government agencies to hear and weigh the evidence before them and the scope of judicial review of their findings were the basic issues.[26]

After quoting section 10 (e) of the National Labor Relations Act, Mr. Justice Stone pointed out that this provision has reference to evidence which is substantial. Substantial evidence, he added, was such evidence as affords "a substantial basis of fact from which the fact in issue can be reasonably inferred. . . . Substantial evidence is more than a scintilla, and must do more than create a suspicion of the existence of the fact to be established."

Was the evidence sufficient to show that the company had refused to bargain with the union? The Labor Board found that it was and supported its findings by drawing certain inferences from the events related at the hearing before the trial examiner. In coming to this conclusion, the board was no doubt assuming that under the Wagner Act its findings as

26 Mr. Justice Black spoke in simple, even elementary, language by way of setting forth what he regarded to be the fundamental issues in the case.

"I believe that 'the inferences to be drawn were for the Board and not the courts,' and that the inferences drawn by the Board were supported by evidence. Courts should not—as here—substitute their appraisal of the evidence for that of the Board.

"The Labor Board, the Federal Trade Commission, the Interstate Commerce Commission, the Securities and Exchange Commission and many other administrative agencies were all created to deal with problems of regulation of ever increasing complexity in the economic fields of trade, finance and industrial conflicts. Congress thus sought to utilize procedures more expeditious and administered by more specialized and experienced experts than courts had been able to afford. The decision here tends to nullify this Congressional effort." 306 U.S. 292, 300-301 (1939).

to the facts were in its discretion. When the Supreme Court set aside the board's decision, it was in effect substituting its judgment for that of the board with respect to the weight to be assigned to the evidence as presented. But the Court's ruling was not altogether devoid of statutory basis. The authority conferred by section 10 (e) is after all a qualified one. Although free to hear and weigh the evidence before it, the Labor Board is under the legal obligation to see to it that its findings as to the facts are supported by the evidence. This conditional authority thus opens the door for litigation to test the weight of the evidence on which the agency rested its conclusions. In this way the courts are free to reexamine the record.[27]

In the Columbian case, Mr. Justice Stone seemed more concerned with the niceties of administrative procedure than with the effective administration of a highly controversial statute.[28] And yet it would be a mistake to judge from this that the present Chief Justice is generally hostile to the work of administrative agencies. Quite the contrary is the case. He

[27] In the jargon of the subject matter, it might be said that the question as to whether the Labor Board's findings as to the facts were supported by the evidence was a "question of law." If the Justices constituting the majority in the Columbian case were polled on the matter, they might have felt confident in the assertion that their decision left undisturbed the Board's authority to determine "questions of fact." But John Dickinson showed us long ago how barren of meaning such fine spun distinctions really are.

"In truth the distinction between 'questions of law' and 'questions of fact' really gives little help in determining how far the courts will review; and for the good reason that there is no fixed distinction. They are not two mutually exclusive kinds of questions, based upon a difference of subject matter. Matters of law grow downward into questions of fact, and matters of fact reach upward, without a break, into matters of law. . . . It would seem that when the courts are unwilling to review, they are tempted to explain by the easy device of calling the question one of 'fact,' and when otherwise disposed, they say that it is a question of 'law.' " *Administrative Justice and the Supremacy of Law in the United States* (Cambridge: Harv. Univer. Press, 1927), p. 55.

[28] This is the more remarkable when it is recalled that the Wagner Act by express provision frees the board from the rigidities of court pro-

may be counted among the friends of the administrative process, but he is a friend whose sympathetic understanding of the problems confronting administrative agencies has not blinded him to some of their shortcomings. He was with Holmes and Brandeis when they pleaded for a greater appreciation of regulatory tribunals as instruments for dealing with modern problems of social control. It was in the rate-valuation cases that he first indicated his sympathetic attitude. In his thorough grasp of the intricacies of the problem and in his unstinted defense of the special competence of the commissions, he has been the peer of Brandeis. Whether voicing the opinion of the Court, concurring separately or dissenting, he has accepted the fact that public service commissions were "informed by experience" and "appointed by law" to deal with the problems of rate-making. He has called for a minimum of judicial interference with their decisions, a view flowing naturally from his belief that in undertaking to determine "judicially" the value of the properties of public utilities, "courts have been projected into the most speculative undertaking imposed upon them in the entire history of English jurisprudence." [29]

Speaking broadly, it may be said that Chief Justice Stone is of the opinion that the primary responsibility for determining administrative questions belongs to the administrative agencies, and not to the courts. He would allow courts but a limited power to review the decisions of regulatory boards and commissions. That power, he has insisted, should be exercised with care, lest the courts in the guise of review find themselves substituting their views for those of the agencies. At times he has not hesitated to exclude the judiciary altogether, as when

cedure. Section 10 (b) provides that "the rules of evidence prevailing in courts of law or equity shall not be controlling."

[29] *West* v. *Chesapeake and Potomac Telephone Co.* of Baltimore, 295 U.S. 662, 689 (1935). See his dissents in such cases as *St. Louis and O'Fallon Ry. Co.* v. *United States,* 279 U.S. 461, 548 (1929). For evidence of the vindication of his views, see his opinion for the Court in *Federal Power Commission* v. *Natural Gas Pipeline Co.,* 315 U.S. 575 (1942).

he spoke for a unanimous court in vindicating the right of Congress to bar the courts from reviewing decisions of the National Labor Relations Board certifying bargaining units.[30] Still it is obvious that these general principles to which he stands committed have not been applied with uniform consistency. What explains the occasional deviations?

At the basis of Chief Justice Stone's approach to administrative problems is his belief that "Courts are not the only agency of government that must be assumed to have capacity to govern." [31] Regarding the regulatory agencies as cooperating partners of the courts in the business of modern administration, he has done much to win for the administrative arm of government a greater appreciation of its rightful place. He has sought to foster the administrative process, but also to restrain it. Some of his present colleagues—notably, Justices Black and Douglas—will be found more often than he ready to accept the administrative determination. Even so, it is fair to say that the present Chief Justice is genuinely sympathetic with the administrative process. But he is enough of a respecter of the "supremacy of law" to be willing to interpose the judicial check whenever it is necessary, at least in his judgment, to keep administrators from transgressing fundamental rights.

[30] *American Federation of Labor* v. *National Labor Relations Board,* 308 U.S. 401 (1940). By a careful analysis of the language of the Wagner Act and its legislative history, Mr. Justice Stone demonstrated that for the purposes of court review Congress intended to distinguish between an "order" of the board restraining an unfair labor practice and certifications in representation proceedings. Congress chose to invest the board with sole authority to determine conflicting claims for recognition as bargaining agents and the courts were barred from reviewing. Only a "final order" prohibiting an unfair labor practice may be appealed to the courts. As to the contention that this interpretation would lead to hardship, particularly in these days of rival unions, Mr. Justice Stone replied that these were arguments which should be "addressed to Congress and not to the courts."

The Supreme Court has recently taken a similar stand in relation to representation certifications by the National Mediation Board. *Switchmen's Union* v. *National Mediation Board,* 320 U.S. 297 (1943).

[31] *United States* v. *Butler,* 297 U.S. 1, 87 (1936).

CHAPTER V

"CENSORING" STATE REGULATION OF ECONOMIC ACTIVITIES

1. *Introductory*

No MORE enlightening revelation of the fundamental issues implicit in social control will be found in judicial utterance than in the numerous due process cases. The traditional dichotomy of freedom versus authority and its more pragmatic qualifications, the influence of classical economics, the clash of economic interests, the impact of modern industrialism on men's conception of private rights and public needs—all are mirrored in the judicial development of due process concepts. Beginning with its first interpretation of the Fourteenth Amendment,[1] it has been apparent that the Supreme Court personnel was divided over these issues no less deeply than men who were not judges have been divided. To the student of constitutional history, however, the absence of unity within the Court is most instructive for its bearing on the nature of judicial review. For however explicable may be the fluctuations in the exposition of the Fourteenth Amendment,[2] their greatest significance derives from the proof they afford of the essentially "legislative" character of judicial power.

From the latter standpoint, the reason Justice Miller gave

---

[1] *Slaughter-House Cases,* 16 Wall. 36, 83 (1873).

[2] Excellent brief accounts of the fluctuations in the interpretation of the Fourteenth Amendment will be found in Edward S. Corwin, "The Supreme Court and the Fourteenth Amendment," *7 Mich. L. Rev. 643* (June, 1909) ; and in Robert E. Cushman, "Social and Economic Interpretation of the Fourteenth Amendment," *20 Mich. L. Rev. 737* (May, 1922).

in the *Slaughter-House Cases* for refusing to apply the Fourteenth Amendment to the legislative authority of the states displayed rare foresight, even if it ultimately proved to be the wrong prognosis. Counsel for the New Orleans butchers had argued that the Fourteenth Amendment was adopted in order to place the ordinary rights of the individual under the guardianship of the National Government.[3] In rejecting this contention, Miller protested that its acceptance by the Supreme Court "would constitute this Court a perpetual censor upon all legislation of the states." He was unable to find in the due process clause of the Fourteenth Amendment any limitation on the power of a legislature to restrict the uses to which private property might be put. And speaking of the meaning of that provision, he declared that "under no construction" of it could the action of the Louisiana legislature be held to be "a deprivation of property" within the meaning of the due process clause.[4]

But Miller's self-denying ordinance never obtained unqualified support from his colleagues. Mr. Justice Field—for whom, Walton H. Hamilton has said, "liberty and property came to be a single word" [5]—was the leader of the group on the Bench which, in numerous dissents, sought to extend due process to the substance of state legislation.[6] The eventual triumph of

[3] The argument of the attorneys for the butchers was based primarily on the effect of the privileges and immunities clause of the Fourteenth Amendment. But the other clauses of the first section of the amendment were also discussed by counsel and court.

[4] Miller proved himself to be an equally false prophet in his estimate of the equal protection clause. "We doubt very much," he predicted, "whether any action of a State not directed by way of discrimination against the negroes as a class, or on account of their race, will ever be held to come within the purview of this provision."

[5] "The Path of Due Process," in *The Constitution Reconsidered*, Conyers Read (Ed.), (New York: Columbia Univ. Press, 1938), p. 180.

[6] Field's efforts in this direction are typified by his dissents in *Munn* v. *Illinois*, 94 U.S. 113, 136 (1877) and *Powell* v. *Pennsylvania*, 127 U.S. 678, 687 (1888). He argued in the latter case that due process "has always been supposed to secure to every person the essential conditions for the pursuit

Field's conception of due process helped to establish the Supreme Court as the ever-present arbiter of state action—a result which Miller thought would be obviated by the principles enunciated in the *Slaughter-House Cases*.[7] More explicitly, due process as a restraint upon substantive legislative power, at least as applied to the states, furnished the Court with the necessary constitutional weapon for overseeing all regulations undertaken by the states in the exercise of their police power. And since the Court refused to define "due process" in any final form,[8] the weapon could be used flexibly, depending upon the predilections of the members constituting the "majority."

The resulting "jurisprudence of concepts," as the reading of substance into due process has been termed, placed the Supreme Court in a particularly strategic position at a time when government regulation was everywhere on the increase. But regulation, especially in the economic field, has always involved a choice among competing claims. Fundamentally,

of happiness and is, therefore, not to be construed in a narrow or restricted sense." at p. 691.

[7] Professor Robert E. Cushman has shown that there were four influences working toward the adoption of the new interpretation of due process. (1) The appointment of five new justices between 1875-85. "When Mr. Justice Miller died in 1890 he left behind him on the bench but one colleague who had sat with him in the *Slaughter-House Cases,* and that colleague, Mr. Justice Field, had from the outset been an outspoken and dogmatic apostle of the new faith." (2) The gradual abatement of Reconstruction issues, and with it a lessening of the fear that a broad construction of the Fourteenth Amendment would enable Congress to dictate to the states regarding their treatment of the Negro; (3) the pressure from the American Bar, reinforced by the persistent clamor on the part of the Justices on the Court led by Field; and (4) the post-Civil War economic transformation of the country which had accelerated demands for government control of business, and the inevitable search for judicial protection against legislative interference. 20 Mich. L. Rev. 737, at pp. 742-43.

[8] The rule of "judicial inclusion and exclusion" in the interpretation of due process was set down by Justice Miller in *Davidson* v. *New Orleans,* 96 U.S. 97 (1878). "There is wisdom," the Court thought, "in ascertaining the intent and application of such an important phrase [due process of law] in the federal Constitution, by the gradual process of judicial inclusion and exclusion, as the cases presented for decision shall require, with the reasoning on which such decisions may be founded." P. 104.

that is to say, social control, whether undertaken by the national or a state government, has entailed a decision as to which of two or more divergent private interests was entitled to public recognition, protection or even positive aid.[9] Thus the application of due process to the regulatory powers of the states made it possible for the Supreme Court to exert a decisive influence on the economic policies adopted by them; for ultimately the interests sought to be reconciled had to be weighed in judicial scales. Abstractions such as "liberty of contract" and the shelter given corporations as "persons" facilitated immeasurably the Court's role as "censor." [10]

The conflict of private interests out of which governmental action grows was discussed with great insight by Mr. Justice Stone early in his tenure on the Court. His opinion in *Miller* v. *Schoene* [11] demonstrates how keenly aware he has been of the roots of modern legislation. Confronted with an unusually drastic curtailment of property rights, he was nevertheless able to see it as necessitated by a "preponderant public concern."

Acting under the authority of a state law, the Virginia state entomologist had ordered the owners of ornamental red cedar trees located within two miles of apple orchards to cut down the trees. This he did in order to prevent the spread to the apple orchards of a rust or plant disease with which the red cedar trees were infected. The cedar rust was destructive

---

[9] This has been so, even though it has been the custom to draw the metaphysical picture in which the "government" is always made to appear as in opposition to the interests of the "individual." And when corporations were interpreted to be "persons" within the meaning of the due-process clause as well as the equal protection of the laws clause, this oversimplified antithesis became even more widespread.

[10] For an interesting reexamination of the old question whether the framers of the Fourteenth Amendment intended to protect corporations, see Howard J. Graham, "The Conspiracy Theory of the Fourteenth Amendment," *47 Yale L. Jour. 371* (Jan., 1938) and *48 Yale L. Jour. 171* (Dec., 1938).

[11] 276 U.S. 272 (1928).

'of apples but had no effect on the value of the ornamental cedar trees.

In his opinion sustaining the Virginia statute, Mr. Justice Stone recited at length the facts or considerations which had led the legislature of that state to protect the interests of apple growers as against the rights of the property owners whose trees were ordered destroyed. First there was the fact, as established by the evidence, that the destruction of the infected trees was the "only practicable method" of preventing the communication of the disease to the near-by apple orchards. But more important was the fact that the value of the red cedar in all of Virginia was small in comparison with the value of the state's apple orchards. Apple growing is one of Virginia's leading industries in which millions of dollars are invested and on which a large part of the population depends for a livelihood. The apples are used locally and large quantities of them are shipped outside the state.

The Virginia legislature had obviously chosen to preserve one class of property in preference to another. "It would have been none the less a choice," asserted Mr. Justice Stone, "if by doing nothing," the state had allowed the damage to the apple orchards to continue. In the face of such a choice, the state was not "exceeding its constitutional powers" when it chose to destroy one class of property in order to preserve another "which, in the judgment of the legislature, is of greater value to the public." He rejected categorically the view that the state was merely choosing between two private interests and protecting one at the expense of the other.

It will not do to say that the case is merely one of a conflict of two private interests and that the misfortune of apple growers may not be shifted to cedar owners by ordering the destruction of their property; for it is obvious that there may be, and that here there is, a preponderant public concern in the preservation of one interest over the other. . . . And where the public interest is involved preferment of that interest over the property interest of the individual, to the extent even of its destruction, is one of the distinguishing characteristics of every exercise of the police power which affects property.

Mr. Justice Stone's reasoning was simple and could lead to but one conclusion. In the process of balancing economic interests, the state was coming to the aid of the one in the survival of which society had the greater stake. Virginia's decision was therefore based on "considerations of social policy" which were reasonable and so did not violate due process.[12]

2. *Price Fixing—Regulation of Business "Affected with a Public Interest"*

In the decade following *Lochner* v. *New York*,[13] the Supreme Court exhibited greater sympathy for the aims of social legislation adopted by the states than its decision in that case foreshadowed.[14] This is the period during which the famous Brandeis brief received official recognition from the Court.[15]

---

[12] Although not explicitly raised, the question whether the cedar owners should have been compensated might well have been the central issue had the Court been divided. Even Holmes and Brandeis once found themselves in sharp disagreement in a case which presented to the Court not too dissimilar a problem. See their opinions in *Pennsylvania Coal Co.* v. *Mahon*, 260 U.S. 393, 416 (1922).

[13] 198 U.S. 45 (1905).

[14] *Muller* v. *Oregon*, 208 U.S. 412 (1908), *Bunting* v. *Oregon*, 243 U.S. 426 (1917), *Miller* v. *Wilson*, 236 U.S. 373 (1915), *Wilson* v. *New*, 243 U.S. 332 (1916), are all illustrative of the trend in this period.

[15] Long before he was appointed by President Wilson to the United States Supreme Court, Louis D. Brandeis fought to win for the factual inquiry its rightful place in the legal process. The brief he presented in *Muller* v. *Oregon,* as counsel for the State of Oregon, was the first of his famous briefs to stress the importance of facts in the disposition of due process questions. Commenting on the Brandeis brief, Mr. Justice Brewer, speaking for the Court in that case, said:

"The legislation and opinions, referred to in the margin, may not be, technically speaking, authorities, and in them is little or no discussion of the constitutional question presented to us for determination, yet they are significant of a widespread belief that woman's physical structure and the

Its approach to due process issues was marked by an awareness of the social and economic conditions which had impelled
the states to act. But during the 1920's there was a reversion
to the more legalistic interpretation which had carried the
day in the Lochner case.[16] This was the Court to which Mr.
Justice Stone came and it was not long before he revealed his
fundamental disagreement with the new trend.

In *Miller* v. *Schoene* Mr. Justice Stone was speaking for
a unanimous Court, but even then there was evidence that
basically a majority of his colleagues did not share his tolerance of state action. The Justice who objected to the test
of "direct" and "indirect" in commerce clause cases could be
expected to protest, sooner or later, against the use of "labels"
in the application of the Fourteenth Amendment. "Affected
with a public interest" was the first of the judicially developed
formulas he challenged.

Since *Munn* v. *Illinois* the test of the constitutionality of
price fixing was whether the business was "affected with a
public interest." The liberals on the Court opposed more than
once the use of so artificial a criterion. "Vague and illusory"
was the way Mr. Justice Stone described it in *Tyson Brothers*
v. *Banton*,[17] decided less than two months after the DiSanto
case. He was dissenting against the decision by the majority
that a New York law regulating the resale price of theater
tickets was a violation of due process inasmuch as the business

functions she performs in consequence thereof justifies special legislation
restricting or qualifying the conditions under which she should be permitted to toil. . . . when a question of fact is debated and debatable and
the extent to which a special constitutional limitation goes is affected by
the truth in respect to that fact, a widespread and long-continued belief
concerning it is worthy of consideration. We take judicial cognizance of
all matters of general knowledge." 208 U.S. 412, 420-21 (1908).

16 *Truax* v. *Corrigan*, 257 U.S. 312 (1921) and *Adkins* v. *Children's Hospital*, 261 U.S. 525 (1923) may be regarded as having inaugurated the
retreat to the older position.

17 273 U.S. 418, 447 (1927).

involved was not "affected with a public interest." [18] To be
subject to price control, Justice Sutherland had said for the
Court, the business must be such "as to justify the conclusion
that it has been devoted to a public use and its use thereby in
effect granted to the public."

Mr. Justice Stone objected to the basis for the decision and
primarily because he thought it made a realistic solution
impossible. The difficulty with the phrase "affected with a public
interest" is that as applied it has become a "convenient expression" for describing those businesses the control of which
has been sanctioned by the Court. As a result, its use makes
it inevitable that the Court must continue "begging the question to be decided." For to hold that only those businesses
affected with a public interest are subject to regulation is but
another way of saying that businesses which may be regulated
are affected with a public interest. Such a term cannot be used
"free of its connotation of legal consequences."

Rather than rely on so unsatisfactory a criterion of constitutionality, Mr. Justice Stone urged the Court to look into
the basic assumption which has served as the justification
for the rule that ordinarily prices may not be controlled.

The constitutional theory that prices normally may not be regulated
rests upon the assumption that the public interest and private right
are both adequately protected when there is "free" competition
among buyers and sellers, and that in such a state of economic
society the interference with so important an incident of the
ownership of private property as price-fixing is not justified and
hence is a taking of property without due process of law.

When, however, the "regulative force of competition" has
broken down and the buyers or sellers are at a disadvantage

---

[18] The New York law declared the price of admission to theaters to
be "affected with a public interest" and made it illegal for anyone to sell
theater tickets at a price which was more than fifty cents above the box-
office price printed on the ticket.

in the bargaining struggle, statutory regulation of price is a permissible means of protecting that part of the community which would suffer from the economic consequences arising from the absence of genuine competition. New York was seeking to deal with exactly such a situation. The unscrupulous activity of the theater ticket speculators was notoriously widespread and the legislature was aware that their victims were helpless.

The remedy for that situation might be dictated by "considerations of economics," Mr. Justice Stone asserted, concerning which, he added, there might be "reasonable differences of opinion." But the Supreme Court, he insisted, is without power to make a choice between the conflicting views, since such a choice would take it from the "judicial to the legislative field." He would have the judicial function end "when it is determined that there is basis for legislative action in a field not withheld from legislative power by the Constitution."

A year later, the Supreme Court was once more confronted with price-control legislation and again Mr. Justice Stone dissented from the prevailing view.[19] He renewed his protest against formalism in constitutional interpretation, but this time he added a positive aspect to his criticism. In the Mc-BRIDE case he developed in detail the factual inquiry for testing the validity of price-control measures.

The majority, with Justice Sutherland as its spokesman, held invalid a New Jersey law regulating the fees charged by private employment agencies to persons seeking employment. As in *Tyson* v. *Banton*, in this case Justice Sutherland explained the Court's action on the familiar ground that the business sought to be regulated (the operation of employment agencies) was not one sufficiently clothed with a public interest

---

[19] *Ribnick* v. *McBride*, 277 U.S. 350, 359 (1928). As in *Tyson* v. *Banton*, so in this case Mr. Justice Stone was joined in his dissent by Justices Holmes and Brandeis.

to permit state supervision of the rates charged for its services. He professed to see no difference between the business of ticket brokers and the business of operating employment agencies.

In an opinion notable for its grasp of economic conditions, Mr. Justice Stone took issue with the majority on all points. Reminding his colleagues that the term "affected with a public interest" is not to be found in the Constitution, he again noted that its meaning can be gathered only from the Court's decisions. And so far as he was able to read those decisions, price regulation by the states was permissible "whenever any combination of circumstances seriously curtails the regulative force of competition, so that buyers or sellers are placed at such a disadvantage in the bargaining struggle that a legislature might reasonably anticipate serious consequences to the community as a whole." This meant, of course, that the validity of price-fixing legislation should be governed by the demands of the public interest. But more specifically, what was to be the "test" by which to judge whether or not a business could be brought under price control? That it was being used by the public generally was not the decisive factor. The "elements" which Mr. Justice Stone thought ought to be considered in ascertaining the existence of the public interest were "the nature of the service rendered, the exorbitance of the charges and the arbitrary control to which the public may be subjected without regulation." [20]

Indeed, his entire opinion in this case stands out as a powerful argument against the use of theoretical or merely legalistic concepts in the solution of constitutional questions.

[20] Mr. Justice Stone said further: "The economic disadvantage of a class and the attempt to ameliorate its conditions may alone be sufficient to give rise to the 'public interest' and to justify the regulation of contracts with its members . . . and obviously circumstances may so change in point of time or so differ in space as to clothe a business with such an interest which at other times or in other places would be a matter of private concern."

He was unable to say *"a priori,"* he tells us, that the business of operating employment agencies lacked the "requisite public interest." He wanted the Court to decide the case in the light of the conditions which had led New Jersey to adopt remedial legislation. Thus he wrote:

> We are judicially aware that the problem of unemployment is of grave public concern; that the conduct of the employment agency business bears an important relationship to that larger problem and affects vitally the lives of great numbers of the population, not only in New Jersey, but throughout the United States; that employment agencies, admittedly subject to regulation in other respects . . . and in fact very generally regulated, deal with a necessitous class, the members of which are often dependent on them for opportunity to earn their livelihood, are not free to move from place to place and are often under exceptional economic compulsion to accept such terms as the agencies offer. We are not judicially ignorant of what all human experience teaches, that those so situated are peculiarly the prey of the unscrupulous and designing.

It had never questioned, Mr. Justice Stone reminded the Court, that the operation of employment agencies was inherently subject to grave abuses because of the helpless position of unemployed persons. He disagreed with Mr. Justice Sutherland's contention that the activity of such agencies was similar to the activity of ticket brokers involved in *Tyson* v *Banton*. There was a "marked difference" between the two businesses. Not only did the fraud which New York had legislated against affect only a small portion of the public, but its regulation was directed to the protection of a luxury. New Jersey, on the other hand, was concerned with a problem which potentially affected most of the population and which obviously concerned a human necessity. Its legislation had a two-fold purpose: "to protect a class unable to protect itself" and "to mitigate the evils which unemployment brings upon the community as a whole."

This sympathetic appraisal of the need for regulating employment agencies led Mr. Justice Stone to espouse a doctrine of "presumption" completely consistent with that view. He demanded that "some presumption should be indulged" that the legislature of New Jersey was acting with a knowledge of the conditions in the state which made it necessary to control the fees charged by employment agencies. Then, interestingly enough, after quoting a statement from Justice Sutherland's opinion in *Tyson* v. *Banton*,[21] he asserted that it was precisely such a "deserved respect for the judgment of the local lawmaker" on which "depends . . . the presumption in favor of constitutionality." The Court should not "oppose" its view of the need for the legislation to that of the local authorities. He would have it accord state legislatures the same respect to which the rule of presumption of constitutionality looks in the case of acts of Congress.[22] Furthermore, the burden of showing that state legislation is unconstitutional is on those who question its validity.

But even if the Court were unwilling to allow presumption of constitutionality in favor of the legislation, Mr. Justice Stone saw another, and no less important, basis for holding it valid. "We need not close our eyes," he told his brethren, "to the available data throwing light on the problem with which the legislature had to deal." Citing *Muller* v. *Oregon* as authority for judicial recognition of the facts underlying

[21] Justice Sutherland had said that the validity of price fixing turns "upon the existence of conditions peculiar to the business under consideration." 273 U.S. 418, 438 (1927). Repeating the quoted phrase several times, Mr. Justice Stone argued that his approach to the case was the one which conformed to this standard.

[22] To illustrate the similarity of treatment for which he was arguing, Mr. Justice Stone quoted the following statement from Justice Sutherland's opinion for the Court in *Adkins* v. *Children's Hospital:* "This Court, by an unbroken line of decisions from Chief Justice Marshall to the present day, has steadily adhered to the rule that every possible presumption is in favor of the validity of an act of Congress until overcome beyond rational doubt." 261 U.S. 525, 544 (1923).

social legislation, he went on to examine at some length the findings of numerous public and private inquiries into the abuses which had led Congress and twenty-one state legislatures to undertake regulation of employment agencies.[23] These findings, the Justice emphasized, afforded "a substantial basis for the conclusion of the New Jersey legislature that the business is peculiarly subject to abuses relating to fee charging, and that for the correction of these the restriction to a reasonable maximum charge is the only effective remedy."

Particularly unacceptable to Mr. Justice Stone was the distinction on which the opinion of the majority appeared to him to depend. Mr. Justice Sutherland had said that if there were evils incident to the business of operating employment agencies they might be regulated but not by fixing reasonable rates for their services. Criticizing this distinction as based "on no real economic difference" and for which he was unable to find any support in the Federal Constitution, he expounded a standard for determining the constitutionality of price fixing which a majority of the Court adopted six years later. He said:

I cannot accept as valid the distinction on which the opinion of the majority seems to me necessarily to depend, that granted constitutional power to regulate there is any controlling difference between reasonable regulation of price, if appropriate to the evil to be remedied, and other forms of appropriate regulation which

[23] According to Mr. Justice Stone, these investigations and reports disclosed the existence of five types of abuses in connection with the operation of employment agencies. These were:

(1) When unregulated, agencies have charged exorbitant fees.

(2) These fees have not infrequently been discriminatory.

(3) Operators of employment agencies have been known to resort to "fee-splitting." They have turned over to the employer or his foreman part of the fee charged to the worker.

(4) In periods of widespread unemployment, private agencies raised their fees.

(5) Only the employee pays for a service of value to employer as well as worker.

curtail liberty of contract or the use and enjoyment of property. Obviously, even in the case of businesses affected with a public interest, other control than price regulation may be so inappropriate as to be arbitrary or unreasonable, and hence unconstitutional. To me it seems equally obvious that the Constitution does not require us to hold that a business, subject to every other form of reasonable regulation, is immune from the requirement of reasonable prices, where that requirement is the only remedy appropriate to the evils encountered. In this respect I can see no difference between a reasonable regulation of price and a reasonable regulation of the use of property, which affects its price or economic return. The privilege of contract and the free use of property are as seriously cut down in the one case as in the other.[24]

With the aid of numerous instances where the Supreme Court had sanctioned legislative control of prices or rates,[25] Mr. Justice Stone continued to argue that the effect upon freedom to contract is the same, whether the regulation is of the price or the goods or services involved in the bargain. He confessed that he would be the first to concede that there might be differences of opinion as to the wisdom of the remedy pre-

[24] A similar doctrine was set forth by Mr. Justice Brandeis in his dissent in *New State Ice Co.* v. *Liebmann,* 285 U.S. 262, 280 (1932). On the ground that the business of selling ice was an ordinary private activity and not one affected with a public interest, the majority in that case held invalid an Oklahoma law requiring persons wishing to engage in such a business to secure a certificate of convenience and necessity. Justice Brandeis, in whose views Justices Stone and Holmes concurred, wrote an elaborate opinion in which he vigorously assailed the artificial standard applied by the Court. His opinion, reading like a profound treatise on economic affairs, says in part:

"The notion of a distinct category of business 'affected with a public interest' employing property 'devoted to a public use' rests upon historical error. In my opinion, the true principle is that the state's power extends to every regulation of any business reasonably required and appropriate for the public protection. I find in the due process clause no other limitation upon the character or the scope of regulation permissible." P. 302.

[25] Other than the regulation of so-called "public callings," he referred to such long accepted legislative curtailments of freedom of contract as the fixing of rates to be charged by grain elevators and insurance companies, the fixing of the fees charged by attorneys practicing before workmen's compensation commissions, the establishment of maximum rents, etc.

scribed by the New Jersey legislature. Nevertheless, he repeated what he had said in *Tyson* v. *Banton*, that for the Court to decide the fate of legislation on the basis of its view of the wisdom or unwisdom of the particular form of the regulation is for it to take "a step from the judicial to the legislative field." He was convinced that such a choice should remain where "it was left by the Constitution,—to the states and to Congress."

These repeated criticisms were not made in vain. In *Nebbia* v. *New York* [26] the Supreme Court repudiated the vague theory by which the constitutionality of price control had been tested. The regulation of prices or rates, Mr. Justice Roberts said for the majority, was one of many methods for restricting liberty and property in the interest of the public and was, therefore, an attribute of the police power of the state. As such, price fixing was subject to the same limitations of due process which generally apply to any other exertion of the police power. "There is no closed class or category of businesses affected with a public interest," he declared; and added, "the function of courts in the application of the Fifth and Fourteenth Amendments is to determine in each case whether circumstances vindicate the challenged regulation as a reasonable exertion of governmental authority or condemn as arbitrary or discriminatory." As to the concept of a business affected with a public interest, it merely meant that a business "for adequate reason, is subject to control for the public good." If regulation is justified by prevailing conditions and is reasonably related to the object sought to be attained by the legislature, it may take the form of control of prices to be charged for the property or services involved. The choice of the method for effectuating the policy is for the legislature to make.[27]

[26] 291 U.S. 502 (1934).

[27] To what extent Mr. Justice Stone's views on price fixing finally prevailed is best indicated by the following language from the opinion by Mr. Justice Roberts in the NEBBIA case: "So far as the requirement of

3. *Minimum Wages for Women*

Thanks to the labors of Louis D. Brandeis, the courts came to accept the physiological differences between men and women as a valid basis for extending special protection to women. His signal success in *Muller* v. *Oregon* led some to suppose that the result reached in that case was of permanent significance. It seemed as though Mr. Justice Brewer's commendation of the Brandeis brief bespoke a judicial mind that would henceforth look with favor upon legislation intended to protect those unable to protect themselves.[28]

Such an attitude, had the Supreme Court continued to apply it, would have made the task of safeguarding the interests of women workers much easier for the nation's legislatures. But any hopes that might have been inspired by *Muller* v. *Oregon* and the related cases that followed it were shattered by Mr. Justice Sutherland's opinion for the Court in *Adkins* v.

due process is concerned, and in the absence of other constitutional restrictions a state is free to adopt whatever economic policy may reasonably be deemed to promote public welfare, and to enforce that policy by legislation adapted to its purpose. If the laws passed are seen to have a reasonable relation to a proper legislative purpose, and are neither arbitrary nor discriminatory, the requirements of due process are satisfied." 291 U.S. 502, 537 (1934).

[28] The abolition of "sweating" and the guarantee of a minimum standard of existence have been the twin objectives of minimum wage legislation in the United States as well as in all other countries which have adopted it. "Minimum Wage Legislation in Various Countries," *Bulletin #467* (Bureau of Labor Statistics).

The fact that women were working in occupations and industries which were for the most part unorganized and paying low wages has been pointed to as justifying protective legislation in their behalf. In addition, the health of women as the "bearers of the race" was said to be of special concern to the community. The connection between "poor wages" and "poor health" and their social effects were developed at length in the brief drawn up by Felix Frankfurter and others in the ADKINS case. With the aid of data gathered from the writings of economists, sociologists and physicians here and abroad, this eleven hundred page brief sought to convince the Court that the District of Columbia minimum wage law was supported by circumstances about which there could be no doubt. *District of Columbia Wage Cases, Brief for Appellants,* 2 vol. (New York, 1923).

Children's Hospital, decided in 1923.[29] In an opinion which, for its refusal to heed social and economic realities, belongs in a class with Justice Peckham's opinion in *Lochner* v. *New York*,[30] Mr. Justice Sutherland found the minimum wage law which Congress adopted for the District of Columbia in 1918 to be an unreasonable interference with freedom of contract. As such it was in conflict with the due process clause of the Fifth Amendment.

In the ADKINS case, the majority were unable to believe that the act of Congress was for the protection of persons who might otherwise be helpless. Instead, they saw the act as "simply and, exclusively a price-fixing law, confined to adult women . . . who are legally as capable of contracting for themselves as men." [31] Under the law, the Minimum Wage Board was to prescribe such standards of minimum wages as were deemed by it to be adequate to provide the necessary cost of living to women workers, sufficient to maintain them in health and to protect their morals. Asserting that "the relation between earnings and morals is not capable of standardization," the Court expressed the view that adequate wages were no insurance for the protection of a woman's morals, any more than they are insurance of a man's honesty. And as to the relation between wages and health, its opinion was that the adequacy of a woman's wages may be determined by such

[29] 261 U.S. 525 (1923).

[30] The majority in that case invalidated New York's bake-shop law principally because it was not convinced that there was any relation between the health of bakery workers and the number of hours they stayed at their tasks. "We think," Justice Peckham declared, "there can be no fair doubt that the trade of the baker, in and of itself, is not an unhealthy one to that degree which would authorize the legislature to interfere with the right to labor and with the right of free contract on the part of the individual, either as employer or employee. . . . To the common understanding, the trade of baker has never been regarded as an unhealthy one." 198 U.S. 45, 59 (1905).

[31] The Court did not question in this case, as it has not questioned in other minimum wage cases, the validity of minimum wages for the benefit of minors.

factors as personal thrift, family conditions, and others which vary with each individual.

There was one feature of the congressional statute, how-ever, which the majority in the ADKINS case found particularly objectionable. That was its failure to relate the minimum wage to the value of the services rendered by the employee. Justice Sutherland remarked that this shortcoming of the law "per-haps more than any other" put upon it "the stamp of invalid-ity." Nor was his opinion without a hint of the type of formula which might have proved acceptable to the Court—at least so it was supposed at the time. Thus he said:

> A statute requiring an employer to pay in money, to pay at prescribed and regular intervals, to pay the value of services ren-dered, even to pay with fair relation to the extent of the benefit obtained from the service, would be understandable.

Acting on this broad suggestion but at different times, eight states [32] drafted their minimum wage laws to meet what was re-garded as the Supreme Court's chief objection to the District of Columbia Minimum Wage Law. The legislature of New York enacted its minimum wage statute in April of 1933. It directed the industrial commissioner of the state to appoint "wage boards" which, after inquiry, were to determine fair wages for women in specific industries. Under its terms, a "fair minimum wage" was to be one "fairly and reasonably commensurate with the value of the service or class of services rendered." It de-fined an "oppressive and unreasonable wage" as one which is "both less than the fair and reasonable value of the services rendered and less than sufficient to meet the minimum cost of living necessary for health."

These were the provisions which many competent authorities, including Solicitor General Henry J. Epstein of New York,

[32] Connecticut, Illinois, Massachusetts, New Hampshire, New Jersey, Ohio, Rhode Island and New York.

believed would furnish an adequate basis for distinguishing the New York statute from the District of Columbia minimum wage law. But when the New York legislation came to be challenged, neither the Court of Appeals of New York nor the United States Supreme Court [33] was able to discern any "material difference" between the two statutes. Denying that the decision in the ADKINS case was influenced by the standard for fixing minimum wages prescribed by the act of Congress, Mr. Justice Butler, speaking for the majority of the Supreme Court,[34] left no doubt as to the basic issue in both the ADKINS case and the New York minimum wage case. Fundamentally, both cases involved the validity of minimum wage legislation for women, and not the constitutional possibilities of any particular brand of minimum wage laws. "The state is without power," declared Mr. Justice Butler in the 1936 case, "by any form of legislation to prohibit, change or nullify contracts between employers and adult women workers as to the amount of wages paid."

Thus within the brief span of a year, the federal government and the states were stripped of the power to regulate wages. Unlike the decision in the Schechter case, however, the ruling in the New York minimum wage case was not by a unanimous Court. Four of the Justices dissented and two of them wrote opinions vigorously questioning the ground taken by the majority as well as its broader implications. Chief Justice Hughes, with whom Justices Brandeis, Cardozo and Stone agreed, dissented because he thought that the New York law was distinguishable from the minimum wage law for the District of Columbia invalidated in the ADKINS case. Declaring that liberty of contract is a "qualified and not an absolute right," he took the position that since the standard embodied in the New York

[33] *Morehead* v. *New York* ex rel. *Tipaldo*, 298 U.S. 587, 631 (1936).

[34] In addition to Justice Butler, Justices Sutherland, McReynolds, Roberts and VanDevanter constituted the majority. The vote of Mr. Justice Roberts was once more decisive.

law required a "fair equivalence of wage and service" it could not be said that the state was acting arbitrarily.

Even though Mr. Justice Stone subscribed to all that Chief Justice Hughes had written, he did not want it to be thought that his vote to sustain the New York law was due to the differences between it and the statute which Congress enacted in 1918 for the District of Columbia.[35] He did not share the Chief Justice's opinion—at least as that opinion can be deduced from the justification he gave for dissenting—that the validity of minimum wage legislation depends upon the standard set up by the legislature for determining a minimum wage. With undisguised sarcasm, he remarked at the outset that he was attaching "little importance" to the fact that the Act of Congress "was aimed only at a starvation wage," whereas the New York law did not "prohibit such a wage unless it is also less than the reasonable value of the service."

Mr. Justice Stone preferred to take the broader ground that the states in the exercise of their police power were free to restrict the terms of a wage contract. Whenever the legislature of a state is impelled by its knowledge of local conditions to provide for such restrictions in order to safeguard the public interest, it is but an incident of its exercise of that power to prescribe the methods for implementing its policy. The choice of a standard, he argued, was a legislative, and not a judicial matter. "The vague and general pronouncement of the Fourteenth Amendment against deprivation of liberty without due process of law," he declared, "is a limitation of legislative power, not a formula for its exercise." Mr. Justice Stone could not construe the liberty guaranteed by that amendment as securing to anyone freedom from the restraints of a law which "reasonable men" consider to be "an appropriate means" for solving problems of concern to the community. It was "grim

[35] Mr. Justice Stone was also speaking for Justices Brandeis and Cardozo.

irony" to speak of the freedom of contract of persons who are compelled by their economic circumstances to sell their services for less than is enough for subsistence.

Mr. Justice Stone renewed his plea that protective legislation be judged in the light of the conditions it is intended to correct. He found two considerations particularly persuasive. The first and more important was the evidence of the effect of starvation wages upon the health and morals of women workers and upon their children.[36] When the legislature's purpose is to prevent the deterioration of the race and the impairment of health and morality, the Justice maintained, the inevitable interference with freedom of contract is but a necessary means to a legitimate end. The other consideration was the fact, established by the experience of the United States and numerous foreign countries, that wage-control measures have been regarded as "an appropriate corrective for serious social and economic maladjustments growing out of inequality in bargaining power." [37] That fact in itself convinced Mr. Justice Stone that minimum wage legislation was not "beyond the bounds of reason."

Such, indeed, was the character of the considerations which prevailed with a majority of the Supreme Court when it upheld the New York Milk Control Act of 1933.[38] And Mr. Jus-

[36] Solicitor General Epstein filed a factual brief in addition to the usual legal brief. Modeled on the pattern of the Brandeis and Frankfurter briefs in behalf of social legislation, his brief sought to defend the minimum wage law by demonstrating: "(1) the need for protecting women in industry in New York State from overreaching and exploitation by employers in certain industries; and (2) the inability of the laundry industry and others to maintain voluntary fair minimum wages because of destructive competition."

[37] Our own Congress, the legislatures of seventeen states, as well as the legislatures of twenty-one foreign countries, have experimented with the regulation of wages. Among the foreign countries are Great Britain and its four dominions.

[38] Among the eight briefs filed in the New York Minimum Wage case was one which Dean Acheson submitted to the Court on behalf of six of the states whose minimum wage laws for women were similar to that of

tice Stone was emphatic in arguing that the reasoning in the
NEBBIA case was irreconcilable with the conclusion reached
in the ADKINS case. He therefore insisted that the ADKINS ruling should not have been allowed to control the Court's decision on the New York minimum wage law, and that the 1923
case should be reconsidered in the light of the Court's more
recent knowledge of the causes of social and economic dislocations. Furthermore, since the Court agreed in the NEBBIA case
—which was the later case—on the necessity to appraise regulatory legislation on the basis of the circumstances under which
it is adopted, Mr. Justice Stone thought that the Court should
adhere to the more recent precedent. He wanted the Court to
reaffirm its stand in the NEBBIA case and to declare that "the
choice of the particular form of regulation by which grave
economic maladjustments are to be remedied is for legislatures
and not the courts" to make.

Since Mr. Justice Stone was of the opinion, moreover, that
the invalidation of the New York Minimum Wage Law could
not be defended on the basis of "history, principles of government, law or logic," it is not surprising to find him taking
his colleagues to task for reading their "economic predilections" into the Federal Constitution. In eloquent language
reminiscent of Holmes' memorable dissent in the LOCHNER case,
he objected vigorously to a doctrinaire approach to constitutional interpretation. Thus in speaking of the conditions which
justified the New York legislature in choosing minimum wages
as an appropriate remedy, he went on to say:

It is difficult to imagine any grounds, other than our own personal
economic predilections, for saying that the contract of employment
is any the less an appropriate subject of legislation than are scores

New York. Mr. Acheson relied heavily on the majority opinion in the
NEBBIA case. Adopting the reasoning of Mr. Justice Roberts in that case,
he argued that "liberty of contract in the field of wages as in any other
field is subservient to the police power."

of others, in dealing with which this Court has held that legislatures may curtail individual freedom in the public interest.[39]

The Court's function under the Fourteenth Amendment, he persisted, is to inquire whether the state has the power to legislate with respect to the particular subject involved in the litigation, but not to weigh the merits of the remedy prescribed by the legislature. Neither is it within the province of courts to resolve doubts about the wisdom of public policy by leaving it to the "blind operation of uncontrolled economic forces" to bring about improvement in conditions. Before concluding, Mr. Justice Stone reaffirmed his conviction that "unless government is to be rendered impotent" legislatures must be left free to choose among alternatives. As Justice Holmes had done in his own way thirty years earlier, so Mr. Justice Stone told his contemporaries on the Court that "the Fourteenth Amendment has no more embodied in the Constitution our preference for some particular set of economic beliefs than it has adopted, in the name of liberty, the system of theology which we happen to approve."

The New York minimum wage case was decided on June 1, 1936. The Justices who dissented in that case waited less than a year to see their views prevail. For on March 29, 1937, the Supreme Court, with Mr. Justice Roberts joining the Chief Justice and Justices Brandeis, Cardozo and Stone to form a bare majority, upheld the minimum wage law which the State of Washington had enacted for the protection of its women workers.[40] It overruled *Adkins* v. *Children's Hospital.* Minimum wage requirements are not an "arbitrary and capricious" remedy for the evils sought to be eliminated, Chief Justice

[39] If such were not the case, then on what theory, Mr. Justice Stone wanted to know, were wages any less subject to control in the public interest than were the hours of work, the time and manner of paying wages, the price of milk, etc.

[40] *West Coast Hotel Co.* v. *Parrish,* 300 U.S. 379 (1937).

Hughes asserted and declared that that was "all" it was necessary to decide.

4. *The States and Economic Security*

Under the unemployment compensation provisions of the Social Security Act,[41] contributors to state unemployment compensation funds were to be entitled to 90 per cent credit on the federal payroll tax. Similar to the scheme that had been used for many years in the inheritance tax field,[42] this tax-credit arrangement was obviously an invitation to the states to cooperate. It was designed, that is to say, to induce the several state legislatures to participate in the social security program by enacting unemployment compensation laws which would meet the standards of the Social Security Board. The Alabama Unemployment Compensation Act, involved in the Carmichael Case, had been approved by the Social Security Board.[43] It levied a tax on the monthly payrolls of employers of eight persons or more.[44]

[41] The Social Security Act became law August 14, 1935. Of the eleven separate titles into which the act is divided, only titles IX and III contain the provisions setting up the unemployment compensation system. *Steward Machine Co.* v. *Davis*, 301 U.S. 548 (1937), upheld the right of the federal government to enact these provisions. On the same day that this case was decided the Supreme Court sustained the Alabama Unemployment Compensation Act which was typical of the complementary state laws contemplated by the Social Security Act. *Carmichael* v. *Southern Coal and Coke Co.*, 301 U.S. 495, 527 (1937).

[42] See *Florida* v. *Mellon*, 273 U.S. 12 (1927).

[43] The CARMICHAEL case was not the first Supreme Court action involving the validity of State Unemployment Compensation laws passed in conformity with the Social Security Act. New York's Unemployment Insurance law had been before the Court several months earlier, but no opinion was written. The Court divided four to four, with Mr. Justice Stone not participating because of illness, and since the New York Court of Appeals had upheld the Act its decision stood. *Chamberlin* v. *Andrews*, 271 N.Y. 1 (1936), affirmed, 299 U.S. 515 (1936).

[44] The major provisions and exemptions of the Alabama statute were summarized by Mr. Justice Stone as follows:

"The Unemployment Compensation Act . . . sets up a comprehensive scheme for providing unemployment benefits for workers employed within

Led by Mr. Justice Stone, a majority of the Supreme Court upheld the Alabama Statute against all the objections with which it had been assailed. True judicial tolerance of legislative discretion is nowhere vindicated more generously than in his lengthy but lucid opinion in the CARMICHAEL case. It was the function of legislatures, not that of courts, he maintained throughout, to select the means of protecting the public interest. And since the alleviation of individual misfortunes is often the sole means for promoting the general welfare, he had no difficulty in perceiving the "rational basis" for the Alabama legislature's choice of methods.

The exemption of employers of less than eight employees, the exclusion of certain specified employments, and the requirement of a lesser contribution from employees were objected to by those who challenged the Alabama law as resulting in a denial of the equal protection of the laws in violation of the Fourteenth Amendment. Mr. Justice Stone was able to see all of these distinctions in the law as the product of reasonable considerations. He began his analysis of the factors justifying the exemptions by pointing out that it was inherent in the exercise of the taxing power that a "state be free to select the subjects of taxation and to grant exemptions." The oft-repeated

the state by employers designated by the Act. These employers include all who employ eight or more persons for twenty or more weeks in the year . . . except those engaged in certain specified employments. (E.g., agricultural labor and domestic service.) It imposes on the employers the obligation to pay a certain percentage of their total monthly payroll into the State Unemployment Compensation Fund. . . . In 1941 and thereafter the rates of contribution by employers are to be revised in accordance with experience, but in no case are they to be less than 1½ or more than 4 per cent of the payroll. . . . After May 1, 1936, each employee is required to contribute 1 per cent of his wages to the fund. . . . The Fund is to be deposited in the 'Unemployment Trust Fund' of the United States Government, . . . and is to be used as requisitioned by the State Commission, to pay unemployment benefits prescribed by the statute, . . . but without any liability on the part of the state beyond amounts paid into or earned by the fund. Benefits are payable from the fund to the employees covered by the Act, in the event of their unemployment, upon prescribed conditions and at prescribed rates."

canon of construction, that "neither due process nor equal protection imposes upon a state any rigid rule of equality of taxation" was still sound.

So long as there were any conceivable set of facts to sustain the conclusion, courts should take it for granted that there was a "rational basis" for differences of degree in taxation. As a limitation on the judicial function this presumption of constitutionality of state statutes was a necessary safeguard for the legislature's freedom of action.

To state the matter in his own language:

A state legislature, in enactment of laws, has the widest possible latitude within the limits of the Constitution. In the nature of the case it cannot record a complete catalogue of the considerations which move its members to enact laws. In the absence of such a record courts cannot assume that its action is capricious, or that with its informed acquaintance with local conditions to which the legislation is to be applied, it was not aware of facts which afford reasonable basis for its action. Only by faithful adherence to this guiding principle of judicial review of legislation is it possible to preserve to the legislative branch its rightful independence and its ability to function.

Starting with this assumption, Mr. Justice Stone went on to indicate some of the considerations which might have influenced the legislature to confine unemployment benefits to certain groups. So far as the exclusion of employers with fewer than eight employees was concerned, he showed that administrative convenience and cost in the collection of the tax might alone be adequate justification. Distinctions of degree, in the form of differences in number, are typical of many distinctions which legislatures are often compelled to make. The number of persons employed in a business bears a "reasonable relationship" to the size of the payroll and to the amount of the tax. Accordingly, the legislature might have decided that the inconvenience and expense of collecting the tax from small employers would be disproportionate to the revenue the tax would yield. Furthermore, since small employers keep inadequate, if any employment records at all, the Unemployment Compensation Commission would experience far greater difficulty in collecting the tax from such employers than from larger firms. Where the line should be drawn in the matter of the size of businesses to be taxed, Mr. Justice Stone contended, is "peculiarly a question for legislative decision."

The principle that the states are free to choose the objects of taxation was the all-sufficient answer to the objection against the exemption of certain specified employments.[45] To judge from the nature of the exceptions contained in the Alabama statute, it was obvious that the legislature had chosen to tax those employing industrial labor only. But when the intention is to promote the public interest, one business may be taxed and another not taxed, especially if the primary purpose is to limit or suppress the one or assist the other. Exemption of charitable institutions and exemptions in behalf of agriculture have been upheld largely on this basis. Thus the exclusion of concerns doing business for less than twenty weeks in the year may have been dictated by the wish of the Alabama legislature to encourage seasonal or unstable industries.

The most instructive phase of Mr. Justice Stone's opinion is his discussion of the purposes to which the revenue derived from the payroll taxes was to be put. From the standpoint of realism in constitutional law, this part of the opinion is the most encouraging, as it is also the most persuasive. It evinces an understanding of the impact of economic forces and a recognition of social change which are all too rare in judicial utterance.

Since the adoption of the Fourteenth Amendment the taxing

---

[45] Agricultural laborers, domestic servants, seamen, insurance agents, close relatives, and those employed by charitable institutions, interstate railways and the national, state or local governments were exempted.

power of the states has been limited to the raising of revenue for public purposes; it may not be exerted to raise funds for purely "private" purposes.[46] So far as the requirements of due process are concerned, however, the states enjoy "free scope" for the exercise of "wide legislative discretion in determining what expenditures will serve the public interest." Mr. Justice Stone made it clear that he would accord to the states as much free play in the exercise of their spending power as he had pleaded for in behalf of the Federal government in his dissenting opinion in the BUTLER case. The Supreme Court has recognized, he asserted, that the public purposes for which a state may secure funds by taxation include appropriations in promotion of the general welfare, and he added:

The existence of local conditions which, because of their nature and extent, are of concern to the public as a whole, the modes of advancing the public interest by correcting them or avoiding their consequences, are peculiarly within the knowledge of the legislature, and to it, and not to the courts, is committed the duty and responsibility of making a choice of the possible methods. . . . As with expenditures for the general welfare of the United States, . . . whether the present expenditure serves a public purpose is a practical question addressed to the law-making department, and it would require a plain case of departure from every public purpose which could reasonably be conceived to justify the intervention of a court.

Turning to the question whether expenditures for the relief of unemployment were expenditures for a lawful public pur-

[46] It may be of interest to note that when the Supreme Court announced for the first time that a state tax imposed for a private purpose was unconstitutional, it did not invoke the due process clause of the Fourteenth Amendment as the basis for the new doctrine. *Loan Association* v. *Topeka*, 20 Wall. 655 (1875). Justice Miller apparently thought that the principle of public purpose in taxation was required by the "essential nature of all free governments."

For a discussion of public purpose in taxation under the due process clause, see *Fallbrook Irrigation Co.* v. *Bradley*, 164 U.S. 112 (1896) and *Green* v. *Frazier*, 253 U.S. 233 (1920).

pose, Mr. Justice Stone went on to say that the widely published facts concerning the economic and social effects of unemployment furnished the necessary basis for the "legislative judgment" represented by the Alabama statute. The depression had already taught the country to appreciate the "profound influence" of unemployment upon the public welfare. All evidence pointed to the fact that unemployment had become a "permanent incident in our industrial system" and that it is influenced by such factors as technological progress, fluctuations in the demands for manufactured goods, and the emergence of new sources of competition. Its grave consequences were felt by the entire community and not alone by those who happened to find themselves without work.

The Southern Coal and Coke Company had complained that the unemployment compensation act was invalid because it was not limited to the indigent or to those not discharged for cause. It opposed the statute on the further ground that its terms did not distinguish between employers with a high unemployment record and those with a low unemployment experience.[47] The degree of the tax, it contended, was the same for all employers subject to it.

In his reply to these objections, Mr. Justice Stone developed an analysis which the proponents of the principles of social insurance would heartily approve. As to the first objection, he pointed out that the effects of unemployment are not confined to the unemployed alone. The entire community feels its catastrophic results. Poverty was not the only effect of unemployment, and the legislature could rightfully seek to forestall "the gathering cloud of evils which beset the worker, his family and

[47] As on many other frontiers, Wisconsin was the pioneer in the United States in the field of unemployment compensation. Its unemployment compensation law was passed in 1931. The amount of the tax imposed under its provisions varies with the employment experience of the employer. The payments made by an employer are credited to him alone and it is only out of these funds that his former employees are paid. Social Security Board. *Information Circular #5* (Nov. 1936).

the community after wages cease and before destitution begins." Indeed, since the basic purpose of unemployment compensation is the prevention of these consequences, the legislature could even decide to extend the benefits of unemployment compensation to workers discharged for misconduct.

He found equally unconvincing the objection that the Alabama statute was arbitrary because of its failure to vary the amount of the tax in accordance with the unemployment experience of the employers to whom it applied. He suggested that this contention sprang from the "misconception" that there must be a causal relationship between the subject of a tax (e.g., the exercise of the right to employ) and the condition (e.g., unemployment) sought to be remedied with the aid of the funds raised by the tax. It assumes, that is to say, that those who pay a tax must be directly benefited by its proceeds or that the taxpayers involved must be responsible for the evil to be remedied by the appropriation.

Mr. Justice Stone rejected these "misconceptions" and in doing so took occasion to recapitulate canons of constitutional construction important in the field of taxation. It was immaterial, in so far as the Federal Constitution was concerned, that some of the employers who paid the payroll tax contributed little or not at all to unemployment and that they would not be benefited by the expenditure. "Nothing is more familiar in taxation," the Justice asserted, "than the imposition of a tax upon a class or upon individuals who enjoy no direct benefits from its expenditure, and who are not responsible for the condition to be remedied." Taxes are not assessed for benefits received; they are, in his now familiar words, "a means of distributing the burden of the cost of government." Declaring that the "most fundamental principle of government" is that "it exists primarily to provide for the common good," he reiterated a view of taxation which he has expounded in numerous other tax cases. It was the principle that the only advantage to which taxpayers are "constitutionally entitled" is that gained from their "enjoyment of the privileges of living in an organized society, established and safeguarded by the devotion of taxes to public purposes." [48]

Mr. Justice Stone considered next the many complex causes of unemployment which would make it difficult for any legislature to apportion equitably the burden of the payroll tax. Remarking that unemployment may be induced by such factors as the struggle among competing employers, tariffs, inventions, fashion changes, or other fluctuations in market or business conditions, he noted that knowledge of these phenomena might have led the Alabama legislature to conclude that the responsibility for unemployment could not be justly apportioned among individual employers. Some of these factors may stimulate the business of one employer and at the same time diminish or even destroy that of another. It is, therefore, conceivable that a business may suffer the most from a condition, such as a depression, for which it is least responsible. The Alabama legislature had good reason for assuming that no one employer could be held responsible for unemployment and that unemployment was "an inseparable incident of modern industry, with its most serious manifestations in industrial production." Accordingly, it could have come to the conclusion that employees would best be protected and the cost of protecting them best be distributed by placing the tax "evenly" on all industrial employers.

Since the scheme represented by the Alabama Unemployment Compensation Act sprang from considerations which were reasonable, it was not the province of the Supreme Court to declare it invalid as arbitrary because it regards another plan

---

[48] The *reductio ad absurdum* inherent in the objection based on the want of relationship between the subjects and the benefits of the payroll tax is indicated by Mr. Justice Stone in one terse sentence: "A corporation cannot object to the use of the taxes which it pays for the maintenance of schools because it has no children."

as more desirable.[49] In Mr. Justice Stone's view, the Constitution does not require any state to apportion the burden of a tax imposed for public purposes. So we find him saying that since the states are free to distribute the burden of a tax without regard to the particular purpose for which it is to be used, "there is no warrant in the Constitution for setting the tax aside because a court thinks that it would have drawn a better statute or could have distributed the burden more wisely. Those are functions reserved for the legislature." [50]

In these days of unprecedented concentration of power in

---

[49] Justice Sutherland, in whose opinion Justices VanDevanter and Butler concurred, filed a dissent in the CARMICHAEL case. While agreeing that the relief of unemployment is an objective "within the constitutional power of the state," they found the particular method by which the Alabama legislature sought to accomplish its objective to be "so arbitrary as to result in a denial both of due process and equal protection of the laws." Justice Sutherland contrasted the scheme which Wisconsin had adopted for crediting to each employer the contributions made by him with the pooling feature of the Alabama statute. Under the Alabama law all employers subject to the payroll tax contributed to a common fund out of which all unemployment benefits were paid. In the view of the dissenters, the imposition of the tax without regard to the amount of unemployment in the plant resulted in an "unequal burden." To them it was plain that "a disproportionately heavy burden will be imposed by the tax upon those whose operations contribute least to the evils of unemployment, and, correspondingly, the burden will be lessened in respect of those whose operations contribute most." They assailed Mr. Justice Stone's opinion for the majority as being inconsistent with the decision in *Railroad Retirement Board* v. *Alton R. R. Co.,* 295 U.S. 330 (1935). That case set aside an act of Congress which required all interstate railroads to contribute payments to a pooled fund out of which pensions were to be paid to employees who reached the age of sixty-five.

[50] As it had been argued against the unemployment compensation provisions of the Social Security Act, so it was contended in this case that state unemployment compensation laws enacted with the cooperation of the federal government were invalid because their adoption was "coerced" by the terms of the federal statute. Concretely, the Alabama Unemployment Compensation Act was assailed as resulting in an unconstitutional surrender of state power. Agreeing that even though it might be assumed that otherwise valid state legislation might be rendered invalid because of the coercive effect of federal action, the Court held in the CARMICHAEL case that the Social Security Act had no such effect on the State of Alabama. "The United States and the State of Alabama are not alien govenrments," Mr. Justice Stone asserted; and added: "They coexist within the same

the national government, it may not be amiss to recall the part played by the states in the solution of the problems which modern industry and finance created for society. Yet it has become so fashionable to deprecate what Harold J. Laski has called "the obsolescence of federalism" [51] that it may perhaps appear as a sign of retrogression even to examine the contributions of our state governments in the field of social policy. The truth is, however, that the first efforts in the United States to mitigate the effects of an industrial economy were those of the states. It was in the "insulated chambers of state legislatures," to use Justice Holmes' meaningful phrase,[52] where the responses to the issues engendered by this economy were first shaped and where were reached the compromises by which conflicting interests and ideas were harmonized.

Action by the states within their reserved spheres, whether limited by the negations of the Fourteenth Amendment or in competition with the national government, has stirred Chief Justice Stone to some of his most compelling expositions of the importance of local treatment of local problems. As areas of decentralized control, the states present fertile opportunities for experimentation with new ideas, techniques and processes in government and economics. Because he is impressed with the urgent necessity of solving the people's problems, Chief Justice Stone would allow the states considerable latitude in the formulation of economic policy. His focus is on the wants and conflicts of society, and with such a starting point it is not surprising to find him proclaiming that the states too have a place in the American scheme of things.

territory. Unemployment within it is their common concern. Together the two statutes now before us embody a cooperative legislative effort by state and national governments for carrying out a public purpose, common to both which neither could fully achieve without the cooperation of the other. The Constitution does not prohibit such cooperation."

[51] *New Republic* (May, 1939), p. 367.

[52] Justice Holmes, dissenting in *Truax* v. *Corrigan,* 257 U.S. 312, 344 (1921).

CHAPTER VI

SAFEGUARDING CIVIL LIBERTIES

1. *Property Rights versus Civil Liberties*

SINCE the days when it became customary to speak of the Supreme Court in terms of the "conservative" majority and the "liberal" minority, it has been apparent that the attitude of some of the liberals toward government regulation of business enterprise was somewhat at variance with their approach to civil liberty issues. Indeed, as compared with their willingness to allow legislatures free play in the formulation of economic policy, their attitude toward legislative restrictions on fundamental civil rights seemed to be, at least at first glance, a contradiction in terms. Great deference for the legislative judgment has marked their thinking in the realm of economic regulation.[1] This inclination to let the legislature have its way, aptly labeled by Professor Corwin "legislative

---

[1] And contrariwise, many of the so-called conservatives on the Bench were at times as intolerant of legislative restrictions on the fundamental rights of man as they were of experimentation with the rights of property. This could certainly be said of men like Chief Justice Hughes and Mr. Justice Sutherland. For a brief but illuminating discussion of this problem, in which he warns against assuming the existence of a "rigid dividing line" between the erstwhile conservative majority and liberal minority on the Supreme Court, see Zechariah Chaffee, Jr., *Free Speech in the United States* (Cambridge: Harv. Univ. Press, 1942), pp. 357-62. See also: Alpheus T. Mason, "The Conservative World of Mr. Justice Sutherland," *XXXII Amer. Pol. Sci. Rev. 443* (June, 1938) and F. D. G. Ribble, "The Constitutional Doctrines of Chief Justice Hughes," *XLI Col. L. Rev. 1190, 1203* (Nov. 1941).

laissez-faire," many of them, including the present Chief Justice, have honored in the breach in the civil rights cases.[2]

What explains these contradictory attitudes? Just as the conservative majority on the Supreme Court was for a long time accused of exalting the rights of property above the rights of man, so today's majority on the Court may be said to be extending relatively greater protection to liberty of mind and conscience.[3] Essaying an explanation some years ago, Mr. Justice Stone suggested that there may be "narrower scope" for the presumption of constitutionality in cases not concerned with ordinary economic activities. The occasion was not a civil liberties case but one in which the Court was sustaining an act of Congress prohibiting interstate shipment of "filled milk."[4] Regulatory legislation touching "ordinary commercial transactions" should be held constitutional, he observed, "unless in the light of facts made known or generally assumed it is of such a character as to preclude the assumption that it rests upon some rational basis within the knowledge and experience of the legislators."

[2] To be sure, Holmes sometimes deferred to the legislative judgment, even though it embodied a scheme of regulation which both liberals and conservatives regarded as inimical to basic civil rights. See his dissenting opinion, in which he was joined only by Justice Sutherland, in *Meyer* v. *Nebraska*, 262 U.S. 390, 412 (1923).

[3] "There is truth," Felix Frankfurter wrote shortly before coming to the Court, "behind the familiar contrast between rights of property and rights of man. But certainly in some of its aspects property is a function of personality, and conversely the free range of the human spirit becomes shrivelled and constrained under economic dependence. Especially in a civilization like ours where the economic interdependence of society is so pervasive, a sharp division between property rights and human rights largely falsifies reality. A good deal of the history of the United States may fairly be summarized as the process, complicated and confused, of bringing to the masses economic freedom commensurate with their political freedom. But the various interests of human personality are not of equal worth. There is a hierarchy of values. . . . *Mr. Justice Holmes and the Supreme Court* (1938), p. 50.

[4] *United States* v. *Carolene Products Co.*, 304 U.S. 144 (1938), at pp. 152-53, n.4.

And tolerant though he would have the Court be of the legislative judgment in the commercial field, Mr. Justice Stone clearly implied that it should be less ready to presume that the legislature knows what it is doing when it seeks to limit rights and conduct lying outside the commercial arena. In this particular case he did no more than hint that presumption of constitutionality should operate less liberally in favor of legislation which "appears on its face" to be within a specific prohibition of the Constitution, such as those of the Bill of Rights or those "deemed equally specific" when held to be protected by the Fourteenth Amendment.[5] "It is unnecessary to consider now," he declared, "whether legislation which restricts those political processes which can ordinarily be expected to bring about repeal of undesirable legislation, is to be subjected to more exacting judicial scrutiny under the general prohibitions of the Fourteenth Amendment than are most other types of legislation." As instances of legislation restrictive of political processes, he cited cases involving limitations on suffrage, restrictions on the dissemination of information, and interferences with political organizations and peaceable assembly. "Nor need we enquire," he added, "whether similar considerations enter into the review of statutes directed at particular religious, or national or racial minorities . . .; whether prejudice against discrete and insular minorities may be a special

[5] With its decision in *Meyer* v. *Nebraska,* the Supreme Court began a process of reconsideration by means of which it has gradually assimilated into the "liberty" guaranteed by the Fourteenth Amendment certain of the "fundamental" rights protected by the first ten amendments against abridgment by Congress. Mr. Justice Stone, it should be noted, helped to form the majority in the 1920's and early 1930's for this judicial expansion of the meaning of liberty. He voted with the prevailing side in such cases as: *Fiske* v. *Kansas,* 274 U.S. 380 (1927), *Near* v. *Minnesota,* 283 U.S. 697 (1931), *Stromberg* v. *California,* 283 U.S. 359 (1931), *Powell* v. *Alabama,* 287 U.S. 45 (1932), *Grosjean* v. *American Press Co.,* 297 U.S. 233 (1936). For an exceedingly lucid discussion of the motivation behind this process of absorption, see Mr. Justice Cardozo's opinion for the Court in *Palko* v. *Connecticut,* 302 U.S. 319 (1937), particularly pp. 325-26.

condition, which tends seriously to curtail the operation of those political processes ordinarily to be relied upon to protect minorities, and which may call for a correspondingly more searching judicial inquiry."

Although by no means clear and direct, if not actually oblique, these observations did contain the key to the alleged contradiction in outlook. Considering their nature, they were hardly calculated to commit the Court to an undeviating course of decision. Still, they suggest a way out, should the Court feel called upon to explain. For Mr. Justice Stone was thereby announcing that he for one felt justified in viewing the economic regulation cases quite differently from those growing out of attempts to curtail the free exercise of the individual's civil rights. He was apparently prepared to assign greater importance to them than to the freedom of action ordinarily impinged upon by economic controls. Without free speech and a free press and the right to assemble, he implied, the political process itself cannot be carried on. To make the enjoyment of these rights more secure and thereby safeguard that process he would presumably impose on the courts a greater responsibility for appraising the legislative judgment.[6]

2. *Protecting the Political Process*

In these days of intense pressure group activity, the processes by which public policy is ultimately shaped cannot be too zealously guarded. Realism in constitutional law would certainly demand recognition by the courts of their great import-

[6] As a purely procedural matter, one result of treating the two classes of cases differently might be for the Court to presume legislation restricting the exercise of civil rights to be unconstitutional until its validity is established. This would throw the burden of proving its validity on those seeking to justify it. With such an approach, the Court would feel freer in scrutinizing the purposes behind such legislation and even the methods chosen for realizing them. For a discussion of these trends, see the Flag Salute cases below, pp. 216-22, 228-34.

ance. Scrupulous care ought to be taken in judging legislation which frustrates their effective operation.

His doctrine of political restraints is probably Mr. Justice Stone's response to this necessity, and his conception of the judicial function in civil rights cases would seem to be an integral part of his development of that doctrine. Because he places high in the "hierarchy" of democratic values the integrity of the instruments of popular action, he is less reticent in exerting the judicial veto in cases concerned with threats to such fundamental liberties as those of the First Amendment. The concurring opinion he wrote in the HAGUE Case [7] is clearly evidence of this inclination, as it is also proof of his desire to extend the protection of those guaranties to as many persons and groups as possible.

The case began as an attempt to stop Mayor Hague of Jersey City from continuing to interfere with the organizing activities of the Committee for Industrial Organization.[8] The Mayor and his subordinates were relying on a city ordinance which prohibited meetings "in or upon the public streets, highways, public parks oₓ public buildings" without a permit from the Director of Public Safety. Under the pretense of seeking to prevent "riots, disturbances, or disorderly assemblage," the police were directed to break up meetings and to stop the distribution of circulars, leaflets and handbills.[9] These repressions were justified on the further ground that the C.I.O. members were Communists or affiliated with Communist groups,

[7] *Hague* v. *Committee for Industrial Organization*, 307 U.S. 496, 518 (1939).

[8] The name was subsequently changed to Congress of Industrial Organizations.

[9] The membership drive launched by C.I.O. organizers in the industries of Jersey City and their campaign to acquaint workers with their rights under the National Labor Relations Act were being obstructed at every turn. Others, including Norman Thomas, who had come to test how far the Hague program of repression would be carried, got their answer when they were forcibly ejected from the City. The American Civil Liberties Union was also kept from holding its meetings in Jersey City.

so that their meetings were said to be called for unlawful purposes. The specific provision invoked was the one which authorized the police not to grant permission for the holding of meetings at which speakers would advocate unlawful changes in the government of the United States or the State.

A majority of the Supreme Court agreed that the injunction against the enforcement of the Jersey City ordinance was properly granted.[10] The question as to which particular constitutional guarantee governed the case, however, found the Court seriously split. Although five separate opinions were written, not one of them had the approval of a majority.

The opinion by Mr. Justice Roberts, concurred in by Mr. Justice Black, invoked the privileges and immunities clause of the Fourteenth Amendment as the relevant constitutional provision. These two Justices took the position that the Jersey City ordinance was "void upon its face" because it abridged the privileges and immunities of citizens of the United States. Freedom to disseminate information concerning the provisions of the National Labor Relations Act, they said, was a privilege or immunity of national citizenship, as was also the right to assemble peaceably for the purpose of discussing the benefits of the act. "Citizenship of the United States would be little better than a name," Mr. Justice Roberts asserted, "if it did not carry with it the right to discuss national legislation and the benefits, advantages, and opportunities to accrue to citizens therefrom." [11]

10 The lower court had undertaken to enumerate the conditions under which the activities interfered with by the Jersey City authorities could be carried on. The Supreme Court struck out this part of the decree and thus reduced it to a simple injunction against the enforcement of ordinances which interfere with the distribution of lawful information and the holding of lawful meetings.

11 As to the right of peaceable assembly, Mr. Justice Roberts relied on the *Slaughter-House Cases* and the decision in *United States* v. *Cruikshank*. He quoted the following sentence from Justice Miller's opinion for the Court in the *Slaughter-House Cases:* "The right to peaceably assemble and petition for redress of grievances, the privilege of the writ of habeas

Mr. Justice Stone, with whom Mr. Justice Reed agreed, objected to this application of the privileges and immunities clause. Neither freedom of speech nor the right of assembly was a privilege of citizens of the United States. Freedom of speech and of assembly, he urged, were rights of personal liberty secured to all persons, without regard to citizenship, by the due process clause of the Fourteenth Amendment.[12] He maintained that there was nothing in the record and briefs to justify the Court in deciding the case on the basis of the privileges and immunities clause, especially since none of the complaining parties had invoked it or presented evidence of citizenship.[13] Neither was it clear that the C.I.O. unions sought to be

corpus, are rights of the citizen guaranteed by the Federal Constitution." 16 Wall. 36, 79 (1873). He quoted also the following language from the Cruikshank case: "The right of the people peaceably to assemble for the purpose of petitioning Congress for a redress of grievances, or for anything else connected with the powers or the duties of the National Government, is an attribute of national citizenship and, as such, under the protection of and guaranteed by, the United States. The very idea of a government, republican in form, implies a right on the part of its citizens to meet peaceably for consultation in respect to public affairs and to petition for a redress of grievances." 92 U.S. 542, 552 (1875).

[12] This was not the first time that Mr. Justice Stone expressed his opposition to the revitalization of the privileges and immunities clause of the Fourteenth Amendment. See his dissenting opinion in *Colgate* v. *Harvey*, 296 U.S. 404, 436 (1935). And since the HAGUE case, he has given further evidence of this opposition. In 1941, he joined Justices Roberts, Frankfurter, Reed and Byrnes in pronouncing the so-called "Okie" law of California to be an unconstitutional burden on interstate commerce. *Edwards* v. *California*, 314 U.S. 160 (1941). The statute in question made it a misdemeanor to bring or assist in bringing an "indigent person" into the state. In eloquent concurring opinions in which they were also speaking for Justices Black and Murphy, Mr. Justice Douglas and Mr. Justice Jackson took the position that the right of free movement from state to state is an attribute of national citizenship protected by the privileges and immunities clause of the Fourteenth Amendment against interference by the states.

[13] Chief Justice Hughes agreed with this point in the Stone opinion, although he concurred in the opinion by Mr. Justice Roberts "with respect to merits." Article IV, Section 2, and the due process and equal protection clauses of the Fourteenth Amendment were the only provisions of the Constitution on which the complainants relied as securing to them the rights of free speech and assembly. Mr. Justice Stone agreed with Mr. Justice Roberts that Article IV, Section 2—"The citizens of each State

established would be in industries subject to the National Labor Relations Act or to the jurisdiction of the National Labor Relations Board. One of the handbills suppressed by the police informed workers that the Wagner Act protected their right to choose the labor union which they wished to represent them in collective bargaining. Mr. Justice Stone referred to this exhibit in the case, but repeated that the injunction which the Court was sustaining was not limited to the protection of the right of citizens to discuss the Wagner Act. The injunction, on the contrary, prohibited "in the broadest terms" interferences with the holding of "any lawful meeting and disseminating any lawful information by circular, leaflet, handbill and placard." Indeed, if all that was at stake was the right of a citizen to disseminate information about national questions, then the decree was too broad in its statement of the activities enjoined.

Taking up the view of the CRUIKSHANK and *Slaughter-House Cases* presented by Mr. Justice Roberts, Mr. Justice Stone reminded us that at the time those cases were decided the judicial expansion of the "content" of the due process and equal protection clauses had not yet taken place. Specifically, the right of assembly was not considered at the time to be part of the liberty protected by the Fourteenth Amendment. That fact, as well as the interpretation of the privileges and immunities clause in the *Slaughter-House Cases*, explained the assertion in the CRUIKSHANK case that the right of assembly was protected by the Constitution against state interference.

If it be part of wisdom to avoid unnecessary decision of constitutional questions [Mr. Justice Stone observed], it would seem to be equally so to avoid unnecessary creation of novel constitutional

shall be entitled to all privileges and immunities of citizens of the several States"—was inapplicable since the "settled view" considered that section as only preventing a state from discriminating against citizens of other states and in favor of its own.

doctrine, inadequately supported by the record, in order to attain an end easily and certainly reached by following the beaten paths of constitutional decision.

This he said by way of indicating the unfortunate effect which the construction put upon the privileges and immunities clause by Mr. Justice Roberts might possibly have. The right of assembly ought not to be discussed in terms which might create the impression that it depended on the individual's status as a citizen of the United States or on his relationship to the national government. He objected to the implication, that is to say, that the right of the C.I.O. members to go to court depended on their citizenship or their action in disseminating information about or in meeting to discuss the National Labor Relations Act. There was nothing in the record to indicate that any of the meetings which were broken up had been called for the purpose of considering the Wagner Act or that the act was actually discussed at these meetings.

Mr. Justice Stone preferred the less complicated view of the District Court, which he regarded as more in keeping with the now established interpretation of the Fourteenth Amendment. The District Court had held that the repressive measures of the Jersey City officials violated the due process clause of the amendment since the liberty it protects guarantees to all persons freedom of speech and of assembly for any lawful purpose. This approach to the suit was seen by Mr. Justice Stone as making the rights with which it was concerned turn on the "real issue" in the case. That issue was whether the court action undertaken by the C.I.O. unions could be maintained "as a suit for the protection of rights and privileges guaranteed by the due process clause." His argument was that the issue was avoided if the outcome was made to depend on the limited range of the privileges and immunities clause. The complaining unions were entitled to bring the suit as individuals under the due process clause as well as act of Congress, regardless of their citizenship and the amount in controversy. The right to do so was conferred upon them by the Civil Rights Act of 1871, the relevant section of which is now part of the United States Code.[14]

One can sympathize with Mr. Justice Stone over his impatience with the use which his brethren were making of a clause of the Constitution which had long ago ceased to have any significance for civil rights. Yet in fairness to Mr. Justice Roberts and those who agreed with him, it should be pointed out that some of the bothersome questions precipitated by their approach to the case were to a certain extent unavoidable. The challenge to the Hague administration had been brought as an original suit in the District Court and the privileges and immunities clause may have made easier the task of resolving a knotty jurisdictional problem.[15] Chief Justice Hughes

[14] Section 1 of the Civil Rights Act of 1871 reads as follows: "Any person who, under color of any law, statute, ordinance of any state, shall subject, or cause to be subjected, any person within the jurisdiction of the United States to the deprivation of any rights, privileges or immunities secured by the Constitution of the United States . . . shall be liable to the party injured in any action at law, suit in equity, or other proceeding for redress." The same section conferred on the district and circuit courts of the United States jurisdiction to hear such suits. Mr. Justice Stone pointed out that even as later modified Congress extended the right to all persons, whether citizens or not, and that the revised provision is now section 43 of Title 8 of the United States Code.

[15] Mr. Justice McReynolds was of the opinion that the United States District Court should have dismissed the suit for want of jurisdiction to review the legality of the action of municipal officers in regulating the use of streets and parks. "There was ample opportunity for respondents," he wrote in his brief dissenting opinion, "to assert their claims through an orderly proceeding in courts of the state empowered authoritatively to interpret her laws with final review here in respect of federal questions." (p. 533.) In his one-sentence dissent, Mr. Justice Butler merely declared that the ordinances involved in the HAGUE case are indistinguishable from the city ordinance regulating the use of the Boston Common upheld in the famous case of *Davis* v. *Massachusetts*, 167 U.S. 43 (1897). That case had come to the Supreme Court from the Supreme Judicial Court of Massachusetts which had also sustained the ordinance in an opinion by Holmes. *Commonwealth* v. *Davis*, 162 Mass. 510 (1895). This opinion by Holmes is reprinted by Professor Lerner, with some comment on its relation to the Justice's reputation as a defender of civil liberties, in his

and Justice Roberts had written opinions in cases in which freedom of speech and of assembly had been held to be rights off personal liberty protected by the due process clause of the Fourteenth Amendment.[16] In view of these earlier statements, it is understandable why Mr. Justice Stone should have felt that their position in the HAGUE case introduced new and unnecessary difficulties. In the HAGUE case, however, they chose to stress that it was a privilege of citizens of the United States to use the streets and parks "for communication of views on national questions," as Mr. Justice Roberts phrased it, and one can be sure that Mr. Justice Stone agreed with the value they placed on that right. What he objected to were the complications inherent in the theory, such as the failure of the record to disclose the citizenship status of those whose rights were being infringed or proving that they had actually met to discourse on the advantages of the Wagner Act. Neither did he think that the jurisdictional problem in the case justified resort to the privileges and immunities clause. He was convinced that the right to bring a suit in the district courts to restrain state and local officers from interfering with freedom of speech and of assembly as guaranteed by the due process clause was conferred by Congress on all persons within the jurisdiction of the United States, whether they were citizens or not.

When the purely technical questions taken up in the HAGUE case are put to one side, there is reason for suspecting that the

recent book, *The Mind and Faith of Justice Holmes* (Boston: Little, Brown & Co., 1943), pp. 106-108.

For a discussion of the procedural problem in the HAGUE case, see Zechariah Chafee, Jr., *Free Speech in the United States* (Cambridge: Harvard Univer. Press, 1941), p. 413, n.77.

[16] See the opinions by Chief Justice Hughes in *Near* v. *Minnesota,* 283 U.S. 697 (1931), *Stromberg* v. *California,* 283 U.S. 259 (1931), *De Jonge* v. *Oregon,* 299 U.S. 353 (1937). See also the opinion by Mr. Justice Roberts in *Herndon* v. *Lowry,* 301 U.S. 242 (1937). Their attitude toward freedom of speech and press are fully described in Chafee, *ibid.,* ch. 11.

views expressed by Mr. Justice Stone were dictated by larger considerations. One cannot read his opinion in that case without becoming aware of the importance he places on public discussion as one of the life streams of the democratic process. It should not come as a surprise to find the author of the political restraints theory discountenancing an interpretation of fundamental human rights which even suggests that any of them are rights which are the special prerogative of the citizen. Starting as he does with the assumption that "no more grave and important issue" can be brought to the Supreme Court than that of freedom of speech and of assembly, he would wish them to be secured to all persons, citizens or not. And if the object is to safeguard the channels through which public affairs are discussed and common action fostered, there is much to be said, especially in a country of immigration, for the wisdom of extending to all, regardless of citizenship, the rights upon which these processes ultimately depend.

But if free public discussion is a prerequisite to group action and political pressure, the integrity of the ballot box touches even more directly the democratic base of government. Pernicious practices at the polls raise a more significant issue than that of honesty in government. In the final analysis, what is really at stake is the extent of the popular basis of our political institutions. However, when called upon to deal with corrupt administration of elections, courts have more often recognized the corruption than its ultimate import for the democratic process.

Even less frequently has the Supreme Court grappled squarely with the deeper implications of a restricted suffrage. One can question, for example, the soundness of the Court's erstwhile classification of the political party as a private organization. To sanction, as the Court did in *Grovey* v. *Townsend*, the right of a political party to exclude a substantial section of the population from participating in the primary, in circumstances where nomination is for all practical purposes equivalent to election, is certainly to slide over the real situation. And yet the result reached in that case had the support of such stalwart champions of democratic rights as Justices Cardozo, Brandeis and Stone.[17]

Since then Mr. Justice Stone has had occasion to speak more frankly. In the opinion he delivered in the CLASSIC case,[18] his last before assuming the duties of Chief Justice, he dealt forthrightly with an old and touchy question. The case started in the United States District Court for the Eastern District of Louisiana with the indictment of several Commissioners of Elections. They were charged with wilfully altering the results of a primary in Louisiana held by the Democratic Party to nominate a candidate for Representative in Congress. The fundamental question the Court was asked to decide was whether the right of voters to participate in a congressional primary and to have their ballots duly counted was a right assured them by the Constitution.[19]

---

[17] *Grovey* v. *Townsend*, 295 U.S. 45 (1935), climaxed the constitutional battle against the "white primary" legislation of Texas which began in the early 1920's. See *Nixon* v. *Herndon*, 273 U.S. 536 (1927) and *Nixon* v. *Condon*, 286 U.S. 73 (1932). The 1935 decision, to be sure, was in line with decisions of the last fifty years. As far back as the decision in the *Civil Rights Cases*, 109 U.S. 3 (1883), the Court had held that the prohibitions of the Fourteenth Amendment do not protect against private discrimination. Presumably, therefore, the Democratic Party of Texas, as a private body, was constitutionally incapable of violating the amendment. Since this was written, the Supreme Court has reversed *Grovey* v. *Townsend*. *Smith* v. *Allwright*, 321 U.S. 649 (1944).

[18] *United States* v. *Classic*, 313 U.S. 299, 329 (1941).

[19] Strictly speaking, there were two questions in the case, at least as stated by Mr. Justice Stone: "The questions for decision are whether the right of qualified voters to vote in the Louisiana primary and to have their ballots counted is a right 'secured . . . by the Constitution' within the meaning of sections 19 and 20 of the Criminal Code, and whether the acts of appellees charged in the indictment violate those sections." Section 19 of the Criminal Code makes it a crime to conspire to injure a citizen in the exercise "of any right or privilege secured to him by the Constitution or laws of the United States." Section 20 outlaws as a crime the action of anyone who "under color of law" is wilfully subjecting or causing to be

It had been settled in the YARBROUGH case [20] that the privilege of voting for national officers was secured by the Constitution to all persons who were otherwise qualified to vote under state law. Asserting that it was essential that elective officials of the federal government should be the "free choice of the people," the Court in that case upheld the power of Congress to protect those eligible to vote for members of Congress against fraud and violence. But for the decision in the NEWBERRY case,[21] therefore, the CLASSIC case could have been disposed of by a citation of the Yarbrough ruling. Coming to the Supreme Court as an appeal from a conviction under provisions of the Federal Corrupt Practices Act of 1910 limiting expenditures in congressional elections, the NEWBERRY case found four Justices of the opinion that those provisions could not be made to apply to campaign expenses incurred in a primary contest. They denied that a primary election was an election within the meaning of the fourth section of Article I of the Constitution authorizing Congress to adopt regulations with respect to the manner of conducting elections for Senators and Representatives.[22]

subjected "any inhabitant of any state . . . to the deprivation of any rights, privileges, or immunities secured or protected by the Constitution and laws of the United States."

[20] Ex Parte *Yarbrough*, 110 U.S. 651 (1884).

[21] *Newberry* v. *United States*, 256 U.S. 232 (1921).

[22] The Court was unanimous in reversing the conviction of Truman Newberry who had spent close to $200,000 in securing the Republican nomination for United States Senator from Michigan in a primary contest with Henry Ford. "The ultimate question for solution," Mr. Justice McReynolds declared in the NEWBERRY case, "is whether, under the grant of power to regulate 'the manner of holding elections,' Congress may fix the maximum sum which a candidate therein may spend, or advise or cause to be contributed and spent by others to procure his nomination." Apparently speaking only for himself and Justices Holmes, Day and Van Devanter, he stated that primaries were unknown at the time the election provisions of the Constitution were adopted so that they were "in no sense elections for an office, but merely methods by which party adherents agree upon candidates whom they intend to offer and support for ultimate choice by all qualified electors." Because they thought that there had been an error in the way the

In the CLASSIC case, the District Court relied on the NEW-BERRY decision and held that as applied to the actions of the elections commissioners, sections 19 and 20 of the Criminal Code were unconstitutional. The government, on the other hand, contended that the right of a qualified voter to have his vote counted in a congressional primary was guaranteed by the Constitution, and that conspiring to rob the voter of that right was a violation of section 19 of the Criminal Code. In falsifying the returns and therefore depriving the voters of that right, the commissioners, since they were state officers, were also guilty of denying equal protection of the laws in violation of the Fourteenth Amendment. When taken together, the government concluded, all these actions were violations of section 20 of the Criminal Code.

Mr. Justice Stone began his opinion for the majority in the CLASSIC case by emphasizing that although the right to vote for members of Congress could only be claimed by those eligible to vote under state law, that right, since it was secured by the Constitution, could be protected by Congress against fraud and violence. And so far as choosing members of the House of Representatives was concerned, the power to safeguard that right was given Congress by section 4 of the legislative article of the Constitution authorizing it to regulate the times, places and manner of holding elections for Representative.

With these long-established principles in mind, all that was

case was submitted to the jury, Chief Justice White and Justices Pitney, Clarke and Brandeis went along with the reversal of the conviction, but were of the opinion that primaries were subject to the regulating power of Congress. Justice McKenna concurred in the opinion by McReynolds, but to judge from the statement announcing his concurrence, it would appear that his vote was largely dictated by the fact that the law under which Newberry was convicted had been enacted prior to the adoption of the amendment providing for popular election of United States Senators. He "reserved" judgment on the power of Congress under the Seventeenth Amendment.

necessary was to examine the election laws of Louisiana, "to ascertain the nature of the right which under the constitutional mandate they define and confer on the voter and the effect upon its exercise of the acts with which appellees [the elections commissioners] are charged." Mr. Justice Stone thought that this inquiry would help the Court determine the answer to three questions:

. . . first, whether the right or privilege is one secured by the Constitution of the United States, second, whether the effect under the state statute of appellees' alleged acts is such that they operate to injure or oppress citizens in the exercise of that right within the meaning of section 19 and to deprive inhabitants of the state of that right within the meaning of section 20, and finally, whether sections 19 and 20 respectively are in other respects applicable to the alleged acts of the appellees.

He found that in Louisiana the direct primary is the only procedure by which candidates for Representative are to be nominated. Conducted at public expense, primary elections are governed by the same provisions for honest counting of the ballots and their accurate recording as is the general election itself. Voting for Representative was in Louisiana limited "as a matter of law" to the candidate nominated at the primary. However, by way of minimizing the importance of the primary contest, the defendants had pointed out that under Louisiana law voters were free on election day to write in the names of those rejected at the primary. Mr. Justice Stone replied to this by declaring that since the names of candidates eliminated at the primary may not be printed on the general election ballot, the effect of the Louisiana primary law is such as to place "serious restrictions upon the choice of candidates by the voters save by voting at the primary elections."

Following the brief review of the statutes of Louisiana, Mr.

Justice Stone took up the two fundamental issues in the CLASSIC case. The first of these, the effect of a Democratic nomination in Louisiana, is set forth by him in a way that makes the disposition of the principal question come almost as an anticlimax.

. . . the practical operation of the primary in Louisiana is and has been, since the primary election was established in 1900, to secure the election of the Democratic primary nominee for the second congressional district of Louisiana. Interference with the right to vote in the congressional primary in the second congressional district for the choice of Democratic candidate for Congress is thus as a matter of law and in fact an interference with the effective choice of the voters at the only stage of the election procedure when their choice is of significance, since it is at the only stage when such interference could have any practical effect on the ultimate result, the choice of the Congressman to represent the District. The primary in Louisiana is an integral part of the procedure for the popular choice of Congressman. The right of qualified voters to vote at the congressional primary in Louisiana and to have their ballots counted is thus the right to participate in that choice.

The right to vote in the primary, where such primary election is by law made an "integral part" of the general election process or effectively controls the final choice at the polls, was construed in the CLASSIC case to be part of the right to vote for members of Congress. The two rights are presumably inseparable, at least in the circumstances disclosed in that case. Both rights are secured by the Constitution and may be protected by Congress against corrupt interference with their exercise. The right to vote for members of Congress includes the right to have one's ballot duly counted in congressional elections.

Addressing himself to the question with which the Court was chiefly concerned—"whether the right to choose at a primary election, a candidate for election as Representative is embraced in the right to choose Representatives secured by Article I, Section 2" [23]—Mr. Justice Stone conceded that the framers of the Constitution "did not have specifically in mind" the direct primary when they adopted that provision. The framers need not have known of the primary as a procedure for nominating candidates for Representative, he asserted, any more than they could have foreseen the use of the commerce clause to regulate interstate telephone, telegraph and wireless communications.

The free choice by the people of their representatives in Congress is "one of the great purposes" of our system of government. That "constitutional purpose" remains, even though the procedure for choosing Representatives may have come to consist of two steps—the preliminary selection of the candidate in a primary and his subsequent election—instead of the single step in the form of a general election such as was known at the time the Constitution was established. Election methods may be new, but the power of Congress to assure a free choice by the people is undiminished. Article I, Section 4, which is the source of Congress' power to protect the electoral process against corruption, extends therefore to congressional primaries.[24]

On the latter point, the principal one in the case, all of the Court's members agreed. Justices Douglas, Black and Murphy dissented, however, against the construction placed by the majority on section 19 of the Criminal Code. They agreed with most of the views expressed by Mr. Justice Stone. Dissenting "with diffidence" for all three, Mr. Justice Douglas

[23] "The House of Representatives shall be composed of members chosen every second year by the people of the several States, and the electors in each State shall have the qualifications requisite for electors of the most numerous branch of the State legislature." *Constitution,* Article I, Sec. 2.

[24] Mr. Justice Stone disposed of the NEWBERRY case by calling attention to the confused alignments in it and concluded that the question whether the power of Congress over elections extends to primaries "has not been prejudged by any decision of this Court."

nevertheless was vigorous in his denunciation of what the Court had done.

When he finally turned to the question whether sections 19 and 20 of the Criminal Code applied to the acts for which the election officials had been indicted, Mr. Justice Stone said that they did, and continued:

Conspiracy to prevent the official count of a citizen's ballot, held . . . to be a violation of section 19 in the case of Congressional election, is equally a conspiracy to injure and oppress the citizen when the ballots are cast in a primary election prerequisite to the choice of party candidates for a Congressional election. In both cases the right infringed is one secured by the Constitution.

It is this final determination in the case which called forth the dissent, and the dissenters too spoke in the name of fundamental rights. They stressed, as had also Mr. Justice Stone, the vital connection between the integrity of elections and the representative character of our institutions. "Free and honest elections are the very foundations of our republican form of government," declared Mr. Justice Douglas. And although he shared Mr. Justice Stone's intolerance of interference with what he himself termed "the sanctity of the ballot," he disagreed with the result reached in the case because he did not think that Congress had created the particular crime charged in the indictment. Reviewing the history of section 19 and its interpretation by the courts, he found that it had been adopted in order to impose severe penalties on those tampering with congressional elections.[25] He thought that the Court was setting a dangerous precedent when it made a criminal statute apply to persons and circumstances for whom it was not clearly meant when enacted.[26]

[25] The penalty was $5000 or ten years imprisonment or both.

[26] Mr. Justice Douglas reminded the majority of the principle that there is no common-law offense against the United States, and quoted the following from an old case: "The legislative authority of the Union must make

It is not enough for us to find in the vague penumbra of a statute some offense about which Congress could have legislated and then particularize it as a crime because it is highly offensive. . . . Civil liberties are too dear to permit conviction for crimes which are only implied and which can be spelled out only by adding inference to inference.

Mr. Justice Douglas left no doubt that he and those who were dissenting with him subscribed without hesitation to the view that the power of Congress over elections also extends to congressional primaries, especially where the primary is made by state law an integral part of the election or effectively influences the ultimate choice. They were in complete agreement with the majority on its interpretation of the constitutional basis of Congress' authority to protect the right of choice in congressional primaries. And they also agreed that that right could be safeguarded against interference on the part of private individuals as well as administrative officers. In essence they were dissenting against what they regarded to be the perilous conclusion reached by the majority, namely, that the Constitution, without specific supplementary congressional legislation on the subject, protects against corruption the procedure by which candidates for Congress are nominated. They refused to construe the Criminal Code broadly enough to make it apply to the particular case and charged that the majority was leaving the "safety zone" in the judicial construction of statutes. Congress did not intend to exercise the power which the Court was now ruling it had. In the absence of an "unambiguous" congressional mandate, the courts were not free to apply stringent criminal statutes merely because the offense charged is serious.

Mr. Justice Douglas saw in the Court's broad interpreta-

an act a crime, affix a punishment to it, and declare the Court that shall have jurisdiction of the offense." *United States* v. *Hudson,* 7 Cranch 32, 34 (1812).

tion of section 19 an abuse of judicial power which, because of its consequences for the accused, was nothing short of an exercise of a "legislative function." Obviously replying to this contention, Mr. Justice Stone observed that it was "hardly the performance of the judicial function" to interpret section 19 in such a way as not to apply it to corruption in congressional primaries, especially in an election situation where the primary is the only effective means of exercising the franchise. "If a right secured by the Constitution may be infringed by the corrupt failure to include the vote at a primary in the official count," he concluded, "it is not significant that the primary, like the voting machine, was unknown when section 19 was adopted." [27]

Minority and majority were thus motivated by a common desire to safeguard important democratic values. What separated them was their disagreement over a choice of lesser evils. Although not minimizing in the least the importance of honesty in the administration of all the interrelated steps in modern elections, the dissenters were concerned with preserving another asset of free institutions. They were irked to see the Supreme Court sanctioning administrative interpretation which had in effect spelled out a crime and sought to punish severely those who committed it on the basis of legislation lacking the "specificity" which criminal statutes should have.

[27] Neither did Mr. Justice Stone think that any inference should be drawn from the fact that Congress failed to extend its provisions to primaries when it adopted the Hatch legislation of 1939-1940. The dissenters, on the other hand, considered this omission to be significant of a congressional desire to leave corruption in primaries to be dealt with by the states. They referred to the action of the Senate in eliminating from the bill provisions adopted by the House which would have punished "pernicious politics" in connection with primaries. Mr. Justice Stone thought that the failure of Congress to extend the provisions of the Hatch Act to congressional primaries was to be explained by the "constitutional doubts" which the NEWBERRY case had raised. But his assertion that these doubts were being "resolved" by the decision in the CLASSIC case begged the question, to say the least, since the dissenting Justices were insisting that Congress did not intend to regulate primaries when it adopted section 19.

As for the majority, impressed as it was with the overriding importance of protecting the right of popular choice, it was quite willing to rely on analysis and deduction in order to find a legislative intention to punish those who tamper with that right.

From the point of view of its vindication of the congressional authority to protect the integrity of the procedures by which members of Congress are chosen, the opinions in the CLASSIC case are probably among the most important since the adoption of the Civil War amendments. Nor would they have been any the less significant if the qualifications for which Mr. Justice Douglas pleaded had prevailed. However, it is possible to overestimate the significance of both opinions. For proper perspective two facts should be borne in mind. The first and probably more important of these is the fact that the determination of the actual qualifications for voting is left by the Federal Constitution to the several states. The other, relating to the setting in which the CLASSIC case arose, is that Mr. Justice Stone put much stress on the fact that in Louisiana the congressional primary was by state law an integral part of the congressional election.

Not much comfort, therefore, can be derived from the CLASSIC case if one is interested in finding constitutional basis for federal legislation prohibiting the payment of a poll tax for voting in national elections. The Court was careful to point out that Congress' power over primaries applied to situations where the primary is by law made an inseparable part of the election or effectively determines the final choice. In the face of that reasoning, it may be difficult to convince even the present Supreme Court that Congress has the power to proscribe payment of a poll tax in congressional elections in a state which requires it of voters in all elections.[28] Each state

[28] Before it could uphold such federal legislation, the Court would be obliged to reconsider, if not actually to reverse, its decision in *Williams* v.

still retains its historic right to fix the qualifications for voting and the election methods incident to the choice of members of Congress. If the primary is part of that mode of choice, Congress may protect it against fraud and violence.

The spectacle in the CLASSIC case of the liberals on the Supreme Court in sharp disagreement over the scope of judicial power proves nothing so much as the essentially subjective character of judicial opinions. Mr. Justice Stone's unhesitating assertion of the Court's prerogative in reading content into an exceedingly ambiguous statute, if inconsistency it be, can be easily explained if it is remembered that the case was concerned with the protection of the political process. He regards the protection of that process and of the rights on which it depends as one of the chief responsibilities of courts. How willing he is to undertake a "searching judicial inquiry" in civil rights cases is best demonstrated by his forceful dissent in the 1940 flag salute case.

3. *Guardian of Liberty: Court or Legislature*

"Whether or not Jehovah's Witnesses leave a mark on the religious history of the United States, they are certainly leaving one on its constitutional history." [29]

The editors of the New York *Times* might well have added that the activities of the Witnesses have furnished the chief grist for the Supreme Court's recent discussion of its own function in constitutional cases. Of particular interest and importance is the considered reexamination of the Court's role

Mississippi, 170 U.S. 213 (1898). That decision sustained the constitutionality of the statutes which Mississippi adopted in 1890 providing for payment of a poll tax and taking of a literacy test. It was their general application which saved them, since the Court was able to say that they did not deny the right to vote on account of race or color. The statistics of the extent to which the poll tax has also disfranchised whites would only serve to weaken the case for the constitutionality of federal legislation forbidding payment of a poll tax in national elections.

[29] New York *Times*, June 19, 1943 (editorial page).

as guardian of civil liberties to which this recurring litigation has led.

In the GOBITIS case,[30] the Court, speaking through Mr. Justice Frankfurter, sustained the constitutionality of a school board regulation requiring pupils and teachers to participate in a daily flag salute ceremony. The Gobitis children, whose parents were members of the sect known as Jehovah's Witnesses, were expelled from the Minersville public school when they refused to salute the American flag. To avoid the necessity of sending them to private schools [31] their father brought suit to enjoin the enforcement of the compulsory flag salute, contending that it violated religious liberty guaranteed by the due process clause of the Fourteenth Amendment. For the Witnesses, the Bible as the revealed will of God is the supreme authority on earth. The Gobitis children were taught to believe that gestures of respect for the symbol of civil authority, such as the flag is, were not allowed by the Bible.[32]

Mr. Justice Frankfurter spoke for all the members of the Court except Mr. Justice Stone. He found that the flag salute requirement did not differ from numerous other regulations of general application which the Court had in the past sustained, even though exemption from them had been sought by those whose religious scruples made it difficult for them to conform.[33] The Gobitis children, the Court stressed, were not

---

30 *Minersville School District* v. *Gobitis,* 310 U.S. 586, 601 (1940).

31 At the time this action was brought, the Gobitis children were ten and twelve years' old respectively and therefore subject under Pennsylvania law to compulsory school attendance.

32 Exodus 20: 4, 5, which according to the Witnesses, is the source of the injunction against the salute to the flag, says:

Thou shalt not make unto thee any graven image, or any likeness of anything that is in heaven above, or that is in the earth beneath, or that is in the water under the earth; thou shalt not bow down thyself to them nor serve them.

The Witnesses regard the flag as an image within the meaning of the scriptures and therefore refuse to salute it.

33 He cited as examples the decision in such cases as *Reynolds* v. *United States,* 98 U.S. 145 (1878); *The Selective Draft Law Cases,* 245 U.S. 366

required to do anything which was not also demanded of all other school children. Such regulations, so long as they are not directed against particular religious groups and do not result in the censorship of religious belief, are proper exertions of the legislative power for the promotion of "that orderly, tranquil, and free society without which religious toleration itself is unattainable." Society's need to foster loyalty and to promote national unity is "an interest inferior to none in the hierarchy of legal values." "National unity is the basis of national security," Mr. Justice Frankfurter asserted, and continued by declaring that the flag is a "symbol of our national unity, transcending all internal differences however large, within the framework of the Constitution."

With the aid of these assumptions, Mr. Justice Frankfurter turned to what he termed "the precise issue" which the Court was called upon to decide. That issue, he said, was "whether the legislatures of the various states and the authorities in a thousand counties and school districts of this country are barred from determining the appropriateness of various means to evoke that unifying sentiment without which there can ultimately be no liberties, civil or religious." In so far as the religious convictions of the Gobitis children conflict with the procedure established by the Board of Education for stimulating loyalty, those beliefs must be subordinated to the needs of training in citizenship. Furthermore, the wisdom of the means by which patriotism can best be promoted in the formative years is not for the Court's "independent judgment." It

(1918); and *Hamilton* v. *Regents,* 293 U.S. 245. (1934). In the REYNOLDS case, the Court sustained an act of Congress prohibiting polygamous marriage in the Territory of Utah. One of the objections to the 1917 Draft Law was that its exemption from military service of religious groups whose tenets forbade participation in war set up a religion in violation of the First Amendment. In the HAMILTON case, the Supreme Court sustained a California statute requiring the students at the University of California to take a course in military science and tactics, and held that those wishing to take advantage of the education offered by the state university cannot set up conscientious objections to the prescribed military training.

cannot weigh the relative merits of the different educational techniques for fostering loyalty without entering the field of "pedagogical and psychological dogma" and in that field the courts "possess no marked and certainly no controlling competence."

In dissenting, Mr. Justice Stone questioned the soundness of practically everything that had been written in the name of the Court. About the only premise in the Frankfurter opinion to which he was willing to subscribe was the importance of inculcating patriotism. What was dictum and buried in a footnote in his opinion in the CAROLENE PRODUCTS Co. case concerning the judiciary's role in civil rights cases is made central in his dissent in the GOBITIS case.

Characterizing the flag salute requirement as "unique in the history of Anglo-American legislation," Mr. Justice Stone charged that it did more than suppress freedom of speech and more than interfere with the free exercise of religion. By it the authorities were compelling children to profess something which they not only did not believe but which violated "their deepest religious convictions." He read the majority opinion as not denying that the regulation infringed freedom of speech and religion but as justifying it as an exercise of the state's power over public education. The state was without power to force expressions which violate the individual's religious beliefs. "The very essence" of the freedom secured by the guarantee of civil liberty, he maintained, is the freedom of the individual from compulsion as to what he shall say, at least where the compulsion is to bear false witness to his religion.

Mr. Justice Stone could see no need for this compulsion. He rejected Mr. Justice Frankfurter's assumption that the Court should refrain from weighing the desirability of the flag salute. There were alternatives.

There are other ways to teach loyalty and patriotism which are the sources of national unity, than by compelling the pupil to affirm that which he does not believe and by commanding a form of affirmance which violates his religious convictions. Without recourse to such compulsion the state is free to compel attendance at school and require teaching by instruction and study of all in our history and in the structure and organization of our government, including the guaranties of civil liberty which tend to inspire patriotism and love of country. I cannot say that government here is deprived of any interest or function which it is entitled to maintain at the expense of the protection of civil liberties by requiring it to resort to the alternatives which do not coerce an affirmation of belief.

It will be seen that Mr. Justice Stone was here asking for an independent judicial examination of the legislative judgment as to what was desirable for the community as a whole.[34] He remarked that most measures of repression have been justified in the name of "righteousness and the public good" and expressed the belief that the framers of the Bill of Rights were not ignorant of the fact that invasions of personal freedom could be cloaked behind legislative declarations as to the public interest to be served. He refused to believe that the men who adopted the explicit guarantees of freedom of speech and of religion intended nevertheless to leave legislatures free to exact the compulsory expression of sentiments which violate sincere religious convictions.

Next came a series of assertions which reaffirm Mr. Justice Stone's conviction that the Supreme Court has a great responsibility as protector of civil liberty. His first comment was that even if his own view that legislatures are without power to compel public expressions contrary to one's religion should be rejected, the Court should nevertheless not "refrain from passing upon the legislative judgment." It is fair to say,

---

[34] Mr. Justice Frankfurter viewed the flag salute required by the school board as if it had been adopted by the legislature of Pennsylvania itself. Mr. Justice Stone accepted this construction.

particularly since he was taking issue with the conception of the judicial function he himself espouses in the economic field, that he was in effect inviting his colleagues to substitute their will for that of the school board, in order to safeguard religious liberty. At the same time, he made it clear that he saw no need for building his own theory of political restraints into the straitjacket of a legal fetish. Advancing beyond the political, he argued that there are even higher values to a free society for the preservation of which the "searching judicial inquiry" may be extended.

By way of indicating that the Court's refusal to exert its veto did not leave religious minorities completely unprotected, Mr. Justice Frankfurter had said that "so long as the remedial channels of the democratic process remain open and unobstructed" personal liberty is most secure "when it is ingrained in a people's habits and not enforced against popular policy by the coercion of adjudicated law." He continued:

> Judicial review, itself a limitation on popular government, is a fundamental part of our constitutional scheme. But to the legislature no less than to courts is committed the guardianship of deeply cherished liberties. . . . Where all the effective means of inducing political changes are left free from interference, education in the abandonment of foolish legislation is itself a training in liberty. To fight out the wise use of legislative authority in the forum of public opinion and before legislative assemblies rather than to transfer such a contest to the judicial arena, serves to vindicate the self-confidence of a free people.

Replying, Mr. Justice Stone called attention to the fact that the Witnesses were a politically helpless minority and spoke of the Frankfurter thesis as representing the "surrender" of the protection of the rights of such small minorities to the "popular will." Citing his own remarks in the CAROLENE PRODUCTS Co. case, he recalled that the Court had previously pointed to the "importance of a searching judicial inquiry into the legislative judgment in situations where prejudice against discrete and insular minorities may tend to curtail the operation of those political processes ordinarily to be relied on to protect minorities." The Court's recent record in civil liberty cases showed that it did not hesitate "similarly to scrutinize" the rights of religious and racial minorities even though "no political process was affected." Even more important than the political process was another asset of free institutions which the Constitution of the United States meant to perpetuate. Mr. Justice Stone wrote:

> The Constitution expresses more than the conviction of the people that democratic processes must be preserved at all costs. It is also an expression of faith and a command that freedom of mind and spirit must be preserved, which government must obey, if it is to adhere to that justice and moderation without which no free government can exist.

We thus have in his dissent in the GOBITIS case Mr. Justice Stone's qualification of his own political restraints doctrine. There are circumstances in which it is not enough that the processes by which the legislative mind may be changed are left intact. When confronted with legislation which stifles the freedom of helpless minorities, the Supreme Court should not hesitate to assume the role of protector, even if in doing so it is supplanting the legislative judgment with its own conception of what is appropriate. He was quite willing to admit that if his view had prevailed it might have caused the Minersville public school some inconvenience in enforcing its program of discipline. To spare the religious sensibilities of children, however, the Court would have been justified in deciding that the inconvenience was not of such "momentous or pressing" consequence as to "outweigh" the importance of protecting religious liberty. In short, Mr. Justice Stone was telling his colleagues that wisdom and justice must be the tests of constitutionality in civil liberty cases.[35].

To judge from subsequent developments, it would appear that some of those who voted with Mr. Justice Frankfurter in the GOBITIS case were none too convinced of the propriety of the compulsory flag salute. Exactly two years later, although the particular litigation in hand did not call for it, three of the Justices who had been with the majority in the GOBITIS case announced that they had come to believe that that case was "wrongly decided." A year later, they were joined by two others. By the time the GOBITIS case was overruled, only three Justices adhered to the views of the majority in that case.

On June 8, 1942, the Supreme Court decided three cases [36] the dissenters in which regarded them as but a "logical extension" of the principles on which the decision in the GOBITIS case had been based. All three were concerned with the validity of municipal ordinances imposing a license tax for the privilege of selling books and pamphlets on the streets or from

[35] Not the least interesting aspect of the GOBITIS case is the widespread criticism which greeted Mr. Justice Frankfurter's part in it. Many were deeply disappointed to see a Justice whose call to the Bench was but a reward for life-long service to the cause of liberalism reveal an attitude which seemed hostile to the rights of minorities. Some professed to see in it a glaring contradiction to the constitutional philosophy he had expounded for more than a quarter of a century. But the fact is that he himself had indicated more than once that he possessed no abiding faith in the ability of the Supreme Court to "guarantee toleration." Writing in the *New Republic* in 1925, editor Frankfurter warned the liberals of the country that "the real battles of liberalism are not won in the Supreme Court," and added that "only a persistent, positive translation of the liberal faith into the thoughts and acts of the community is the real reliance against the unabated temptation to straitjacket the human mind." He reminded his readers of the "heavy price" which must be paid for the Supreme Court's "occasional services to liberalism," such as the nullification of protective labor legislation. *Law and Politics,* Occasional Papers of Felix Frankfurter, MacLeish and Prichard, ed.; (New York: Harcourt, Brace & Co. 1939), pp. 195-97.

[36] The principal case was *Jones* v. *Opelika,* 316 U.S. 584,600 (1942). The other two were *Bowden* v. *Fort Smith* and *Jobin* v. *Arizona.*

house to house. Opelika, Alabama, Fort Smith, Arkansas, and Casa Grande, Arizona, defended these levies as applied to the activities of Jehovah's Witnesses in selling the printed propaganda of the sect as taxes for general revenue purposes.[37] The members of Jehovah's Witnesses involved in each of these cases had been convicted and fined for selling literature without first securing a license and paying the required tax.

Dividing five to four, the Supreme Court in an opinion by Mr. Justice Reed held that since these taxes were general and nondiscriminatory they could be demanded of persons selling religious literature on city streets. The exactions did not infringe freedom of speech or press or the free exercise of religion. Describing the efforts of Jehovah's Witnesses in selling their literature as "partaking more of commercial than religious or educational transactions," Mr. Justice Reed summed up in one sentence the principle upon which the Court was resting its decision: "When proponents of religious or social theories use the ordinary commercial methods of sales of articles to raise propaganda funds, it is a natural and proper exercise of the power of the state to charge reasonable fees for the privilege of canvassing."

Dissenting against this ruling were Chief Justice Stone and Justices Murphy, Black and Douglas. Although he thought that the ordinance in each of the three cases was "on its face" an interference with the freedoms guaranteed by the First Amendment, the Chief Justice found the Opelika ordinance particularly objectionable and directed a large part of his criticism to it. One of its provisions authorized the licensing authorities to revoke without notice licenses which they had

37 The Opelika ordinance levied a ten-dollar annual tax on all book agents and a five-dollar annual tax on transient distributors of books. In addition, there was a fifty-cents "issuance fee" on the license. In Fort Smith, the tax was twenty-five dollars per annum, ten dollars a week and two-fifty a day. The Casa Grande exaction was twenty-five dollars per quarter.

previously granted. Mr. Justice Reed had considered the objection to this provision, but had taken the view that the danger that the license might be improperly revoked was "far too slight" to justify the Court in holding the whole ordinance invalid.

But Chief Justice Stone found the Court's disposition of the complaint against the revocation provision of the Opelika ordinance to be inconsistent with the decision in an important case handed down four years earlier.[38] He described the Opelika ordinance as constituting a "more callous disregard" of the right of free expression than that which the Court had before it in *Lovell* v. *Griffin*. Under the Griffin ordinance, the defendant might have secured a license if she had applied for it. At least she was not required to pay for the privilege of free speech. In Opelika, one was prohibited from distributing literature unless he paid a year's taxes for the privilege, and in addition the license granted him could be revoked at the whim of the local officials.

Chief Justice Stone thought that all three cases raised but one central issue. The issue was "whether a flat tax, more than a nominal fee to defray the expenses of a regulatory license, can constitutionally be laid on a non-commercial, non-profit activity devoted exclusively to the dissemination of ideas educational and religious in character, to those persons who consent to receive them." He objected to the Court's charac-

---

[38] *Lovell* v. *City of Griffin*, 303 U.S. 444 (1938). In this case, the Supreme Court unanimously declared unconstitutional a municipal ordinance prohibiting the distribution of "circulars, handbills, advertising, or literature of any kind" without first obtaining the written permission from the city manager. It reversed the conviction of Alma Lovell, a member of Jehovah's Witnesses, who had been sentenced to imprisonment for fifty days in default of a fifty dollar fine for distributing a religious magazine and other pamphlets without the required permit. In his opinion for the Court, Chief Justice Hughes stressed the fact that the Griffin ordinance conferred administrative discretionary authority over the circulation of printed matter which was in essence a means for imposing "previous restraint" on the dissemination of ideas.

terization of the exactions as "fees." So to describe them was to imply that they were passed to defray expenses incident to the enforcement of the licensing system; whereas, their amount "without more" proved that they were adopted for revenue-raising purposes.[39] He was willing to assume, "for argument's sake," that a nominal fee for a regulatory license would not be invalid. But he showed that none of the ordinances set up machinery for regulating the time, place and manner of distributing the books and pamphlets, nor were any of them passed to maintain law and order. In all three cases, the legislative objective was to ban the distribution of literature, unless one wishing to exercise the privilege paid in advance a tax "fixed in amount" which was not measured either by the extent of his activities under the license or by the amount which he collects for or devotes to religious purposes in the exercise of the licensed privilege.

Since many of the defendants were "transient distributors of literature" who may come to a town for a day or two, it should be obvious that for them the exaction may actually be prohibitive. Recalling that the tax in each case was spoken of by the state courts as a levy on business employment, he insisted that the activities of Jehovah's Witnesses were no mere business or commercial transactions. They were engaged in disseminating their religious views, and in the course of their evangelism they offered to sell books and pamphlets, but only to raise funds for their religious movement. Sometimes the literature was given gratis. The Witnesses have organized non-profit charitable corporations to publish their literature and nobody derives profit from its publication or sale.

[39] Under the Opelika ordinance, there was in addition to the tax a fifty-cent "issuance fee" and only the latter, the Chief Justice pointed out, could conceivably be regarded as needed to defray the cost of administering the licensing system. He also noted that in each instance the state courts thought that the real issue was whether the city enjoyed the power to tax the distribution of religious literature, and not whether a nominal exaction could be demanded to administer the licensing law.

If taxes devised for transactions not protected by the Bill of Rights could be applied to the dissemination of ideas, they might serve as a "ready instrument" for destroying that right. Chief Justice Stone expected few to deny that a license tax imposed specifically on the dissemination of ideas would violate freedom of speech and argued that the offense of the tax in each of the three cases was no less far reaching. As applied to the exercise of religious freedom, its "vice" was that it was levied and paid in advance of the activities taxed and that it was "applied at rates well calculated to suppress those activities, save as others may volunteer to pay the tax." When demanded of Jehovah's Witnesses, these taxes were in their operation an exaction for the dissemination of ideas or at best a charge for the privilege of collecting funds for religious purposes. Emphasizing that freedom of press and religion are specifically guaranteed by the Constitution, Chief Justice Stone asked the Court to extend to those freedoms at least the same protection from burdensome taxation which it has extended to interstate commerce under the "more general phraseology" of the commerce clause. And whatever doubts may exist concerning the Supreme Court's power "unaided by congressional legislation" to protect interstate commerce against such tax burdens, he thought that none should question its function under the "explicit guarantees of freedom of speech, press and religion." He concluded his opinion with these words: "In its potency as a prior restraint on publication, the flat license tax falls short only of outright censorship or suppression. The more humble and needy the cause, the more effective is the suppression."

In a joint dissent, Justices Black, Douglas and Murphy characterized the taxes upheld by the Court as a "device" for suppressing the free exercise of religion by a minority group. The validation of these taxes was but a "logical extension" of the principles of the Gobitis opinion, and since they had joined in that opinion they took occasion to announce that they had come to believe that the earlier case was also "wrongly decided." They expressed the fear that the OPELIKA and GOBITIS opinions placed the free exercise of religion in a "subordinate position." Chief Justice Stone too feared that a way had been found "despite constitutional guarantees" for suppressing freedom of speech, press and worship, especially since the taxes sustained by the Court had been imposed in small communities and upon "peripatetic religious propagandists."

But the dissenters were not to harbor this fear for long. In less than a year the Supreme Court reversed itself when it held on May 3, 1943, that Jehovah's Witnesses could not be required to pay a license fee for the distribution of religious literature.[40] The Court at the same time overruled its decision in the OPELIKA case.[41] Mr. Justice Douglas spoke for a majority of five in setting aside the license tax requirements of Jeanette, Pennsylvania.[42] This time the Court held that the distribution of pamphlets, as a form of evangelism, "occupies the same high estate under the First Amendment as do worship in the churches and preaching from the pulpit." It has the same "claim to protection as the more orthodox and conventional exercises of religion." [43]

[40] *Murdock* v. *Pennsylvania,* 319 U.S. 105, 117 (1943).

[41] *Jones* v. *Opelika,* 319 U.S. 103 (1943).

[42] The Court's junior member, Wiley Blount Rutledge, joined Chief Justice Stone and Justices Black, Douglas and Murphy to form the majority. Mr. Justice Byrnes, who had resigned to become Director of the Office of Economic Stabilization, had voted against the Witnesses in the 1942 OPELIKA case.

[43] In a dissent in which he was objecting to both the ruling in the MURDOCK case and the one upsetting the Opelika ordinance, Mr. Justice Reed again emphasized the commercial character of the activities involved in the sale of religious books and pamphlets.

". . . even if the distribution of religious books was a religious practice protected from regulation by the First Amendment, certainly the affixation of a price for the articles would destroy the sacred character of the transaction. The evangelist becomes a book agent.

"The rites which are protected by the First Amendment are in essence

In the MURDOCK case and the others decided the same day, the Court remained silent on the compulsory flag. salute issue. But its decision in those cases and the alignments revealed on that day presaged a change of view. A month later, the expected reversal was announced. By a six-to-three vote, the Supreme Court struck down the flag salute requirement of the West Virginia Board of Education and overruled *Minersville School District* v. *Gobitis.*[44]

The majority in this case was composed of the Chief Justice and Justices Jackson, Black, Douglas, Murphy and Rutledge. Justices Black, Douglas and Murphy, who were with the majority in the GOBITIS case, came over to the views expressed by Mr. Justice Stone in that case. Dissenting were Justices Frankfurter, Reed and Roberts. Mr. Justice Jackson and Mr. Justice Rutledge came to the Court since the decision in the 1940 case.

On June 9, 1942, the West Virginia State Board of Education adopted a resolution requiring pupils and teachers to participate in the flag salute ceremony which was made a regular part of school activities. Refusal to salute the flag was made an act of insubordination and was to be followed by expulsion. The expelled child was to be considered unlawfully absent and therefore a delinquent. His parent or guardian was rendered liable to prosecution. Appellees, members of Jehovah's Witnesses, challenged the constitutionality of the requirement, complaining that as applied to them it infringed their religious freedom and freedom of speech in violation of the First and Fourteenth Amendments.

This action enabled the Supreme Court to reconsider the

spiritual—prayer, mass, sermons, sacrament—not sales of religious goods." 319 U.S. 105, 132 (1943). Justices Frankfurter, Jackson and Roberts joined in this dissent, with Mr. Justice Frankfurter filing a separate dissenting opinion.

44 *West Virginia Board of Education* v. *Barnette,* 319 U.S. 624, 646 (1943).

Gobitis decision. Four opinions were written in the case, and all give evidence of the extent to which the real issue dividing the Justices was the nature of the judicial function itself. The majority opinion of Mr. Justice Jackson, the joint concurring opinions of Justices Black and Douglas, the separate concurring opinion of Mr. Justice Murphy, and the dissenting opinion of Mr. Justice Frankfurter, all may be read as essays primarily concerned with the role of the Supreme Court in safeguarding civil liberties. Before it could hold the compulsory flag salute to be valid, Mr. Justice Jackson asserted, it would be necessary for the Court to declare that "a Bill of Rights which guards the individual's right to speak his own mind, left it open to public authority to compel him to utter what is not in his mind."

Almost before the circumstances in the immediate case were fully set forth, Mr. Justice Jackson turned to the question of the Court's competence. He quoted the passages from Mr. Justice Frankfurter's Gobitis opinion in which the latter had questioned the special competence of the Court and had pleaded for a greater recognition of legislatures and public opinion as guardians of fundamental rights. Mr. Justice Jackson then argued that the "very purpose" of the Bill of Rights was "to withdraw certain subjects from the vicissitudes of political controversy, to place them beyond the reach of majorities and officials and to establish them as legal principles to be applied by the courts." He denied that the Court's duty to enforce the Bill of Rights need be justified by any claim of "marked competence" to deal with the invasion of rights. The task of applying guarantees framed in the eighteenth century to the problems and needs of the twentieth century may be "one to disturb self-confidence," but it is precisely because conditions have changed that precedents sometimes lose their reliability and the Court is "cast" upon its own "judgment." "We act in these matters," Mr. Justice Jackson stated, "not by authority of our competence but by force of our commissions. We cannot because of our modest estimates of our competence in such specialties as public education, withhold the judgment that history authenticates as the function of this Court when liberty is infringed." And as to what he termed "the very heart of the Gobitis opinion," namely, that since national unity is the basis of national security legislatures may determine the means for fostering the necessary loyalties, all that the Court was now deciding was that the compulsory flag salute was not one of the "permissible means" for the promotion of national unity. The Court could perceive no danger, especially since those being coerced were as harmless as Jehovah's Witnesses, that the "social organization" would disintegrate if patriotism were fostered by voluntary rather than by compulsory programs of education.[45]

One of the main points of controversy in the BARNETTE case was the question as to whether the explicit guarantees of the First Amendment require a more rigorous performance of the judicial function. To the extent that the majority and the minority were in disagreement over this issue, they were, of course, also divided on the need for Chief Justice Stone's conception of the "more searching judicial inquiry" in the civil liberties area. The majority was stating categorically that the criterion of constitutionality is much more definite when the legislation conflicts with the Fourteenth Amendment because it also conflicts with the freedoms of the First Amend-

---

[45] Concurring jointly, Justices Black and Douglas explained that they had joined with the Court in the GOBITIS case because of their "reluctance to make the Federal Constitution a rigid bar against state regulation of conduct thought inimical to the public welfare." Since then "long reflection" had persuaded them that while the principle by which they were guided was sound, the same could not be said for the way it was applied in the particular case. They had come to believe that the compulsory flag salute was a "handy implement for disguised religious persecution." Concurring separately, Mr. Justice Murphy made it known that "reflection" had convinced him that "as a judge" he had "no loftier duty or responsibility than to uphold spiritual freedom to its furtherest reaches."

ment than when only the Fourteenth Amendment is the relevant constitutional limitation. Wrote Mr. Justice Jackson:

> Much of the vagueness of the due process clause disappears when the specific prohibitions of the First [Amendment] become its standard. The right of a state to regulate, for example, a public utility may well include, so far as the due process test is concerned, power to impose all of the restrictions which a legislature may have a "rational basis" for adopting. But freedom of speech and of press, of assembly, and of worship may not be infringed on such slender grounds. They are susceptible of restriction only to prevent grave and immediate danger to interests which the state may lawfully protect.

Denying that the Constitution endowed the Supreme Court with "greater veto power" when confronted with one issue of freedom than with another, Mr. Justice Frankfurter contended that there was "no warrant" in the legal basis of the Court's power for assigning to it "different roles." The extent of its authority is not determined by the particular provision of the Constitution on which reliance has been placed. So far as the scope of judicial power is concerned, the right not to have one's property taken without just compensation enjoys the same "constitutional dignity" as the guarantee against unreasonable searches and seizures, and that guarantee is no less important than the freedoms of the First Amendment:

> In no instance is this Court the primary protector of the particular liberty that is invoked. . . . Each specific amendment, in so far as embraced within the Fourteenth Amendment, must be equally respected, and the function of this Court does not differ in passing on the constitutionality of legislation challenged under different amendments.[46]

[46] The distinction between judicial review of economic regulation and judicial enforcement of such explicit guarantees as those of the First Amendment has been succinctly summarized as follows: "To hold that the Fourteenth Amendment was intended to and did provide protection from

Associating himself with the Holmes theory of toleration of legislation, Mr. Justice Frankfurter reiterated his view that it was not within the province of the Supreme Court to pass judgment on the appropriateness of legislative measures.[47] The judge's "opinions about the wisdom or evil of a law" should not influence his decision. For the only opinion that is pertinent is "whether legislators could in reason have enacted such a law."

Declaring that he would have preferred to associate himself with the "libertarian views" of the majority—"representing as they do the thought and action of a lifetime"—Mr. Justice Frankfurter told us that he could not conscientiously join his brethren unless he were prepared to read into the Constitution his òwn "private notions of policy." Since all agreed that the development of good citizenship was a "legitimate legislative

state invasions of the right of free speech and other clearly defined protections contained in the Bill of Rights, . . . is quite different from holding that 'due process,' an historical expression relating to procedure, . . . confers a broad judicial power to invalidate all legislation which seems 'unreasonable' to courts. In the one instance, courts proceeding within clearly marked constitutional boundaries seek to execute policies written into the Constitution; in the other, they roam at will in the limitless area of their own beliefs as to reasonableness and actually select policies, a responsibility which the Constitution entrusts to the legislative representatives of the people." Justices Black, Douglas and Murphy, jointly concurring in *Federal Power Commission* v. *Natural Gas Pipeline Co.*, 315 U.S. 575 (1942), at pp. 600-601, n. 4.

47 Mr. Justice Frankfurter quoted one sentence from an opinion of Justice Holmes which he regarded as summing up the essence of the American constitutional system and the democratic nature of our society. "It must be remembered," Justice Holmes had written, "that legislatures are ultimate guardians of the liberty and welfare of the people in quite as great a degree as the courts." *Missouri, Kansas and Texas Ry. Co.* v. *May,* 194 U.S. 267, 270 (1904). Commenting on this statement, Mr. Justice Frankfurter said: "He [Holmes] was stating the comprehensive judicial duty and role of this Court in our constitutional scheme whenever legislation is sought to be nullified on any ground, namely, that responsibility for legislation lies with legislatures, answerable as they are directly to the people, and this Court's only and very narrow function is to determine whether within the broad grant of authority vested in legislatures they have exercised a judgment for which reasonable justification can be offered."

end," he was unable to believe that the liberty guaranteed by the Fourteenth Amendment empowered the Court to keep a state from using the flag salute ceremony as one of the means for attaining that end. "The lawmaking authority," he stated, "is not circumscribed by the variety of religious beliefs, otherwise the constitutional guarantee would be not a protection of the free exercise of religion but a denial of the exercise of legislation." Moreover, reasonable men might conclude that requiring all children to share in a common demonstration of respect for the flag was not so serious a disregard of the religious scruples of some of the children as to outweigh in importance society's concern in promoting good citizenship. If that is the conclusion reached by "reasonable legislators," courts are without power to insist that the state choose other means, unless they are to assume the powers of a "super legislature."

Commenting on the divergent views in the BARNETTE case, the editors of the New York *Times* expressed sympathy for the layman who was bound to be confused by the able reasoning contained in the majority and minority opinions.[48] But even more distracting than the disagreement over the constitutionality of the compulsory flag salute must be the conflicting conceptions of their own function as set forth by the Justices. These expositions give the case a significance beyond the vindication of the rights of an eccentric religious minority.

Unless one is prepared to argue that the position taken by the minority was due to their concern for inculcating patriotism and to nothing else, it should be obvious that their dissent reflects a fundamental difference of opinion with respect to the scope of the Supreme Court's power in constitutional cases. Three members of the Court, Justices Frankfurter, Reed and Roberts, take the view that the reach of judicial review is the

48 "The Court on the Flag Salute," New York *Times*, June 19, 1943 (editorial page).

same, whether the challenge is to legislation regulating economic activities or to legislation allegedly infringing fundamental civil rights. In both instances, they would deny to the Court any authority to pass judgment on the propriety or wisdom of the legislative action. The other five Associate Justices agree with Chief Justice Stone that the test of constitutionality in civil rights cases must be much more penetrating. His theory of the "more searching judicial inquiry" enjoys today majority support and may therefore be said to be the position of the Court. This is the true significance of the Supreme Court's action in overruling its decision in the GOBITIS case.

The present majority is thus frank to admit that where civil rights are concerned, it is prepared to decide cases on the basis of its view as to whether the particular scheme chosen by the legislature is desirable or necessary. In this field, the "rational basis" of the legislation, a criterion so vital in the economic field, is not determinative of the legislative power. For the sake of preserving the maximum assertion of the liberties guaranteed by the Bill of Rights, the Court will even suggest possible alternatives for achieving otherwise permissible legislative purposes.

One final observation is perhaps in order. However justified one might have been twenty years ago in calling into question the "social value" of judicial review, when weighed by its losses and gains, there was no such ground for concern in the flag-salute cases. Toleration of social legislation by the Court which decided these cases is a far cry from the complacency exhibited by the conservative majority in the 1920's in the field of economic regulation. Such a tribunal, cordial as it is in its reception of measures of economic control, might well appraise with special care legislative action directed against groups not in a position to exert much influence on the legislative process.

4. *Civil-Military Relations*

Every war raises anew the problem of the relationship between the military and the civilian authorities. In the name of military expediency, actions may be taken which seem to challenge that supremacy of civilian over military rule which is an essential of constitutional government. Civil administration of criminal justice, itself an important safeguard of civil liberty, may be one of the first casualties in emergency situations. Where the accused civilian is charged with conduct inimical to public security or to the effective prosecution of a war, there will always be those ready to urge the wisdom of summary action.

Motivated by considerations of safety, chief executives and military commanders may be tempted to by-pass the courts, for fear lest the more protracted ways of the judicial process turn out to be avenues of escape for the guilty. The Civil War saw the greatest excesses in this regard. It was not until the struggle was over, however, that the Supreme Court was afforded an opportunity to define the limits of the jurisdiction of the military in time of war. In the famous MILLIGAN case,[49] the Court was confronted with a demand for the release of a civilian who had been convicted by a military commission in a part of the country which was not within the actual theater of military operations. Milligan, a civilian residing in Indiana and charged with inciting to insurrection, was ordered apprehended and tried by the commander of the military district of Indiana. He was sentenced to be hanged by a military tribunal set up by authority of President Lincoln. The Supreme Court was unanimous in deciding that in the particular case the trial of Milligan by military authority was illegal. Five of the Justices held that the constitutional guarantee of trial by jury forbade both Congress and the President to substitute

[49] Ex parte *Milligan*, 4 Wall. 2, 132 (1866).

trial by military commission for trial in the civil courts in places where the civil authorities were able to function.[50] Said Mr. Justice Davis, speaking for the Court:

If, in foreign invasion or civil war, the courts are actually closed, and it is impossible to administer criminal justice according to law, then, on the theatre of active military operations, where war really prevails, there is a necessity to furnish a substitute for civil authority, thus overthrown, to preserve the safety of the army and society; and as no power is left from the military, it is allowed to govern by martial rule until the laws can have their free course. As necessity creates the rule, so it limits its duration; for, if this government is continued after the courts are reinstated, it is a gross usurpation of power. Martial rule can never exist where the courts are open, and in the proper and unobstructed exercise of their jurisdiction. It is also confined to the locality of actual war.

The principles enunciated in the MILLIGAN case were among the grounds on which reliance was placed by the lawyers designated by President Roosevelt to defend the Nazi saboteurs. In their effort to secure the release of the accused by habeas corpus, they cited the MILLIGAN case as basis for the contention that the saboteurs, and particularly Haupt, had been unconstitutionally denied indictment by grand jury and trial by a petit jury.[51] Born in Germany, all eight had been to the United States, but had returned to the Reich between 1933 and 1941. They had been trained in a school of sabotage and were under orders from an officer of the German High Com-

[50] Chief Justice Chase and Justices Wayne, Swayne, and Miller, although concurring in the judgment of the Court, were of opinion that while the President could not in his own right set up military tribunals for the trial of civilians, he could do so when authorized by congressional legislation. The Chief Justice argued that Congress had not only failed to authorize trial of civilians by military commissions, but "by the strongest implication prohibited them." 4 Wall. 2, 141 (1866).

[51] Only seven of the eight captured men joined in the petition for the writ of habeas corpus presented to the District Court for the District of Columbia. The eighth, Dasch, had apparently turned state's evidence and did not join in the petition.

mand to destroy war industries and war facilities in this country. Sometime in June, 1942, they landed from German submarines on the eastern seaboard of the United States. They had with them supplies of explosives, fuses, and incendiary and time devices. Changing to civilian dress, they buried their supplies, their money and their German Marine Infantry uniforms which they wore on landing. The group landing on the Long Island coast proceeded to New York City, and the group which came ashore on the Florida coast proceeded to Jacksonville and Chicago. On June 27, the Director of the Federal Bureau of Investigation announced their arrest.

In his capacity as Commander in Chief in time of war, President Roosevelt issued two proclamations on July 2nd. One of these declared that "all persons who are subjects, citizens, or residents of any nation at war with the United States or who give obedience to or act under the direction of any such nation, and who during time of war enter or attempt to enter the United States . . . through coastal or boundary defenses, and are charged with committing or attempting or preparing to commit sabotage, espionage, hostile or warlike acts, or violations of the law of war, shall be subject to the law of war and to the jurisdiction of military tribunals." It denied to all such persons access to the courts. By the other proclamation, the President appointed a military commission consisting of eight high-ranking generals and directed it to try the eight Nazis for offenses against the law of war and the Articles of War. Attorney General Biddle and the Judge Advocate-General of the Army were directed to prosecute and Colonel Kenneth C. Royall and Colonel Cassius M. Dowell were assigned as defense counsel.

The secret proceedings before the military commission began on July 8, 1942, and lasted until August 3rd.[52] On July

---

[52] Specification one of the charges on which the eight Nazis were placed on trial before the military commission charged that all of them "being

27—after the presentation of evidence to the military commission was completed but before the verdict was reached— there came the dramatic announcement that the United States Supreme Court would meet in special term to hear appeals for the discharge of the saboteurs.[53] The case was argued July 29-30 and decided the next day. In the brief *per curiam* opinion filed on July 31, the Court simply stated that the saboteurs were charged with an offense which the President was authorized to order tried before a military commission, that the Commission had been lawfully constituted, and that the petitions for habeas corpus had failed to show cause for discharging the prisoners. However, since it would take some time to prepare a full opinion, the Chief Justice announced that such an opinion would be submitted at some future date. The full opinion, written by Chief Justice Stone, was filed on October 29, 1942.[54]

We are told in the official Supreme Court reports that the Court met to hear the case of the Nazi saboteurs "pursuant to a call by the Chief Justice having the approval of all the Associate Justices." [55] To judge from the form of this statement, it would appear that the initiative in convening the Court in special term was taken by Chief Justice Stone. But whether or not this assumption is correct, a far more important aspect of the case, which intrigued many observers, was

enemies of the United States and acting for . . . the German Reich, a belligerent enemy nation, secretly and covertly passed in civilian dress, contrary to the law of war, through the military and naval lines and defenses of the United States . . . and went behind such lines, contrary to the law of war, in civilian dress . . . for the purpose of committing . . . hostile acts, and, in particular, to destroy certain war industries, war utilities and war materials within the United States."

53 For a discussion of the question concerning the Supreme Court's jurisdiction to entertain the suit and for a fuller account of all the known facts in the case, see Robert E. Cushman, "The Case of the Nazi Saboteurs," XXXVI *Amer. Poli. Sci. Rev.* 1082 (Dec. 1942).

54 Ex parte *Quirin,* 317 U.S. 1 (1942). Mr. Justice Murphy, who was at the time on leave with the Army, did not participate in the case.

55 317 U.S. 1, 5 (1942).

the question as to why the country's highest court should
have seen fit to assemble in time of war for the sole purpose
of examining the legality of the procedure by which a group
of ruthless saboteurs bent on crippling the country's war effort
were being tried. The Court was not unaware that this might
be the immediate public reaction. And so at the very outset
of his full opinion, the Chief Justice made known the reasons
for the Court's action.

In view of the public importance of the questions raised by their
petitions and of the duty which rests on the courts, in time of war
as well as in time of peace, to preserve unimpaired the constitutional
safeguards of civil liberty, and because in our opinion the public
interest requires that we consider and decide these questions without any avoidable delay, we directed that petitioners' applications
be set down for full oral argument at a special term of this
Court, . . .

Defense counsel employed arguments which add up to three
major contentions. The first was that neither the Constitution
nor any legislation passed by Congress empowered the President to order tried by military tribunal persons charged with
such offenses as those with which the saboteurs were charged.
In view of that fact, their second contention was that the
prisoners should have been tried by the ordinary civil courts,
where they would have been entitled to all the safeguards extended to the accused in federal criminal prosecutions by the
Fifth and Sixth Amendments, including indictment by grand
jury and trial by jury. Finally, they urged upon the Court
that the President's order setting forth the procedure to be
followed by the military commission and the procedure actually
adhered to by the commission were in conflict with Articles
of War enacted by Congress.

In agreeing to decide these contentions, the Court made it
plain that it was not concerned with the innocence or guilt

of the accused men. This Chief Justice Stone stated explicitly and his entire opinion substantiates it. The sole reason for taking the case was to decide whether the President's proclamations could be applied in the circumstances revealed by the case.

There is nothing in the Proclamation to preclude access to the courts for determining its applicability to the particular case. And neither the Proclamation nor the fact that they are enemy aliens forecloses consideration by the courts of petitioners' contentions that the Constitution and laws of the United States . . . forbid their trial by military commissions.

Passing to what he obviously regarded as the main issue raised by the petitions for habeas corpus, namely, "the basis of the Commission's authority," the Chief Justice showed that the authority of the military tribunal was derived from the war powers of Congress and the President. Among them is the power conferred on Congress by the Constitution to "define and punish . . . offenses against the law of nations." [56] The law of war is a recognized part of the law of nations. The Articles of War adopted by Congress not only provide for the trial and punishment by court-martial of members in the armed services, but also "recognize the military commission appointed by military command as an appropriate tribunal for the trial and punishment of offenses against the law of war not ordinarily tried by court-martial." [57] By Articles 38

[56] Article I, Sec. 8. "The Congress shall have the power (10) to define and punish piracies and felonies committed on the high seas, and offenses against the law of nations."

[57] "By the reference in the 15th Article of War to 'offenders or offenses that . . . by the law of war may be triable by such military commissions,' Congress has incorporated by reference as within the jurisdiction of military commissions, all offenses which are defined as such by the law of war, and which may constitutionally be included within that jurisdiction. Congress had the choice of crystallizing in permanent form and in minute detail every offense against the law of war, or of adopting the system of common law applied by military tribunals so far as it should be recog-

and 46 the President is authorized to lay down the procedure to be followed by military commissions.

From the very beginning of its history, this Court has recognized and applied the law of war as including that part of the law of nations which prescribes for the conduct of war, the status, rights and duties of enemy nations as well as enemy individuals. . . . Congress . . . has exercised its authority to define and punish offenses against the law of nations by sanctioning . . . the jurisdiction of military commissions to try persons for offenses which, according to the rules and precepts of the law of nations, and more particularly the law of war, are cognizable by such tribunals. And the President, as Commander in Chief, by his proclamation in time of war has invoked that law.

In creating the military commission, the President was exercising the power conferred on him by Congress as well as his constitutional authority as Commander in Chief to wage war. But the Court declined to say whether President Roosevelt could have taken this action without the sanction of Congress. It was deciding the broader question whether the federal government had the authority under the Constitution to require trial by military commissions of violations of the law of war.

The law of war draws a distinction between the armed forces and the peaceful populations of belligerent countries and also between "lawful" and "unlawful" combatants. Lawful combatants are subject to capture and detention as prisoners of war; unlawful combatants are also subject to capture and detention, but "in addition they are subject to trial and punishment by military tribunals for acts which render their belligerency unlawful." It has long been recognized that there are classes of unlawful belligerents not entitled to be treated as prisoners of war, and among these are combatants who do not "wear fixed and distinctive emblems." By the 15th Article

nized and deemed applicable by the Courts. It chose the latter course." From the opinion of Chief Justice Stone.

of War Congress has provided for their trial and punishment by military commissions. A universally recognized example of unlawful belligerency is the action of enemy individuals in passing secretly and without uniforms through the military lines of a country at war for the purpose of destroying war industries and facilities. In the language of Chief Justice Stone: "Our government has recognized that those who during time of war pass surreptitiously from enemy territory into our own, discarding their uniform upon entry, for the commission of hostile acts involving destruction of life or property, have the status of unlawful combatants punishable as such by military commission."

Specification 1 of the charges against the saboteurs accused them of such unlawful belligerency in violation of the law of war, and the Court was satisfied that the charge was "not merely colorable or without foundation." And trial by military commission for such offenses against the law of war is unaffected by such consideration as that the alleged acts of unlawful belligerency were not directed against the armed forces of the country, or that the accused is an American citizen, or that the acts of destruction were never consummated.[58] Unlawful belligerency is not confined to hostile acts immediately directed against the armed forces. "Modern warfare is directed at the destruction of enemy war supplies and the implements for their production and transportation quite as much as at the armed forces." Nor is it significant that the unlawful combatant charged with offenses against the law of war happens to be an American citizen. "Citizens who associate themselves with the military arm of the enemy government, and with its aid, guidance and direction enter this country bent on

[58] Haupt, one of those who joined in the petition for habeas corpus, claimed that he was an American citizen by virtue of the naturalization of his parents when he was five years old. All claimed that they did not intend to go through with their work of destruction and that they agreed to accept the mission only as a means of escaping from Germany.

hostile acts are enemy belligerents within the meaning of the Hague Convention and the law of war."

It is equally immaterial that the saboteurs had not actually committed any of the acts of destruction for which they were sent to the United States by the German government. Their mere coming to these shores and passing secretly and without uniform through our military lines for the purpose of committing hostile acts was in itself a violation of the law of war triable and punishable by military commission.[59]

Having found that the saboteurs were charged with offenses against the law of war which were universally subject to trial and punishment by military commission, Chief Justice Stone considered next the contention that the Constitution of the United States required that they be tried in the civil courts. Recalling that indictment by grand jury and trial by jury were an integral part of the administration of criminal justice at the time the Constitution was adopted, he pointed out that these safeguards for accused persons were unknown to military commissions. These procedures applied only to criminal trials in the civil courts and it was not the purpose of paragraph 2 of Article III nor the Fifth and Sixth Amendments to enlarge the right to trial by jury beyond what it was then understood to be.[60] The relevant provisions of Article III and the Fifth and Sixth Amendments "cannot be taken to have

[59] Chief Justice Stone stated that even when committed by citizens of the United States, offenses against the law of war such as those with which the saboteurs were charged were distinct from the crime of treason as defined by the Constitution, "since the absence of uniform essential to one is irrelevant to the other."

[60] Article III, paragraph 2: "The trial of all crimes, except in cases of impeachment, shall be by jury; . . ."

Amendment V: "No person shall be held to answer for a capital, or otherwise infamous crime, unless on a presentment or indictment of a grand jury, except in cases arising in the land or naval forces, or in the militia, when in actual service in time of war or public danger; . . ."

Amendment VI: "In all criminal prosecutions, the accused shall enjoy the right to a speedy and public trial by an impartial jury of the State and district wherein the crime shall have been committed, . . ."

extended the right to demand a jury to trials by a military commission or to have required that offenses against the law of war not triable by jury at common law be tried only in the civil courts." [61] The Court concluded that the Fifth and Sixth Amendments did not diminish the constitutional power to try offenders against the law of war by military tribunal and that since the saboteurs were charged with a crime not triable by jury at common law they had been "lawfully placed on trial by the Commission without a jury."

As for the seemingly contrary ruling in the MILLIGAN case, the Chief Justice distinguished that case by stressing that the principles enunciated there grew out of the facts peculiar to it and were inapplicable to the case of the Nazi saboteurs.[62] In the MILLIGAN case itself the Court was careful to point out, we were reminded, that Milligan was a civilian, for twenty years resident in a state which was not in rebellion and that he was not an enemy belligerent entitled to be treated as a prisoner of war or subject to the penalties prescribed for unlawful belligerents. "We construe the Court's statement as to the inapplicability of the law of war to Milligan's case as having particular reference to the facts before it."

[61] Defense counsel had contended that the exception in the Fifth Amendment concerning cases arising in the land and naval forces had the effect of foreclosing any other exceptions. They therefore insisted that since the saboteurs were not charged with acts relating to the land or naval forces they were entitled to be tried by jury. Chief Justice Stone replied that this contention "misconceived" the purpose of the exception. Its objective was "to authorize the trial by court-martial of the members of our Armed Forces for all that class of crimes which under the Fifth and Sixth Amendments might otherwise have been deemed triable in the civil courts." As examples of exceptions in addition to the one contained in the Fifth Amendment he cited petty criminal cases and criminal contempt cases. These have never been subject to the requirements of the Fifth and Sixth Amendments.

[62] The part of the opinion by Justice Davis in the MILLIGAN case which defense counsel stressed, particularly in behalf of Haupt, was the assertion that the laws and usages of war "can never be applied to citizens in states which have upheld the authority of the government, and where the courts are open and their process unobstructed."

To the victims of the lawlessness which the Nazis call "Aryan justice," it must have been indeed astounding to behold America's highest court interrupting a proceeding before a military tribunal created by the Chief Executive. Even in peacetime the Court's action would have been startling. The fact that it was taken in time of an all-out war made it that much more significant of the Court's determination to be vigilant when fundamental constitutional liberties are alleged to be at stake. But aside from any emotional satisfaction which the spectacle might have afforded, the principles enunciated by the Court were in no sense extraordinary, unless it be their vindication of the legal superiority of the civil courts even in total war. Yet all that the opinion by Chief Justice Stone seems to hold is that even in wartime courts may intervene for the purpose of ascertaining whether trial by military authority is applicable to the particular case. They will not sit in judgment on the innocence or guilt of the accused persons, but will look to see whether the procedure by which guilt or innocence is sought to be established violates constitutional limitations. In the case before it, the Supreme Court found that the acts with which the saboteurs were charged represented offenses against the law of war which the Constitution of the United States authorizes to be tried by military tribunal.

As much as Chief Justice Stone in the QUIRIN case manifests his great concern for the inviolability of constitutional liberties even in time of war, his opinion is no less notable for its grasp of the exigencies of waging modern total war. And by his opinions in the cases arising from the Army's evacuation of the Japanese from our west coast he displayed even greater sympathy for the "war-waging branches" of the Government.[63] Indeed, this case can be read more for its unfolding

---

[63] *Hirabayashi* v. *United States,* decided June 21, 1943, 320 U.S. 81. The companion case of *Yasui* v. *United States* decided the same day, merely applies the principles of the HIRABAYASHI case. 320 U.S. 115.

of Chief Justice Stone's conception of the nature of the war powers than for anything else. This is so particularly because the Court refused to pass on the constitutionality of the evacuation and resettlement of persons of Japanese ancestry.

Hirabayashi was born in the United States in 1918 of Japanese parents and at the time of his arrest was a senior at the University of Washington. He was convicted for violating a statute passed by Congress on March 21, 1942, which made it a misdemeanor to disobey the regulations of a military commander in a military area. The indictment consisted of two counts. The first charged him with failing to report to a Civilian Control Station contrary to a civilian exclusion order, and the second charged him with failing to stay at home between the hours of 8 P.M. and 6 A.M. contrary to a curfew order issued by the military commander of the Western Defense Command. Asserting that he disregarded the restrictions prescribed for persons of Japanese ancestry because he thought that by complying with them he would be waiving his rights as an American citizen, Hirabayashi objected to the law under which he was indicted on two grounds. It violated the Fifth Amendment and was an unconstitutional delegation of legislative power. But these objections were overruled and he was convicted by a jury in the United States District Court and given a three months sentence on each count of the indictment, the two sentences to run concurrently. When the appeal from his conviction reached the Ninth Circuit Court, that court certified certain questions of law to the United States Supreme Court. At the very beginning of his opinion Chief Justice Stone indicated that the Court had decided to pass on the constitutionality of the curfew order only and to leave unresolved the more important issue with respect to the relocation of the Japanese residents.

On February 19, 1942, President Roosevelt issued Executive Order #9066 authorizing the Secretary of War or military commanders designated by him to establish military areas "from which any or all persons may be excluded, and with respect to which, the right of any person to enter, remain in, or leave shall be subject to whatever restrictions the Secretary of War or the appropriate military commander may impose in his discretion." The next day Secretary of War Stimson designated Lieutenant-General J. L. De Witt as military commander of the Western Defense Command, Fourth Army.

On March 12, General De Witt issued Public Proclamation #1, reciting that the entire west coast because of its geographical location was particularly subject to attack, invasion and the peril of sabotage and espionage. It also announced that steps would be taken to protect that part of the country against these dangers and that certain persons might be excluded from certain areas within the Western Defense Command. On March 24, General De Witt began to issue a series of civilian exclusion orders, one of which applied to Hirabayashi. It directed that all persons of Japanese ancestry, citizens and aliens alike, be excluded from a specified section of military area #1 in Seattle, which happened to include the part of the city in which Hirabayashi resided. One member of each family and each individual living alone, to whom the order applied, were required to report on May 11 or May 12 to a designated Civil Control Station in Seattle. On March 27, the military commander issued Public Proclamation #4 providing for the evacuation and resettlement of Japanese within the area.

The Supreme Court construed the act which Congress passed on March 21, 1942, as ratifying and confirming Executive Order #9066 on which these regulations were based. It concluded that the act "contemplated and authorized" the curfew order. Accordingly, the issue to be decided was not whether Congress could have authorized the President to promulgate the executive order, but whether acting together the President and Congress possessed the "constitutional authority" to impose the curfew order and to authorize military commanders to issue such an order on the basis of their appraisal of the need for it. The Court decided that the law of March 21 and Executive Order #9066 were "each an exercise of the power to wage war conferred on Congress and the President." [64] Nor did the case raise any issue of martial law or trial by military commission, since Hirabayashi had been convicted in the civil courts and made to suffer penalties prescribed by Congress itself.[65]

Thus in the HIRABAYASHI case the Court confined its attention to the single inquiry whether the national government, through the cooperative action of Congress and the President, possessed the power under the Constitution to impose the curfew restriction "as an emergency measure." Quoting Charles Evans Hughes to the effect that the war power of the national government is "the power to wage war successfully," [66] Chief Justice Stone declared that the power "extends to every matter and activity so related to war as substantially to affect its conduct and progress." Since the Constitution endows Con-

---

[64] As in the QUIRIN case, so here too, the Court refused to answer the question whether the President, acting alone, could have taken the action complained of.

[65] This was apparently said to meet the contention that in the absence of a "proper declaration of martial law" the military authorities exceeded their power when they issued the order involved in the case. See brief for appellant filed by Messrs. Frank L. Walters, Harold Evans and Osmond K. Fraenkel, p. 8. The American Civil Liberties Union, on the other hand, agreed that even without a declaration of martial law citizens and aliens whose presence in military zones is considered a menace to national security may be removed from such areas. It objected, however, to the basis of the classification represented by the curfew and exclusion orders and insisted that "except in cases of immediate emergency, the necessity for such removals should be determined by civilian authorities, and such removals should be carried out by civilian authorities." Brief Amicus Curiae, *American Civil Liberties Union*, p. 2.

[66] Charles Evans Hughes, "War Powers Under the Constitution," *42 A.B.A. Rep. 232*, 238 (1917).

gress and the President with the power to wage war "in all the vicissitudes and conditions of warfare," it has "necessarily given them wide scope for the exercise of judgment and discretion in determining the nature and extent of the threatened injury or danger and in the selection of the means for resisting it." Furthermore, where the circumstances call for the exercise of "judgment and discretion and for the choice of means" by the war-making departments of the Government, "it is not for any court to sit in review of the wisdom of their action or substitute its judgment for theirs."

The rest of Chief Justice Stone's opinion is for the most part a recapitulation of the events following the attack on Pearl Harbor. His view was that the actions complained of must be judged against the background of the conditions which confronted the President and Congress in those critical months. After reciting the Japanese successes in the early months of 1942, he informed us that our military authorities knew at the time that by these successes the Japanese had gained a naval superiority in the Pacific which might have made it possible for them to seize Pearl Harbor, the last barrier between Japan and our west coast. Consequently, he thought that "reasonably prudent men" responsible for the defense of the country had "ample ground" for believing that the danger of invasion was real, and that in taking steps to meet it they were justified in considering "our internal situation."

However, since only persons of Japanese ancestry were subject to the curfew restriction, it was necessary for the Court to decide whether "in the light of all the facts and circumstances" there was any basis for the conclusion that the order as applied would help protect the west coast against sabotage and espionage and the threat of invasion. Counsel for Hirabayashi had argued that the curfew should have been applied to everybody in the military area or to no one. "Constitutional government, in time of war, is not so powerless," the Chief

Justice declared, as to compel military authorities to choose between inflicting "obviously needless hardship on the many" or doing nothing in the face of threatened danger.

Chief Justice Stone discussed in some detail the two major considerations which he thought justified the Western Defense Command in taking extraordinary precautions, including the limiting of certain restrictions to persons who happened to be of Japanese extraction. First of all, there was the fact of the concentration in military areas #1 and #2 of vast ship-building facilities and airplane plants and the location in California and Washington of important army and navy bases. The other consideration had to do with the suspicion that Japanese in the west coast states maintained close ties with Japan. In March, 1942, the threat of sabotage and espionage was still real. Germany's invasion of western Europe had proved the danger of the "fifth column" as had also the surprise attack on Pearl Harbor. At a time when invasion by Japanese forces seemed imminent, it was part of the responsibility of the military authorities to take into account the consequences of the "ethnic affiliations" with the invading enemy of persons resident in the danger zone. Not only did the great majority of the persons of Japanese ancestry in the United States reside in California, Oregon and Washington, but they were concentrated in or near Seattle, Portland and Los Angeles, all three cities in military area #1. The members of this particular racial group have remained for the most part unassimilated, and the military authorities were not unaware of their many ties with the land of their forefathers. Among the factors which have prevented the assimilation of the Japanese as an integral part of the white population, Chief Justice Stone noted the economic discrimination against them, the sending of their children to Japanese language schools and for part or all of their education to Japan itself, the maintenance by Japan of a system of dual citizenship, and the association of many prominent persons of Japanese descent with Japanese consulates in this country. The Chief Justice wrote in the HIRABAYASHI case:

> Whatever views we may entertain regarding the loyalty to this country of citizens of Japanese ancestry, we cannot reject as unfounded the judgment of the military authorities and of Congress that there were disloyal members of that population, whose number and strength could not be precisely and quickly ascertained. We cannot say that the war-making branches of the government did not have ground for believing that in a critical hour such persons could not readily be isolated and separately dealt with, and constituted a menace to the national defense and safety, which demanded that prompt and adequate measures be taken to guard against it.[67]

Hirabayashi did not quarrel with the contention that since sabotage is most readily committed in the hours of darkness a curfew was an appropriate safeguard against it. He insisted, however, that the restriction was unconstitutional because it discriminated against citizens of Japanese ancestry in violation of the Fifth Amendment. To this Chief Justice Stone replied that if the restriction was an appropriate exercise of the war power it is no objection that it curtailed the citizen's freedom. Also, unlike the Fourteenth Amendment, the Fifth Amendment contains no equal protection clause and it "restrains only such discriminatory legislation by Congress as amounts to a denial

[67] All the briefs, whether filed directly for Hirabayashi or in behalf of organizations who entered the case to vindicate his contentions, took the position that machinery should have been established for determining the loyalty of each person subject to the exclusion and curfew orders. The American Civil Liberties Union called for the establishment of "hearing boards" to pass upon each individual's claim for exemption. While conceding that such procedures, even though usual in civil administration, could not be demanded by each person before complying with the orders, Mr. Justice Douglas indicated in his concurring opinion that he for one believed that after complying, each person of Japanese ancestry should have been afforded an opportunity to be heard for the purpose of establishing his loyalty.

of due process." This was not the first time that the Supreme
Court implied that the equality clause gives greater protection
against discrimination than does the due process clause of the
Fifth Amendment.[68] It is regrettable, however, that the Court
has not been more enlightening on the precise distinctions.
Whether or not the principle is sound, considering the vital
connection in which it was being applied in the HIRABAYASHI
case, the Court might have ventured to explain more fully.

Declaring that "distinctions between citizens solely because
of their ancestry are by their very nature odious to a free
people whose institutions are founded upon the doctrine of
equality," the Chief Justice asserted that these considerations
would have been "controlling" were it not for the fact that
at a time of danger of sabotage and espionage and threatened
invasion the military commanders must reckon with the loyalty
of the population in the danger zone. Merely because discrimi-
nations on the basis of race are ordinarily unlawful, it does
not follow that Congress and the President are without power
to classify citizens of one racial group differently from others.
If in the circumstances of war and threatened invasion that
group seems to menace the country's security more than others,
the military authorities may treat them as distinct from the
rest of the population.[69]

[68] Nor was it the first time that Chief Justice Stone addressed himself
to the problem. Only five months earlier he had declared: "Unlike the
Fourteenth Amendment, the Fifth contains no equal protection clause and
it provides no guaranty against discriminatory legislation by Congress."
Detroit Bank v. *United States,* 317 U.S. 329, 337 (1943). Despite the many
suggestions of differences in the degree of the protection against discrimination afforded by due process and equal protection, no case has held that
the particular congressional legislation being sustained would have been invalidated were the Fifth Amendment to contain an equal protection clause.
In *Truax* v. *Corrigan,* Chief Justice Taft indicated that the equal protection clause of the Fourteenth Amendment extends greater protection than
is afforded by due process. 257 U.S. 312, 340 (1921).

[69] One of the cases cited by Chief Justice Stone as involving a comparable situation is *Clarke* v. *Deckebach,* 274 U.S. 392 (1927). In an opinion
by Mr. Justice Stone himself, the Court in that case upheld a Cincinnati

Since the two sentences imposed on Hirabayashi were to run concurrently and since it was sustaining his conviction for the violation of the curfew restriction, the Court saw "no occasion" for reviewing his conviction for failing to report to the Civil Control Station. It also refused to pass on the government's contention that compliance with the order to report at a Civilian Control Station would not necessarily be followed by confinement in a relocation center. The Court thus declined even to consider the one objection on which all the briefs filed against the actions of General De Witt placed the greatest emphasis, namely, that the enforced evacuation of persons of Japanese descent was a denial of that minimum equal protection of the laws implicit in the due process clause of the Fifth Amendment.[70]

Summing up, it may be said that the HIRABAYASHI case was decided more on the basis of criteria which Chief Justice Stone has espoused in the commercial field than on the basis of principles for which he has called in the civil rights cases. The Court was concerned primarily with the question whether the conditions within the knowledge of the military authorities afforded "a rational basis" for their action in limiting the curfew to persons of Japanese ancestry. Whether in like cir-

---

ordinance requiring the licensing of pools and billiard rooms and prohibiting the issuance of licenses to aliens. Asserting that even though the Fourteenth Amendment forbids "plainly irrational" discrimination against the alien, Mr. Justice Stone had maintained that it did not follow that "alien race and allegiance may not bear in some instances such a relation to a legitimate object of legislation as to be made the basis of a permitted classification." There was "rational basis" for the legislative judgment that the operation of billiard and pool rooms by aliens constituted a special menace to society and the public welfare, and the Court possessed no such knowledge of local conditions as to enable it to say that the legislature was wrong.

[70] As to the complaint that Congress abdicated its legislative function when it passed the act of March 21, 1942, the Court held that the legislative power of Congress is not unduly delegated when executive and administrative officers are authorized to find the facts on the basis of which they are to apply standards and definitions set down by Congress.

cumstances the Court would have reached a similar conclusion was "irrelevant." It was merely deciding that under the conditions in which it was applied the curfew order was a reasonable exercise of the war powers of the national government.

CHAPTER VII

CONCLUDING: AN ENLIGHTENED VIEW OF THE JUDICIAL FUNCTION

. . . Mr. President, the nomination by the President of Mr. Justice Stone to become Chief Justice of the United States is a very proper and commendable recognition of the ability, courage, and wisdom of Mr. Justice Stone, who has served as Associate Justice of the Supreme Court for quite a number of years.

When Mr. Stone was appointed an Associate Justice of the United States Supreme Court, many years ago, I opposed the confirmation of his nomination and voted against it. In the years that have passed I became convinced, and am now convinced, that in my opposition to the confirmation of his nomination I was entirely in error.

I am now about to perform one of the most pleasant duties that has ever come to me in my official life when I cast a vote in favor of his elevation to the highest judicial office in our land. . . .[1]

WITH THIS tribute and by voting for confirmation, George W. Norris was rectifying what he regarded as a great wrong. In 1925 Senator Norris lectured the Senate on the dangers of the appointment when President Coolidge nominated Harlan Fiske Stone of New York to be an Associate Justice of the Supreme Court. Already incensed by the way Coolidge was filling high offices with men imbued "with the viewpoint of special interests and the corporations," he bitterly attacked the Stone ap-

[1] *87 Cong. Rec. 5618-19* (1941).

pointment, charging that the President was adding to the Supreme Court a man who "has spent all his life in an atmosphere of big business, of corporations, of monopolies and trusts." Such an individual, Norris sought to persuade the Senate, would inevitably carry his point of view as a corporation lawyer into his work on the Bench.[2]

Sixteen years later, when another President elevated Mr. Justice Stone to a still higher place, the Senator was as lavish in his praise as he had been unrelenting in his opposition on the earlier occasion. Basically, the factors explaining this change of heart were no doubt the same as those which may have moved President Roosevelt to name as Chief Justice the man whose big business connections impelled Senator Norris to oppose his original appointment to the Court.[3]

The background of the men Mr. Roosevelt has placed on the Supreme Court is the visible evidence of what he considers to be primary in the qualifications for service on the Court. Of the seven Associate Justices serving by appointment of Mr. Roosevelt, only Mr. Justice Rutledge came to the Bench with the kind of previous judicial experience which could be considered as preparation for service on the high court. James F. Byrnes, who was appointed in 1941 and resigned a year later, was also new to the jurist's art. But all eight had indicated their support of major New Deal domestic policies.

[2] "After all, the viewpoint that takes possession of the human being and becomes a part of his very life, and if he is intrusted with the decision of questions where the ordinary citizen must come in contact with those who have power of wealth and political influence he is capable, while acting conscientiously and honestly, of more injury to humanity than the man who lacks some of his ability. The viewpoint of the individual goes with him through life. The viewpoint is part of the man, is part of the judge; and the judge does not lose his individuality if he has a certain viewpoint as a citizen, but maintains it after he is on the bench." *66 Cong. Rec. 3053* (1925).

[3] Only once before had a sitting Associate Justice been elevated to the Chief Justiceship. In 1910, Associate Justice Edward D. White was nominated by President Taft to be Chief Justice.

The "politics" of a prospective member of the Supreme Court seems to be as decisive for Franklin D. Roosevelt as we know it was for Theodore Roosevelt. In a letter to Senator Lodge in 1902, relevant to the appointment of Judge Holmes to the Supreme Court, Theodore Roosevelt wrote:

In the ordinary and low sense which we attach to the word "partisan" and "politician," a judge of the Supreme Court should be neither. But in the higher sense, in the proper sense, he is not in my judgment fitted for the position unless he is a party man, a constructive statesman, constantly keeping in mind his adherence to the principles and policies under which this nation has been built up and in accordance with which it must go on; and keeping in mind also his relations with his fellow statesmen who in other branches of the government are striving in cooperation with him to advance the ends of government.[4]

In this sense, the "politics" of Mr. Justice Stone must have been entirely to Mr. Roosevelt's liking. For in the years that intervened between his appointment as an Associate Justice and his elevation to the Chief Justiceship, Harlan Fiske Stone had established himself as a leader of that liberal jurisprudence of which Holmes and Brandeis were the trail-blazers.

Powerful as may be the impact of a man's background upon his conduct as a judge, there have been judges who have risen above their environment. Holmes was such an exception. Born and bred aristocrat though he was, as a judge he was able most of the time to keep himself from reading his own sympathies "prematurely into the law." [5]

This observation about Holmes applies also to the present Chief Justice, at least in so far as his experience as a corpora-

---

[4] Quoted in Frankfurter, *Mr. Justice Holmes and the Supreme Court*, p. 21.

[5] "It is a misfortune if a judge reads his conscious or unconscious sympathy with one side or the other prematurely into the law, and forgets that what seemed to him to be first principles are believed by half his fellow men to be wrong." Holmes, *Collected Legal Papers,* p. 295.

tion attorney could have been expected to condition his attitude toward the issues likely to come before the Supreme Court. The reputation he has earned for himself as one of the great liberal jurists of our day is therefore that much more remarkable and for the same reason that much more worthy of commendation. When a man has himself "felt the sting of poverty," it is no tribute to his humanitarianism if his sympathy is on the side of the poor. According to the Norris formula, moreover, all of Harlan Fiske Stone's immediate background might well have inclined him toward those in our society who need no special protection. Not only has he not been imprisoned by his past, but by his labors on the Court he has demonstrated that the responsiblility implicit in the exercise of judicial power, even as the responsibility inhering in high executive office, may serve to evoke latent qualities of statesmanship. In the language of James Bradley Thayer, it may be said that the present Chief Justice is destined to be reckoned among the judges who "perceived" that our constitutions have made of them "coadjutors with the other departments in the business of government." [6] And who can measure the subtle influence upon him of the priceless companionship of Holmes and Brandeis and of Cardozo?

Chief Justice Taft had welcomed Mr. Justice Stone's coming to the Court and even boasted that he had "rather forced the President into his appointment." But by 1929 his good opinion of the new Justice had given way to disappointment, and the cause was the Chief's discovery that the Court's junior member was too often in the company of Holmes and Brandeis. "He [Stone] is a learned lawyer in many ways, but his judgments I do not altogether consider safe," Taft wrote in the spring of that year, explaining, "He definitely has ranged himself with Brandeis and with Holmes in a good many of

[6] Thayer, *Cases on Constitutional Law* (Cambridge: George H. Kent, 1895), pp. V-VI.

our constitutional differences." [7] And we have the word of Cardozo's biographer that "Most devoted to Cardozo of all the Justices at Washington . . . was Harlan Stone.[8]

Mr. Justice Brandeis once remarked that the Constitution was as "big as the minds of men." In his approach to the great issues of our day, Chief Justice Stone has shown that his is no static conception of the Constitution. He has revealed a mind which, while full of admiration for the fundamental law of the land as first formulated, has been able to see it as an instrument of enduring usefulness. That our Constitution is more "tool" than "testament," to borrow an apt phrase from a recent book, is certainly one of the cardinal articles of his constitutional faith.[9] His conception of the Court as "the implement of government" under the Constitution has been in the great tradition of Marshall, whose admonition, "We must never forget that it is a Constitution we are expounding," he has often quoted. And in speaking of the judiciary's function in drawing new authority from old provisions, he has expounded a view of the Constitution which, even for its similarity of language, has the Marshallian ring to it:

. . . in determining whether a provision of the Constitution applies to a new subject matter, it is of little significance that it is one with which the framers were not familiar. For in setting up an enduring framework of government they undertook to carry out for the indefinite future and in all the vicissitudes of the changing affairs of men those fundamental purposes which the instrument itself discloses. Hence we read its words, not as we read legislative codes which are subject to continuous revision with the changing course of events, but as the revelation of the great purposes which were

[7] Henry F. Pringle, *The Life and Times of William Howard Taft* (New York: Farrar & Rinehart, 1939), II, 1043-44.

[8] George S. Hellman, *Benjamin N. Cardozo* (New York: Whittlesey House, 1940), p. 222.

[9] Beryl H. Levy, *Our Constitution: Tool or Testament?* (New York: Alfred A. Knopf, 1941).

intended to be achieved by the Constitution as a continuing instrument of government.[10]

"The final cause of law is the welfare of society," Cardozo once wrote.[11] With this instrumental conception of law the present Chief Justice is completely in accord. Viewing law as "not an end, but a means to an end," he is of the opinion that it performs its function best "only when it is suited to the way of life of a people." Hence he sees as the major problem of modern jurisprudence "the reconciliation of the demands that law shall at once have continuity with the past and adaptability to the present and the future." [12]

Where Chief Justice Stone differs from Marshall, whom he has called the Great Chief Justice, is in his view of the methods by which constitutional cases should be decided. Indeed, his constant concern with the techniques of adjudication is one of the distinctive features of his work on the Court. It is true, of course, that in his advocacy of a more eclectic methodology he was preceded by Holmes and Brandeis, to say nothing of the whole school of sociological jurisprudence. But it must also be noted that he has stopped, perhaps more often than any other member of the Court, to take stock of the processes by which it was adjudicating.

Almost from the beginning of his judicial career, Chief Justice Stone has inveighed against the use of legalistic formulas and labels in the disposition of constitutional cases. Marshall was able to settle great questions of constitutional power with the aid of sweeping generalizations. He frowned upon judicial concern with the minutiae of detail, particularly economic data, surrounding a given case. The present Chief Justice, on

---

[10] *United States* v. *Classic*, 313 U.S. 299, 316 (1941).

[11] *The Nature of the Judicial Process* (New Haven: Yale Univ. Press, 1921), p. 66.

[12] Stone, "Common Law in the United States," *L. Harv. L. Rev.* 4, 11, 20 (Nov. 1936).

the other hand, has played a conspicuous part in the struggle to get the Court to decide cases not on the basis of legal logic but on actual experience. What Walton H. Hamilton said of him in 1932 continues for the most part to be true: "Stone pries critically into a concept and wonders if it is not in itself question-begging." [13] His objection to the kind of "arid constitutionalism" of which Parrington spoke is that it keeps judges from informing themselves of all they should know if they are interested in having a realistic basis for their decisions. Modern constitutional questions ought not to be determined in terms of legal or political abstractions.

Chief Justice Stone has stressed the necessity of deciding constitutional cases with the aid of the fullest available information, whether the facts are "within the range of judicial notice" or were developed at the trial.[14] This method he has applied in numerous cases and has summarized with simplicity its importance for the judicial process:

The questions which come to us are rooted in history and in the social and economic development of the nation. To grasp their significance our study must be extended beyond the examination of precedents and legal formulas, by reading and research in fields extra-legal, which nevertheless have an intimate relation to the genesis of the legal rules we pronounce.[15]

[13] Frankfurter (Ed.), *Mr. Justice Brandeis* (New Haven: Yale Univ. Press, 1932), p. 174.

[14] See the brief memorandum in which he and Mr. Justice Cardozo jointly concurred in *Bordens Farm Products Co.* v. *Baldwin,* 293 U.S. 194, 213 (1934).

[15] Stone, "Fifty Years' Work on the United States Supreme Court", *53 A.B.A. Rep. 259,* 278 (1928). In the same address will be found a pointed reminder to the bar of its responsibility for bringing to the bench the facts underlying social legislation:

"Lawyers, who, in the presentation of a negligence case, would prove with meticulous care every fact surrounding the accident and injury, in this field [social legislation cases] too often go little beyond the challenged statute and the citation of authorities in supposedly analogous cases. The court is thus often left to speculate as to the nature and extent of the social problems giving rise to the legislative problem, or to discover

His opinions abound in informative footnotes setting forth such relevant data as legislative history, the findings of inquiry groups and the fruits of research generally.[16] His exposition of the issues in a case reveals a conscious effort to diminish the scope of the judicial check as much as possible. Very often he will state at the outset of his opinion the exact question raised by the record. Assertions such as "the question for decision is," "we are asked to decide whether," and "it is enough for present purposes to say" occur frequently in Chief Justice Stone's opinions.

A possible explanation for his emphasis on facts, it has been suggested, is that he is conscious that most constitutional issues are raised "in suits between individuals." The importance he attaches to the need for deciding constitutional cases "in relation to the persons and circumstances of the particular case" was cited as proof of his use of common law methods.[17] This analysis was soon confirmed by the Justice himself. He has called our attention to the essential similarity in the way constitutional law and common law have evolved:

While there are variations in the nature of the subject-matter of judicial inquiry, they involve no necessary variation of the method

them by its own researches. Intimate acquaintance with every aspect of the conditions which have given rise to the regulatory problems are infinitely more important to the court than are the citation of authorities or the recital of bare formulas." Pp. 271-72.

16 Chief Justice Stone has also used footnotes as the forum for the discussion of new principles, as he did in the BARNWELL case regarding the political restraints doctrine. Later the ideas may reappear in the text. This is precisely what happened in the GERHARDT and O'KEEFE cases. It may well be that new doctrine is treated in footnotes when he is unable to bring his colleagues along and later when the discussion in conference reveals greater acceptance of those views he takes the bolder action of incorporating the thesis in the body of his opinions. Since he was speaking only for himself in the GOBITIS case, it is understandable why he was able to elaborate so freely the idea first stated in a footnote in the CAROLENE PRODUCTS Co. case.

17 Dowling, Cheatham and Hale, "Mr. Justice Stone and the Constitution," *XXXVI Col. L. Rev. 351*, 380 (March, 1936).

by which the common law has been accustomed to solve its problems. Its method of marking out, as cases arise step by step, the
line between the permitted and the forbidden, by the process of
appraisal and comparison of the experiences of the past and of the
present, is as applicable to the field of public law as of private.
Courts called upon to rule on questions of constitutional power
have thus ready at hand a common-law technique suitable to the
occasion.[18]

This preoccupation with the factual foundations of public
policy is, needless to say, no mere manifestation of academic
interest in rich detail. The method has definite strategic significance for the judicial function in constitutional cases.
Obviously, it would be omitting much history and many psychological factors to attribute mechanical jurisprudence to
the absence of pragmatic tests of constitutionality. It is nevertheless true that even judges who were accustomed to view
statutes "in isolation" or "in vacuo," as Cardozo expressed
it,[19] were occasionally moved to accept the legislative judgment because of the overwhelming factual support for it.
Brewer's approbation of the Brandeis brief in *Muller* v. *Oregon*
is a case in point.

In any event, that "underlying questions of fact may condition the constitutionality of legislation" [20] is a principle which
Chief Justice Stone has done much to vindicate. This practical
approach to the decision of constitutional cases has served
as a kind of *modus vivendi* for nurturing greater judicial tolerance of legislative action, especially in the economic field. In
economic matters, he believes that wide latitude must be allowed
for the legislative appraisal of conditions and for the legislative choice of methods. "Out of a decent respect to an inde-

[18] *L Harv. L. Rev. 4*, 23 (Nov. 1936).
[19] *The Nature of the Judicial Process*, p. 81.
[20] The quoted words are from the opinion of Mr. Justice Brandeis in
O'Gorman v. *Hartford Fire Insurance Co.*, 282 U.S. 251, 257 (1931).

pendent branch of the government," he has said, "legislative
acts must be taken to be based on facts which support their
constitutional validity unless the contrary reasonably appears." [21] A natural corollary to this "salutary principle of
decision" is that the responsibility for showing that the legislation is invalid rests on those who challenge it, and Chief Justice
Stone has stated it quite explicitly. "It is a salutary principle,"
he wrote in 1935, "that the burden of establishing the unconstitutionality of a statute rests on him who assails it." [22] These
views help explain why he found himself so often in disagreement with the conservatives on the Court with respect to the
validity of assailed social legislation. It has been truly said
of him that if his name should find a place among the great
dissenters "it will not be so much because he believed the legislatures so often right as that he conceived it less his province
to say at any time that they were wrong." [23]

In common with other liberal jurists, Chief Justice Stone has
insisted that it is not the "business of courts to sit in judgment
on the wisdom of legislative action." [24] As an appeal for judicial humility and objectivity, the principle is understandable
enough, particularly when seen in the light of the circumstance
that judges were striking down statutes largely because of
their aversion to the economic or social theory they embodied.
To maintain, however, that "courts are concerned only with
the power to enact statutes, not with their wisdom," [25] is to
ignore how tenuous the distinction really is between questions
of wisdom or policy and questions of power. It will doubtless
always be true, as Charles Evans Hughes observed some time
ago, that men "holding strong convictions as to the unwisdom

21 *Colgate* v. *Harvey*, 296 U.S. 404, 440 (1935).
22 *Metropolitan Casualty Ins. Co.* v. *Brownell*, 294 U.S. 580, 584 (1935).
23 *XXXVI Columbia L. Rev.* 351, 380 (1936).
24 *United States* v. *Butler*, 297 U.S. 1, 78 (1936).
25 *Ibid.*

of legislation may easily pass to the position that it is wholly unreasonable." [26]

There is in fact a curious dualism (some would say contradiction) to the liberal conception of the judicial function. This is as true of Chief Justice Stone as it was of Holmes, Brandeis and Cardozo. As legal realists, all recognize the essentially subjective character of the judicial process which, in the United States, is further accentuated by the broad, undefined phraseology of the vital clauses of the Constitution. Mr. Justice Holmes summed up this psychological imponderable in one short sentence: "The decision will depend on a judgment or intuition more subtle than any articulate major premise." [27]

And yet despite this analysis of the real roots of judicial decisions, all four have chided their colleagues for reading into the Constitution private notions of public policy. To be sure, judges who are convinced that a progressive society must be free to engage in necessary experiments are naturally disturbed when such efforts are blocked by narrowly conceived interpretations of constitutional provisions.[28] It is such interpretations, furthermore, which help to create the impression that the Constitution itself is a barrier to social progress. The "caveat"

[26] *The Supreme Court of the United States* (Long Island: Garden City Publishing Co., 1936), p. 38.

[27] *Lochner* v. *New York,* 198 U.S. 45, 76 (1905).

[28] No more striking illustration of the fundamental clash in social outlook which often separated the conservative majority from the liberal minority on the Supreme Court is needed than the debate between Justice Holmes and Chief Justice Taft in *Truax* v. *Corrigan* regarding the relation of the Constitution to social experimentation. "There is nothing that I more deprecate [Justice Holmes declared while dissenting in that case] than the use of the Fourteenth Amendment beyond the absolute compulsion of its words to prevent the making of social experiments that an important part of a community desires, in the insulated chambers afforded by the several states, even though the experiments may seem futile or even noxious to me and to those whose judgment I most respect." 257 U.S. 312, 344 (1921). This was no doubt said in reply to the assertion of the Chief Justice (who spoke for the majority) that "The Constitution was intended —its very purpose was—to prevent experimentation with the fundamental rights of the individual." *Ibid.,* p. 338.

which Felix Frankfurter addressed to the judiciary in 1930 will always be timely:

> The need for rigorous objectivity, for scrupulous alertness, against confounding personal convictions upon ephemeral policies with enduring principles of right and wrong, becomes all the more manifest when we consider the exact scope of issues that must frequently solicit the judgment of the Court.[29]

When applied to the function performed by the Supreme Court, however, the criticism directed against certain Justices for translating personal views into constitutional law may be misleading, if not actually productive of unfortunate consequences.[30] Nor is this said in the name of logical consistency. The truth of the matter is that the artificial dichotomy between questions of mere wisdom and questions of power may itself contribute to lay ignorance concerning the nature of judicial review. Considering the extent of popular acquiescence in the authority exercised by the Supreme Court, too much cannot be said for depicting that authority in its true light, as a power which enables the Court to control the activities of government —national, state and local.[31] Its veto is all the more decisive

[29] *Law and Politics*, p. 35.

[30] In his brilliant essay on "The Jurist's Art" written on the occasion of the nationwide celebration of the seventy-fifth birthday of Mr. Justice Brandeis, Walton H. Hamilton reminded us that the truism that the judge cannot be separated from the man applies also to such "self-restrained" jurists as Holmes and Brandeis. He wrote:
"Although he is intellectually aware and the most self-restrained of judges, the universe of ideas which lives in Mr. Justice Holmes' head is an essential ingredient in his constitutional law. The very conception of the instrumental character of the mechanism of justice makes the intellectual views of the man dominant in the opinions of Mr. Justice Brandeis." Frankfurter (Ed.), *Mr. Justice Brandeis,* p. 183.

[31] In terms of political and legal theory, one of the best statements on the exact scope of the power exercised by the Supreme Court is to be found in an article which Professor John Dickinson (who is now general counsel of the Pennsylvania Railroad) contributed to the *Political Science Quarterly* in 1927. Speaking of the "location" of sovereignty in the United States, he wrote: "All the organs of a sovereign power function as parts of

in view of the essential ambiguity of important constitutional clauses and the rigidity of the formal amending process, not to mention the powerful pressures which can be counted on to mobilize resistance to needed constitutional reform. Add to this the popular identification of the Supreme Court with the Constitution—an American "myth" of extraordinary tenacity which has been shaken, but never shattered, when the people have been aroused over some unpopular decision—and the factors explaining the highly strategic position of the Court speak for themselves. And while the fact that the Court's great power is exercised negatively may render hazardous any final judgment as to its exact strength as a directing force in our society, it should not for that reason discourage, much less preclude, candid analysis.

It is difficult to believe that any useful or genuinely patriotic purpose can be served by obscuring the personal equation in judicial review.[32] "Every discussion of the Constitution of the

a single system with an ultimate organ, the Supreme Court, to define authoritatively the sphere of each and to restrain each within its sphere. It is the presence of such an organ with the ultimate power to pass authoritatively upon questions of disputed competence which binds the multiplicity of law-pronouncing organs into a single unified system and preserves sovereignty by making it possible to secure a final authoritative determination of what is and what is not law." And to the argument that a decision of the Supreme Court may be recalled by an amendment to the Constitution, Professor Dickinson replied that even if resort is had to the amending power to reverse the Court "the last word remains with the Court through its power to establish authoritatively the validity and meaning of the amendment." "A Working Theory of Sovereignty," *XLII Poli. Sci. Quart. 524,* 540-41 (1927).

[32] For some, it would seem, awareness of the subjective elements in the act of constitutional interpretation seems to depend on whether or not they approve of the results reached. This is amply illustrated in the speech which Frank J. Hogan, a former president of the American Bar Association, delivered before the 1939 meeting of the Association. Obviously disturbed by the way in which the Supreme Court was at the time redefining "constitutional limits," Mr. Hogan wanted to know "if the Constitution is to be construed to mean what the majority at any given period in history wish it to mean, why a written Constitution and deliberate processes of amendment?" But apparently unaware of any contradiction he also said: "Recognizing that many of the historic dissents of Holmes and

United States," Charles A. Beard has said, "proceeds . . . with reference to some conception or conceptions already in the minds of those who participate in it. Every discussion occurs at some time and in some place." [33] For more than fifty years now, the dominant issue in American constitutional law has been the relation of government to business. To deny that in its response to this issue the Court has been acting as arbiter of public policy, is to endeavor to refute the irrevocable history of the whole period. That the conservative majority on the Court for a long time adhered to economic orthodoxy in interpreting relevant constitutional provisions was also a vital factor in this history.[34] The same can also be said with respect to the alleged "retreat to the Constitution" started in the spring of 1937.

As the "unacknowledged legislators" of the nation, to paraphrase Shelley, there rests on the Justices of the Supreme Court no small responsibility for frankly avowing that the Court is engaged in judicial law-making. Of course, not even jurists given to boldness of speech are free to discuss public affairs in the manner of non-judicial policy-makers. Realism in constitutional law stops short of that; judicial utterance is inevitably circumscribed by the forms and jargon of the trade. Yet only by acknowledging that the Supreme Court is a political institution performing a political function can we hope to escape from naïve notions as to the nature of our Constitution and to foster a more informed public understanding

Brandeis have now been transferred from the minority to the majority side of the Court, the day must come when the future chroniclers of our judicial history, in according unstinted praise to the rugged sturdiness of McReynolds and Butler, shown in their courageous efforts to preserve landmark after landmark of the law, will likewise record that their ringing dissents in this day become rules of decision in a later generation." *64 A.B.A. Rep. 478,* 479 (1939).

[33] "Historiography and the Constitution," reprinted in Conyers Read (Ed.), *The Constitution Reconsidered,* p. 159.

[34] See Max Lerner, "The Supreme Court and American Capitalism," *42 Yale L. Jour. 668* (March, 1933).

of the Court's place in the American system of government. Rather than deny, it would be better to proclaim that the Court does indeed exercise "the powers of a super-legislature." [35] Perhaps then more of the Court's members might more often give heed to what Max Lerner has vividly characterized as Mr. Justice Stone's "agonizing cry *de profundis*"— "the only check upon our own exercise of power is our own sense of self-restraint." [36]

It is in the civil liberty sphere that Chief Justice Stone would allow, if not indeed encourage, the exercise of judicial discretion. He draws a distinction between the Court's limited role in reviewing legislation affecting business activities and its much more penetrating scrutiny of measures which operate to repress "freedom of the human mind and spirit." Fundamentally, this contrast is implicit in the Holmes-Brandeis theory of toleration of legislation. Justice Holmes deviated more frequently than did "Brother Brandeis." But though both deferred to the legislative judgment more often than not, neither Justice hesitated to restrain the legislature when he was convinced that "liberty of the mind" was at stake.

To Chief Justice Stone, however, must be given the credit for raising the distinction to the level of explicit constitutional doctrine. The judicial function in passing judgment on the validity of legislation embodying economic policy stops with the determination that the legislature had a "rational basis" for adopting the challenged regulation.

Chief Justice Stone has succeeded in committing the Court

---

[35] Mr. Justice Brandeis dissenting in *Burns Baking Co.* v. *Bryan*, 264 U.S. 504, 534 (1924).

Of all the analogies, Professor Henry Steele Commager's characterization of the Court as a "continuous constitutional convention" is most realistic, as it is peculiarly accurate. Its inescapable inference is, of course, that since constitutional law is the Constitution, the Supreme Court in effect exercises constituent powers. "Constitutional History and the Higher Law," Conyers Read Collection, p. 231.

[36] *Ideas Are Weapons* (New York: The Viking Press, 1939), p. 464.

to the proposition that its veto power is greater in respect to litigation growing out of attempts to curtail fundamental civil rights, particularly the four freedoms of the First Amendment. In favor of safeguarding liberty of the mind, he is prepared to weigh the legislative restriction in the light of possible alternatives and to substitute the Court's view of what is necessary or appropriate in the given circumstances for that of the legislature. It is this aspect of the Chief Justice's conception of the judicial function which has come under the fire of Mr. Justice Frankfurter.

Mr. Justice Frankfurter would confine the judicial inquiry in constitutional cases to the single issue "whether legislators could in reason have enacted such a law." [37] He insists that this should be the sole test of constitutionality, irrespective of the character of the governmental action or the "phase of liberty" with which the case may be concerned. His opinions in the GOBITIS and BARNETTE cases are fervent pleas for "judicial self-restraint" and for the "free play of the democratic process." He argues that so long as all the "effective means of inducing political changes are left free," civil liberty is best safeguarded when men are free to "fight out the wise use of legislative authority in the forum of public opinion and before legislative assemblies." [38]

With all respect due so valiant a defender of human rights as Mr. Justice Frankfurter proved himself to be long before coming to the Supreme Court, one may nevertheless question

[37] Dissenting in *West Virginia State Board of Education* v. *Barnette,* 319 U.S. 624, 647 (1943).
[38] Professor Henry Steele Commager has published an elaborate defense of the Frankfurter position. *Majority Rule and Minority Rights* (New York: Oxford University Press, 1943). Professor Commager seeks to show that history justifies Mr. Justice Frankfurter's long-range view that a circumscribed judicial power and freer rein for legislatures serve the interests of popular democracy, including civil rights. For this reason, he finds that the Justice's GOBITIS and BARNETTE opinions are in the best tradition of Thomas Jefferson's faith in the people.

the soundness of his conclusions in the flag salute cases. For more than a quarter of a century, he strove to illuminate the threat to democratic politics inherent in the abuse of judicial power. It is entirely fitting, therefore, that he should seek to give practical effect to a life-long belief now that he is in a position to help direct the use of that power.

In the final analysis, his attitude toward the flag salute issue springs from his conviction that the courts cannot ulti- mately guarantee toleration in the United States. However, it is one thing to preach this profoundly important truth, but it is a very different matter (and a dangerous concession to consistency) for the Supreme Court, when dealing with a case of intolerance, to disregard the consequences of its action. None but the naïve-minded and perhaps some of the more avid admirers of judicial supremacy would contend that the Court can replace the hearts and minds of the people as the real guardians of "cherished liberty."

Whether the Supreme Court should retain its power of judi- cial review is, of course, a legitimate matter for debate. And much of Mr. Justice Frankfurter's impassioned dissent in the BARNETTE case would have been far more relevant if that were the question before the country. It would be unfair, however, to attribute to him a desire to see judicial review abolished. Quite the contrary is true. Not only does he not call for its "rejec- tion" but sees much good in it.[39]

Another difficulty with Mr. Justice Frankfurter's position in the flag salute cases is that it poses non-existent alterna- tives. Realistically, the problem is not whether we shall substi-

---

[39] Thus he declared in the BARNETTE case: "One's conception of the Con- stitution cannot be severed from one's conception of the judge's function in applying it. The Court has no reason for existence if it merely reflects the pressures of the day. Our system is built on the faith that men set apart for this special function, freed from the influences of immediacy and from the deflections of worldly ambition, will become able to take a view of longer range than the period of responsibility entrusted to Con- gress and legislatures." 319 U.S. 624, 665 (1943).

tute judicial supervision for "eternal vigilance." No one is suggesting that "adjudicated law" alone can assure good will toward dissident groups.

"The essence of religious liberty," Mr. Justice Frankfurter tells us, demands that "no religion shall receive either the state's support or incur its hostility." Granted that this is a sound principle, the question still is: What should the Court do when it has before it regulations requiring of the members of a religious minority public affirmation of that which is forbidden by their religion and from which they might well be exempted without palpable harm to the community? If the issue concerned a group which was not the object of violent persecution, Mr. Justice Frankfurter's emphasis on society's stake in the cultivation of civic loyalties as the foundation of "national cohesion" would probably find few dissenters. But the question of a compulsory flag salute must be viewed against the background of the sober fact that the specific group concerned is a helpless and harmless religious minority which has incurred the active hostility of numerous communities. So seen, the all important aspect of the controversy is the effect of the Court's decision on the treatment of that minority.[40] If it be said in reply that such considerations would involve the Court in matters of wisdom, the answer must be that "evaluation of interest and appraisal of their need for protection" [41] are a partial

[40] Contrasting the issue of a compulsory flag salute with the problem in *Meyer* v. *Nebraska,* Max Lerner has well summarized the objections to the result in the Gobitis case under three headings:

". . . first, the salute to the flag, however important its symbolic value, seems substantially a good deal less important as a means to social cohesiveness than the exclusive use of English in teaching in the schools; second, the value subordinated in the Gobitis case—the complete freedom of conscience—seems considerably more important than the right to have a child taught in German in the schools. Third, the instances of mob violence against members of the Jehovah's Witnesses sect that followed the Gobitis decision indicated that the need for protecting them as a minority was a real one." *The Mind and Faith of Justice Holmes,* p. 320.

[41] The quoted words are those of Professor Noel T. Dowling from an article he wrote soon after Mr. Justice Stone was elevated to the Chief

assurance that the "world's most mighty court" will exercise its power with some thought to the social consequences of judicial action.

It is doubtless true, as the Court was fond of saying in the race segregation cases, that human prejudice will not be eradicated by legislative fiat. And the same could be said about the power of courts. But Holmes taught us long ago that to generalize is to omit. Deeply ingrained habits and attitudes will not be exorcised by any single step, regardless of the department of government from which it emanates. Yet, since courts and legislatures are also in society, faith in improvement through orderly progress would suggest that what they do or refrain from doing may have a telling effect on the mental climate of the community.

Courts are in a position to influence public thinking; and when the tribunal is the United States Supreme Court, its weight in that regard is immeasurably greater. As Professor Frankfurter himself observed some years ago: "The influence of the Court permeates even beyond its technical jurisdiction." [42] When the particular situation is such that the Court by its own decision may lessen or intensify persecution of a given minority, the spirit of the Bill of Rights would seem to leave it but one course of action. The basis of its responsibility was defined by Mr. Justice Jackson when he declared: "We act in these matters not by authority of our competence but by

---

Justiceship. Addressing himself to the "deeper reasons" for the recent shifts in constitutional doctrine he wrote: "The Court is not, as some would believe, merely withdrawing from the constitutional arena and leaving the field open for legislative action. It has been reexamining its position in this governmental scheme in an effort to determine where it may appropriately interpose a judicial check, and where it should stay out. And this has involved, I believe, a greater recognition of the play of opinion and of the estimates of the wisdom of legislative action, of evaluation of interests and appraisal of their need for protection, than the Court is wont to admit." "The Methods of Mr. Justice Stone in Constitutional Cases," *XLI Columbia L. Rev. 1160,* 1164 (Nov., 1941).

[42] *Law and Politics,* p. 30.

force of our commissions." [43]

Mr. Justice Frankfurter was among those who criticized the erstwhile conservative majorities for exalting property rights above the "rights of man" in their interpretation of constitutional guarantees. Now that the Court sees no incompatability between the rights of private property and public control of business enterprise, a similar "laissez-faire" attitude toward measures restrictive of civil rights may itself encourage intolerance. The Court has an opportunity to contribute to the solution of a major conundrum of the twentieth century: Can a government bent on assuring economic security to the masses be relied on to respect their civil and political rights?

Civil liberty is not so secure that the country can dispense with the appellate services of the Supreme Court. America has its serious danger spots where liberty of the individual and of the group is concerned; but America is also a land whose court of last resort enjoys tremendous prestige. While the Supreme Court alone cannot guarantee toleration, it can serve as a valuable ally in the fight against intolerance.

When it overruled the GOBITIS decision, the Court emphatically endorsed Chief Justice Stone's view of its special duty in guarding civil liberties. Within a period of three years, the lone dissenter in the GOBITIS case saw his ideas embodied in an opinion to which only three Justices took exception. It is already obvious, however, that his notable success in this field

[43] Mr. Jackson has indicated that he has few illusions as to the real nature of judicial review and has discussed the problem with no little insight:

"For a century every contest with the Supreme Court has ended in evading the basic inconsistency between popular government and judicial supremacy. None of the really influential critics of the Court have proposed destroying it or impairing its powers, and none have been able to suggest a hopeful formula for controlling it. None of the leaders of American democracy have yet been willing to risk democracy without some judicial restraint. So now, as always before, the struggle against judicial excess has ended by leaving it to the Justices themselves to correct the errors of the Court." *The Struggle for Judicial Supremacy,* p. vii.

is no guide to the present alignments on the Court, which are by no means that clearly defined.

History is repeating itself; and the calm and unanimity which some anticipated from a Court dominated by men appointed by the same President have given way to dissension and frequent articulation of differences. That the divergences are deeply felt is revealed by the caustic tone of many of the utterances. The new groupings are bound to try the Chief Justice's qualities of leadership, as the new issues are destined to test the resilience of his liberalism. Whatever posterity may judge his ultimate contribution to be, at the moment the American people owe Chief Justice Stone much for helping significantly to vindicate a more enlightened view of the judicial function.

TABLE OF CASES

*Adams Manufacturing Co. v. Storen, 82-85, 88, 90
*Adkins v. Children's Hospital, 166n., 171n., 175-78, 181
Alabama v. King and Boozer, 46n.
Allen v. Regents of University System, 33n.
American Federation of Labor v. National Labor Relations Board, 159n.
Associated Press v. National Labor Relations Board, 125n.

Bailey v. Drexel Furniture Co., 106n., 122n.
Baldwin v. Seelig, 96n.
Baltimore National Bank v. State Tax Commission, 38
Bingaman v. Golden Eagle Western Lines, 75n.
Borden's Farm Products Co. v. Baldwin, 261n.
Bowman v. Chicago & N.W. Ry. Co., 54n.
Brooks v. United States, 132n.
Brown v. Maryland, 49n., 50-51, 52-54
Brush v. Commissioner, 26n., 35, 36
Brushaber v. Union Pacific R.R. Co., 35n.
Bunting v. Oregon, 165n.
Burns Baking Co. v. Bryan, 269n.
*Burnet v. Coronado Oil and Gas Co., 23-24

California v. Thompson, 92n.
*Carmichael v. Southern Coal and Coke Co., 183-92
*Carter v. Carter Coal Co., 123-24
Chamberlin v. Andrews, 183n.
Champion v. Ames, 130
Chicago Board of Trade v. Olsen, 121n.
Civil Rights Cases, 205n.
Clark Distilling Co. v. Western Maryland Co., 55n.

* The asterisk indicates that the case is discussed in some detail.

Clarke v. *Deckebach*, 252n.

Clarke v. *Paul Gray, Inc.*, 75n.

*Clyde Mallory Lines v. *Alabama*, 69-71, 73

Colgate v. *Harvey*, 199n., 264n.

Collector v. *Day*, 9, 30, 31n., 34-37 *passim*, 41

Compania General de Tabacos de Filipinas v. *Collector*, 93n.

Cooley v. *Board of Port Wardens*, 39n., 51-52, 61

*Cudahy Packing Co., Ltd, v. *Holland*, 146-52

Davis v. *Massachusetts*, 202n.

Davidson v. *New Orleans*, 162n.

De Jonge v. *Oregon*, 203n.

Detroit Bank v. *United States*, 252n.

*DiSanto v. *Pennsylvania*, 56-60, 65, 92, 166

Dobbins v. *Erie County*, 6n., 9, 36

Edelman v. *Boeing Air Transport, Inc.*, 67

*Educational Films Corp. of America v. *Ward*, 17-20

Edwards v. *California*, 199n.

Evans v. *Gore*, 35n.

Ex parte Milligan, 235-36, 244

*Ex parte Quirin, 236-45, 248

Ex parte Yarbrough, 206

Fallbrook Irrigation Co. v. *Bradley*, 187n.

Federal Land Bank v. *Priddy*, 29n.

Federal Power Commission v. *Natural Gas Pipeline Co.*, 158n., 232n.

*Fisher's Blend Station v. *State Tax Commission*, 76-78, 81n., 82

Fiske v. *Kansas*, 195n.

Florida v. *Mellon*, 183n.

Fox Film Corporation v. *Doyal*, 19n.

Gibbons v. *Ogden*, 48-50, 130

Gillespie v. *Oklahoma*, 23-24

*Graves v. *New York* ex rel, *O'Keefe*, 36-41, 44, 46, 47, 262n.

Green v. *Frazier*, 187n.

Greiner v. *Lewellyn* 14n.

Group #1 Oil Corp. v. *Bass*, 24, 41n.

Grosjean v. *American Press*, 195n.

Grovey v. *Townsend*, 205n.

Gwin, White & Prince v. *Henneford*, 85-88

Hague v. *Committee for Industrial Organization*, 197-204

Hale v. *Bimco Trading Co.*, 96n.

Hamilton v. *Regents*, 217n.

Hammer v. *Dagenhart*, 122n., 130

Helson v. *Kentucky*, 66

Helvering v. *Gerhardt*, 25-36, 40, 41n., 262n.

Helvering v. *Mountain Producers Corp.*, 25n., 41n.

Helvering v. *Powers*, 26n., 33, 35

Herndon v. *Lowry*, 203n.

Hirabayashi v. *United States*, 245-54

Home Insurance Co. v. *New York*, 14n.

Houston E. & W. Ry. Co. v. *United States*, 113n., 133

Indian Motorcycle Co. v. *United States*, 21-23

Ingels v. *Morf*, 73-75

In re *Rahrer*, 55n.

Interstate Buses Corporation v. *Blodgett*, 67-69, 74

James v. *Dravo Contracting Co.*, 13n., 41n.

Jones v. *Opelika*, 316 U.S. 584 (1942), 221-27

Jones v. *Opelika*, 319 U.S. 103 (1943), 227n.

Kentucky Whip and Collar Co. v. *Illinois Central R.R. Co.*, 55n., 132n.

Leisy v. *Hardin*, 54n., 55

License Cases, 51

Loan Association v. *Topeka*, 187n.

Lochner v. *New York*, 165, 166, 176, 181, 265n.

Long v. *Rockwood*, 18n., 19

Lovell v. *City of Griffin*, 224

*Macallen Co. v. Massachusetts, 13-20

Marbury v. Madison, 3n.

*Massachusetts v. Mellon, 99n., 101-103

McCarroll v. Dixie Greyhound Lines, 94n.

*McCulloch v. Maryland, 1n., 2n., 5-10, 18n., 28-29, 38, 50

*McGoldrick v. Berwind-White Coal Mining Co., 88-91, 95

*Metcalf & Eddy v. Mitchell, 10-13, 14, 41n.

Metropolitan Casualty Ins. Co. v. Brownell, 264n.

Meyer v. Nebraska, 194n., 195n., 272n.

*Miller v. Schoene, 163-66

Miller v. Wilson, 165n.

*Minersville School District v. Gobitis, 216-22, 226-29, 262n., 270-72, 274

Missouri, Kansas & Texas Ry. Co. v. May, 232n.

*Morehead v. New York ex rel. Tipadlo, 99n, 178-82

*Morf v. Bingaman, 71-74

Morgan v. United States, 298 U.S. 468 (1936), 140n.

Morgan v. United States, 304 U.S. 1 (1937), 140n.

Mulford v. Smith, 116n., 132n.

Muller v. Oregon, 165n., 171n., 175, 263n.

Munn v. Illinois, 161n., 166

*Murdock v. Pennsylvania, 227-28

Nashville, Chattanooga & St. Louis Railway Co. v. Wallace, 67

*National Labor Relations Board v. Columbian Enameling & Stamping Co., 152-57

National Labor Relations Board v. Fansteel Metallurgical Corp., 152n., 153

National Labor Relations Board v. Friedman-Harry Marks Clothing Co., 124n.

National Labor Relations Board v. Fruehauf Trailer Co., 124n.

National Labor Relations Board v. Jones and Laughlin Steel Corp., 124n., 125n.

National Labor Relations Board v. Sands Manufacturing Co., 152n., 153

Near v. Minnesota, 195 n., 203

Nebbia v. New York, 174, 181

*Newberry v. United States, 206-207, 210, 213
New State Ice Co. v. Liebmann, 173n.
New York ex rel. Cohn v. Graves, 40n.
New York ex rel. Rogers v. Graves, 36, 41
Nixon v. Condon, 205n.
Nixon v. Herndon, 205n.
Northwest Airlines v. Minnesota, 97n.

O'Gorman v. Hartford Fire Insurance Co., 263
Ohio v. Helvering, 26n., 33
*Opp Cotton Mills, Inc., v. Administrator, 142-45
Osborne v. United States Bank, 114n.

Pacific Co. v. Johnson, 20n.
Palko v. Connecticut, 195n.
Panama Refining Co. v. Ryan, 140n.
Panhandle Oil Co. v. Mississippi, 17n., 21, 23, 46n.
Pennsylvania Coal Co. v. Mahon, 165n.
Philadelphia & S.M. Steamship Co. v. Pennsylvania, 87n
Pittman v. Home Owners' Loan Corporation, 46n.
Plumley v. Massachusetts, 59n.
Pollock v. Farmers Loan and Trust Co., 35n.
Postal Telegraph-Cable Co. v. Richmond, 93n.
Powell v. Alabama, 195n.
Powell v. Pennsylvania, 161n.

Railroad Retirement Board v. Alton R.R. Co., 99n., 191n.
Reynolds v. United States, 216n.
*Ribnick v. McBride, 168-74
Robbins v. Shelby County Taxing District, 53-54, 65

St. Joseph Stockyards Co. v. United States, 137n.
St. Louis and O'Fallon Ry. Co. v. United States, 158n.
*Schechter Brothers Poultry Corp. v. United States, 99n., 122-24,
    127, 141n., 178
Scott v. Sandford, 2n.
*Slaughter-House Cases, 160-63, 198n., 200

Smith v. *Allwright*, 205n.

South Carolina v. *United States*, 26n., 31n., 33

South Carolina State Highway Department v. *Barnwell Bros., Inc.*, 60-65, 94n., 262n.

Sprout v. *City of South Bend*, 64n., 95n.

Stafford v. *Wallace*, 121n.

State Tax Commission v. *Van Cott*, 41n.

Steward Machine Co. v. *Davis*, 119, 183n.

Stromberg v. *California*, 195n., 203n.

Sunshine Anthracite Coal Co. v. *Adkins*, 120n., 124

Switchmen's Union v. *National Mediation Board*, 159n.

Texas & New Orleans R.R. Co. v. *Brotherhood of Ry. & SS. Clerks*, 121n.

Texas v. *White*, 45n.

The Selective Draft Law Cases, 216n.

Truax v. *Corrigan*, 166n., 192n., 252n., 265n.

Tyson Brothers v. *Banton*, 166-68, 170-71

United States v. *Butler*, 98-119, 159n., 187, 264n.

United States v. *California*, 32n.

United States v. *Carolene Products Co.*, 194n., 218, 220, 262n.

United States v. *Classic*, 205-15, 260n.

United States v. *Constantine*, 99n., 108n.

United States v. *Cruikshank*, 198n., 200

United States v. *Darby*, 128-35, 142

United States v. *E. C. Knight Co.*, 122

United States v. *Hudson*, 212n.

United States v. *Morgan*, 307 U. S. 183 (1939), 140

United States v. *Morgan*, 313 U. S. 409 (1941), 140n.

United States v. *Perkins*, 14n.

Virginian Railway Co. v. *System Federation #40*, 125n.

Washington, Virginia and Maryland Coach Co. v. *National Labor Relations Board*, 125n., 126n.

Welton v. *Missouri*, 88n.

West v. *Chesapeake and Potomac Telephone Co.,* 158n.
West Coast Hotel Co. v. *Parrish,* 182
West Virginia Board of Education v. *Barnette,* 228-34, 270-72
Western Livestock v. *Bureau of Revenue,* 76, 78-83
Western Union Telegraph Co. v. *Kansas,* 76n.
Weston v. *Charleston,* 6n., 9n., 43n.
Whitfield v. *Ohio,* 55n.
Williams v. *Mississippi,* 214n.
Wilson v. *New,* 121n., 165n.
Woodruff v. *Parham,* 53, 90

Yasui v. *United States,* 245n.

INDEX

Acheson, Dean G., 180n.
administrative process, definition of, 136n.
Agricultural Adjustment Act of 1933, 100-101
Agricultural Adjustment Act of 1938, 116n.
Aiken, Charles, 125n.
Alabama Unemployment Compensation Act, 183-92
American Bar Association, 94n., 267n.
American Bar Association Reports, 94n., 97n., 141n., 261n., 268n.
American Civil Liberties Union, 197n., 248n., 251n.
American Federation of Labor, 153
American Political Science Association, 138n.
American Political Science Review, 138n., 193n., 238n.
Articles of Confederation, 42
Articles of War, 239-42
assembly, right of, 196, 197-204
Attorney General's Committee on Administrative Procedure, 136n., 138, 150n.

Beard, Charles A., 268
Beveridge, Albert J., 3n., 6n., 7n.
Biddle, Attorney General Francis, 237
Bituminous Coal Act of 1937, 123
Bituminous Coal Conservation Act of 1935, 123
Black, Justice Hugo L., 35-36, 83-85, 87-88, 95n., 96, 154n., 155, 156n., 159, 198, 199n., 210, 223, 226, 227n., 228, 229, 230n., 232n.
Bradley, Justice Joseph P., 10n., 34n., 53-54, 65-66

Brandeis, Justice Louis D., 14n., 17n., 18n., 20n., 23n., 24n., 35, 43, 57, 64n., 92n., 95n., 137n., 154n., 158, 165n., 173n., 175, 182, 205, 207n., 257, 258, 259, 260, 265, 266n., 268n., 269
Brandeis brief, 165, 175, 180n., 263
Brewer, Justice David J., 165n., 175, 263
Bryce, James, 1
Bureau of Internal Revenue, 44n.
Butler, Justice Pierce, 17n., 19n., 20n., 35n., 36n., 47, 56, 89n., 178, 191n., 202n., 268n.
Byrnes, Justice James F., 199n., 227n., 256

California "caravan" laws, 73, 75n.
Cardozo, Justice Benjamin N., 20n., 99n., 108n., 119, 182, 195n., 205, 258, 259, 260, 261n., 263, 265
Chafee, Zechariah, Jr., 193n., 203n.
Chamberlain, Joseph P., 138n.
Chase, Chief Justice Salmon P., 45n., 236n.
Cheatham, Elliott E., 262n.
Child Labor Law, 132n.
civil liberty cases, judicial review in, *see* Stone
Civil Rights Act of 1871, 202
Civil War, 162n., 235
Clarke, Justice John H., 23n., 93, 207n.
Clayton Anti-Trust Act, 133n.
Coasting License Law of 1793, 49
collective bargaining, *see* Stone
Collier, Charles S., 111n.
Columbia Law Review, 96n., 151n., 193n., 262n., 264n., 272n.
combatants, lawful and unlawful, 241-43

Commager, Henry Steele, 269n., 270n.

commerce clause cases, judicial function in, *see* Stone

Committee on Ministers' Powers, 138

"competitive federalism," 135n.

Congress: consent of, 45-46, 55, 94n.; intent of, 29-30, 45-46, 147-48; silence of, 38-39, 51-52, 87, 89-90

Congress of Industrial Organizations, 197, 199

contractural power of federal government, 111n.

Coolidge, President Calvin, 255

Corrupt Practices Act of 1910, 206

Corwin, Edward S., 3, 107n., 114, 121n., 135n., 160, 193

Curtis, Justice Benjamin R., 52

Cushman, Robert E., 160n., 162n., 238n.

Davis, Justice David, 236, 244n.

Day, Justice William R., 132n., 206n.

DeWitt, Lieutenant-General J. L., 247, 253

Dicey, A. V., 4

Dickinson, John, 157n., 266n.

District of Columbia Minimum Wage Law, 175-78

Douglas, Justice William O., 88n., 95n., 120, 123, 148-52, 159, 199n., 210-15, 223, 226-28, 229, 230, 232n., 251n.

Dowell, Colonel Cassius M., 237

Dowling, Noel T., 96n., 138n., 262n., 272n.

"dual federalism," 135n.

due process of law, 64, 93, 160-93, 199-201, 216, 245-54

employment agencies, regulation of, 168-74

Epstein, Solicitor General Henry J., 37, 177-78, 180n.

equal protection of the laws, 161n., 184, 205n., 207n., 252-53

equity, 140

Evans, Harold, 248n.

Fair Labor Standards Act, 128-33, 142-52

Federal Bureau of Investigation, 237

Federalists, 42, 50

Federal Trade Commission, 147

Field, Justice Stephen J., 88, 161-62

Fifth Amendment, 174, 243-44, 251-52

First Amendment, 197, 230-31, 270

Flag Salute Cases, 216-22, 228-34, 270-72

"flexible" tariff clause, 145n.

Ford, Henry, 206n.

Fourteenth Amendment, 40n., 63, 160-61, 166, 174, 182, 184, 186-87, 195, 199n., 200, 205n., 209, 216, 228-34 251, 265n.

Fraenkel, Osmond K., 248n.

Frankfurter, Justice Felix, 3n., 36n., 47n., 49n., 50, 51n., 55, 88n., 95n., 97, 154n., 175, 180, 194n., 199n., 216-22 228-29, 231-34, 266, 270-72, 274

freedom of religion, 215-34, 270-72

freedom of speech and press, 196, 197-204, 224n., 226

Fuller, Chief Justice Melville W., 55, 122

Gellhorn, Walter, 151n.

general welfare clause, 103-108, 118-19, 187

George Washington Law Review, 111n.

Graham, Howard J., 163n.

grain exchanges, 121n.

gross receipts taxes, constitutionality of, 76-91, 95-96, 97n.

Guffey Coal Act, *see* Bituminous Coal Conservation Act of 1935

Hague, Mayor Frank, 197

Haines, Charles G., 138n.

Hale, Robert L., 262n.

Hamilton, Alexander, 105

Hamilton, Walton H., 161, 261, 266n.

Harlan, Justice John M., 59n., 130

Harvard Law Review, 16n., 49n., 50n., 51n., 260n.

Hatch Act, 213n.
Hays, Paul R., 138n.
Hellman, George S., 259n.
Hepburn Amendment, 138n.
Hewart, Lord Chief Justice, 139n.
High Court of Australia, 47n.
Hogan, Frank J., 267n.
Holmes, Justice Oliver Wendell, 2,
    17n., 18n., 23n., 26, 43, 47, 57n.,
    76, 93, 158, 165n., 181, 182, 192,
    194, 202n., 206n., 232, 257, 258, 260,
    265, 266n., 267n., 269, 273
Home Owners Loan Corporation,
    36-37, 46n.
Hoosac Mills Corporation, 101
Hughes, Chief Justice Charles E.,
    13n., 20n., 25n., 35, 46n., 91, 99n.,
    122-23, 141n., 152n., 178-79, 182,
    193n, 202, 224, 248, 264
Hunt, Gaillard, 104n.

Indiana Gross Income Tax Act, 82-
    83
industry committees, 142n., 144
Interstate Commerce Commission,
    138n.

Jackson, Justice Robert H., 37, 98,
    101n., 199n., 228-31, 273, 274n.
Japanese - Americans, evacuation
    from west coast, 245-54
Jefferson, Thomas, 270n.
Jehovah's Witnesses, 215-34, 270-72
Johnson, Justice William, 43n.
judicial inclusion and exclusion, rule
    of, 162n.
judicial objectivity, 45, 117, 181-82,
    264-66
"jurisprudence of concepts," 162

laissez-faire, 120-21, 193
Landis, James M., 136
Laski, Harold J., 192
law of nations, 240
law of war, 239-44
Lerner, Max, 202n., 268n., 269, 272n.
Levy, Beryl H., 259n.
liberty of contract, 163, 176
Lincoln, President Abraham, 235

Linfield, Seymour L., 151n.
Lodge, Senator Henry Cabot, 257
Lottery Law, 132n.

MacDonald government, 138n.
MacLeish, Archibald, 222n.
Madison, James, 104, 106
Mann Act, 132n.
Marshall, Chief Justice John, 1-10,
    18n., 28, 30, 42, 43, 48-54, 114n.,
    130, 259, 260
martial law 235-36, 248
Mason, Alpheus T., 193n.
Maternity Act of 1921, 99n., 101-102
McKee, Samuel, Jr., 105n.
McKenna, Justice Joseph, 207n.
McReynolds, Justice James C., 18n.,
    20n., 35n., 36n., 47n., 91, 125n.,
    202n., 206n., 268n.
Melder, Eugene F., 96n.
Michigan Law Review, 160n., 162n.
military commissions, trial by, 235-
    45
Miller, Justice Samuel F., 53, 160-
    63, 187n., 236n.
minimum wages, objectives of, 175n.,
    180n.
multiple taxation theory, 76-91, 95-
    96, 97n.
Murphy, Justice Frank, 88n., 199n.,
    210, 223, 226, 227n., 228, 229, 230,
    232n., 238n.

Nation, 152n.
National Association of Manufac-
    turers, 125
National Bank, 6
National Income Tax Magazine, 16n.
National Industrial Recovery Act,
    99n., 122, 141n.
National Labor Relations Act, 124-
    27, 133, 151-59, 197n.
National Labor Relations Board,
    127-28, 151-59
National Mediation Board, 159n.
Nazi saboteurs, case of, 236-45
Nelson, Justice Samuel, 9, 10n., 31n.
Newberry, Truman, 206n.
New Deal: agricultural program,

98-119; implications of, 121; industrial recovery program, 99n., 122-23, 124, 127, 141; labor relations, 124-27, 133, 151-59; social security, 119, 183; Supreme Court reorganization plan, 98, 125n.; Wage and Hour Law of 1938, 128-33, 142-52

New Republic, 192n., 222n.

New York City sales tax, 89, 96

New York Court of Appeals, 178, 183n.

New York Milk Control Act, 174, 180

New York Minimum Wage Law, 179-82

New York State Tax Commission, 36

New York *Times,* 45n., 215n., 233n.

New York Unemployment Insurance Law, 183n.

Norris, Senator George W., 255-56, 258

Office of Economic Stabilization, 227n.

"Okie" Law of California, 199n.

Parrington, Vernon L., 261

Peckham, Justice Rufus W., 176

Pinckney, William, 7

Pitney, Justice Mahlon, 23n., 207n.

police power, nature of, 163-65

"political" questions, 99n.

political restraints, doctrine of, 9-10, 30, 32n., 45, 61, 197, 221, 262n.

Political Science Quarterly, 266n.

poll tax, abolition of, 214-15

Port of New York Authority, 27, 44n.

Powell, Thomas Reed, 16n., 118

presumption of constitutionality, 25, 64, 92-95, 171, 185, 194, 196n., 264

"previous restraint," 224n., 226

Prichard, E. F., Jr., 222n.

primaries, congressional power over, 205-215

Pringle, Henry F., 259n.

prison-made goods, 55

privileges of national citizenship, 161n., 198, 199n., 200-202

processing taxes under A.A.A., 100

"proprietary" functions of government, 26n., 33, 37

psychoanalysis in constitutional law, 108

public purpose in taxation, 186-88

Pure Food and Drug Act, 132n.

questions of "fact" versus questions of "law," 153n., 157n.

railroads, federal regulation of, 113n., 121n., 122, 125n., 133

Railway Labor Act, 125n., 133

rate valuation, 158

Read, Conyers, 161n., 268n., 269n.

Reed, Justice Stanley F., 88n., 97n., 103-104, 199, 223-24, 227n., 228, 233

Report on Manufactures, 105

reversals, reasons for, 23-24

Ribble, F. D. G., 58n., 193n.

Roberts, Justice Owen J., 13n., 20n., 33n., 35, 82-83, 91, 97n., 98-119, 174, 182, 198, 199n., 200-202, 228, 233

Roosevelt, President Franklin D., 98-99, 121, 128, 135, 137, 236, 237, 241, 256-57

Roosevelt, President Theodore, 257

Root, Elihu, 141

Royall, Colonel Kenneth C., 237

Rutledge, Justice Wiley B., 97n., 227n., 228, 256

Safety Appliance Act, 32n., 133

Seventeenth Amendment, 207n.

Shelley, Percy B., 268

Sixteenth Amendment, 35-36

Sixth Amendment, 243-44

social legislation, judicial review of, *see* Stone

Social Security Act, 119, 183

Social Security Board, 183, 188

sovereignty, nature of in U. S., 1n., 8n., 266n.

state prohibition laws, 54–55
statutory construction, 139–40, 146–52
Stevenson, Andrew, 104n.
Stimson, Henry L., 247
stockyards, federal power to regulate, 121n.
Stone, Chief Justice Harlan F., advice to lawyers, 261n.; against "blind adherence" to precedent, 23–24; appointment to the Supreme Court, 255–56; biographical sketch, *see* Prefatory Note; on collective bargaining, 152–57; on Congress' power over primaries, 205–15; on Constitution, 221, 259–60; criticism of legal formalism, 58, 91–92, 166, 169, 260; on danger of multiple taxation, 76–91, 95–96, 97n.; on dissent by Holmes in Child Labor Case, 131; divergence from Marshall, 10, 28–29, 43, 55–56, 260; on flag salute issue, 218–22; on importance of factual inquiry in constitutional cases, 10, 44, 56, 58–59, 91–92, 94, 171–72, 260–64; intergovernmental tax immunity, basic approach to, 10, 25, 34–35, 39–41, 43–44; on judicial function in commerce clause cases, 62–65, 92–95, 97; on judicial review of social legislation, 62, 116–19, 168, 173–74, 269–70; on judicial "self-restraint," 116–19, 269; on *McCulloch* v. *Maryland,* 28–29; on the "more searching judicial inquiry" in civil rights cases, 193–96, 215, 218–22, 233–34, 253–54, 269–70, 274; on need for administrative discretion, 142–45, 253n.; political restraints doctrine, 30, 32n., 45, 61, 197, 221, 262n.; on presumption of constitutionality, 25, 64, 68–69, 92–95, 171, 185, 194, 196n., 264; on privileges and immunities clause, 198, 199n., 200–202; on reach of federal commerce power, 128–35; on spending for

"general welfare," 110–16, 118–19, 187; on similarity between common law and constitutional law, 262–63; on subpoena power, abuses of, 146–52; on Tenth Amendment, effect of, 134; on unemployment, 170, 187–89
Story, Justice Joseph, 104n., 105
subpoena power, *see* Stone
supremacy of national action, 28, 38, 46, 50, 107–108, 135
Supreme Court of Canada, 47n.
Supreme Court reorganization plan, *see* New Deal
Sutherland, Justice George, 15–17, 18n., 19–20, 36n., 66, 99, 124, 167, 168–76, 191n., 193n., 194n.
Swayne, Justice Noah H., 236n.

Taft, Chief Justice William H., 252n., 256, 258, 265
Taney, Chief Justice Roger B., 51
Tenth Amendment, 107, 121, 124, 128, 134–35
Thayer, James Bradley, 258
Thomas, Norman, 197n.
Transportation Act of 1920, 138n.
treason, 243n.
trial by jury, exceptions to, 243–44
Triborough Bridge Authority, 44n.

Unemployment, 170, 187–89
United States Criminal Code, 205–207, 210–13
United States Code, 202

Van Devanter, Justice Willis, 19n., 20n., 21, 191n., 206n.
Virginia Law Review, 96n.

Wage and Hour Law, *see* Fair Labor Standards Act
Wage and Hour Division, 142–52
Wagner Act, *see* National Labor Relations Act
Walter-Logan Bill, 137n.

Walters, Frank L., 248n.
War of 1812, 5
war powers, 245-54
War Revenue Act of 1917, 11
Washington "business activities" tax, 85
Wayne, Justice James M., 236n.
Webb-Kenyon Act, 55
Webster, Daniel, 7, 48n.

White, Chief Justice Edward D., 31n., 207n., 256n.
"white" primary, 205n.
Wilson Act, 55
Wilson, President Woodrow, 165n.
Wisconsin Unemployment Insurance Law, 188

Yale Law Journal, 163n., 268n.